Ex Líbrís

Randy Manning

The Cult of the
MOTHER-GODDESS

The Cult of the
MOTHER-GODDESS

E. O. JAMES

D.Litt., Ph.D., F.S.A., Hon. D.D. St Andrews

*Professor Emeritus of the History of Religion in the
University of London. Fellow of University College
and Fellow of King's College, London*

BARNES
&NOBLE
BOOKS
NEW YORK

This edition published by Barnes & Noble, Inc.

1994 Barnes & Noble Books

ISBN 1-56619-600-0

Printed and bound in the United States of America

M 9 8 7 6 5 4 3 2 1

CONTENTS

Contents 9

PREFACE

THE re-examination of the archaeological and documentary material now available concerning the myth and ritual of the Middle East and the Eastern Mediterranean in which I have been engaged in recent years has revealed the unique position occupied by the Goddess cult in this tradition. Its prominence and prevalence, in fact, were such that it seemed to require more detailed investigation than it has received if the part it has played throughout the ages, especially in Near Eastern religions, was to be correctly estimated. Clearly it was an essential element very deeply laid in the long and complex history of the body of beliefs and practices which centred in and around the mysterious processes of fecundity, birth and generation, alike in nature, the human species and in the animal kingdom.

Whether or not the Mother-goddess was the earliest manifestation of the concept of Deity, her symbolism unquestionably has been the most persistent feature in the archaeological record of the ancient world, from the sculptured Venuses of the Gravettian culture in the Upper Palaeolithic and the stylized images of the decorated caves, to the emblems and inscriptions of the cult when it became established in the Fertile Crescent, Western Asia, the Indus Valley, the Aegean and Crete between the fifth and third millennia B.C. Moreover, it is now becoming increasingly evident that in its dispersal from its cradleland in the Southern Russian steppe and Western Asia, it was destined to have a widespread influence and to play a very significant role in the subsequent development of the Ancient Near Eastern religions from India to the Mediterranean from Neolithic times to the Christian era.

With the rise of agriculture and the domestication of animals as the figure of the Goddess became more clearly defined, and with the growing consciousness of the duality of male and female in the generative process, from being the Unmarried Mother personifying the divine principle in maternity she became associated with the Young God as her son or consort. While she remained the dominant figure the cult assumed a twofold aspect in the seasonal drama in which both partners in procreation played their respective roles, until ultimately, after the syncretistic Magna Mater had emerged, it acquired a mystical and theological content in Christendom. Then it was interpreted in terms of the Church as the Mater Ecclesia, and the Virgin Mother of the incarnate Son of God as the Madonna.

A theme and cultus of such persistence and permanent significance cannot be lightly dismissed. While the subject has been investigated and discussed in a variety of different contexts, anthropological, archaeological, philological, psychological and theological, so far as I am aware no single volume has been devoted to the elucidation of the Goddess cult as such in relation to the archaeological and documentary data now available. Its widespread influence is becoming increasingly recognized, particularly in the Near East and the Eastern Mediterranean, but its origin, development, diffusion and purpose present a set of problems more complicated and obscure than would appear at first sight. These are brought under review in this inquiry in an attempt to estimate the part played by the cult and its principal figures, and to determine the purpose of the rites and their associated beliefs. While the psychological aspects of the subject lie outside my province, nevertheless it may be hoped that an objective examination of the factual evidence concerning the practices which not infrequently have been the means of affording an emotional outlet at critical junctures in the life of the community and of its individual members, will be of some interest for those engaged in these and in other interpretations of the phenomena, in the related disciplines.

E. O. JAMES

Oxford

CHAPTER I

The Antecedents of the Goddess Cult

THE PALAEOLITHIC CULTUS

AN adequate supply of offspring and food being a necessary condition of human existence, the promotion and conservation of life have been a fundamental urge from Palaeolithic times to the present day which has found magico-religious expression in a very deeply laid and highly developed cultus. Exactly when and where it arose is still very obscure, but it was from Western Asia, the South Russian plain and the valley of the Don that female figurines, commonly called 'Venuses', in bone, ivory, stone and bas-relief, often with the maternal organs grossly exaggerated, were introduced into Eastern and Central Europe at the beginning of the Upper Palaeolithic by an Asiatic migration in what is now known as the Gravettian culture; the former Upper Aurignacian. The diffusion-centre of the blade-tool, or gravette, from which it takes its name, was Western Asia and the Eurasiatic steppes. Thence it appears to have made its way into Europe through the loess-lands of the Danube to Moravia and Austria, where it became associated with the Brünn type of *Homo sapiens*, to whom in this region the statuettes have been assigned.

Sculptured Female Statuettes

It was, however, essentially in Eastern Europe and Western Asia that bone and ivory were employed for tool-making and the fashioning of human figures of the Venus variety with pendulous breasts, broad hips, rotund buttocks and excessive corpulency suggestive of pregnancy. Thus, examples of this type have been found at Kostienki, Gagarino, Mezine, and especially at Malta near Lake Baikal in Siberia, where their production was on a considerable scale and included a highly conventionalized figure.[1] As the technique was diffused from the Southern Russian steppe to Central and Western Europe it tended to become cruder and more conventionalized. In the squat type the face was seldom portrayed though the ivory statuette of a girl from the Grotte du Pape, Brassempouy, in the Landes (belonging to the Middle Aurignacian rather than to the Gravettian culture) was an exception to this rule. Here the face was fashioned and, as in the example in oölitic lime/ stone from Willendorf, near Vienna, the hair was braided. In the Willendorf Venus, while the arms are only very slightly indicated, the abdomen is prominent and the buttocks are strongly developed. Traces of red ochre occur in the porous limestone, and the emphasis clearly was on the sexual features of the nude figure. In the same level a more elegant form in ivory from the tusk of a mammoth was discovered in 1926.[2] In the Haute Garonne a skilfully executed curious ivory figurine from Lespugne with the legs fused tapering to a point and huge breasts, has a sort of loincloth from the buttocks to the back of the calves of the legs.[3] This represents another variety of the technique in contrast to the slim Magdalenian figure, called the 'immodest Venus', from Laugerie/Basse, Dordogne.

To the north/east of Willendorf Dr Absolon in 1929 brought to light a Venus near Unter Westernitz to the south of Brno in Moravia which occupies an intermediate position between the slim and grotesque varieties.[4] This was followed by further discoveries at Wisternitz (Vestonice) between 1934 and 1937 of a number of plastic anthropomorphic caricatures modelled in ground and burnt mammoth/bones mixed with loam and fat like the Venuses, together with a small ivory head carved in the form of a sculptured portrait of a human being, believed by Keith to represent a woman showing a fine animated face,[5] in striking contrast to the crude plastic carica/ tures and the particular figurines which sufficed for cult purposes. Normally all that mattered in these cases was to emphasize the maternal organs and so they were grossly exag/ gerated, as in the examples that have been considered. Similar statuettes have been recovered from Sireuil in the Dordogne, the Grimaldi caves on the Franco-Italian frontier at Mentone, and in Italy they have been found in Emilia at Savignano sul Panaro.⁶

In a rock-shelter at Laussel in the valley of the Beune near Les Eyzies in the Dordogne, the well-known figure of a nude woman, apparently pregnant, holding in her right hand the horn of a bison, was carved in relief on a block of stone about eighteen inches high. The body had been coloured with red pigment, so widely used in Palaeolithic ritual as a life-giving agent, the surrogate of blood. The face was featureless and egg-shaped, though the head in profile was turned towards the horn. On the ground were four other similar reliefs, two of which had horns and the head turned in their direction. One was a male figure, apparently in the act of shooting with a bow and arrow (if such weapons were in use in Palaeolithic times), and another has been interpreted either as an accouchement or as a copulation.⁷ But an inspection of the original relief at the house of Madame Lalanne at Bordeaux some years ago did not convince the present writer that a copulation was indicated. An erotic element may have been inherent in the tradition, but childbirth rather than conception seemed to be the purpose of the representation, the main purpose of the cultus having been the giving of life through the outward signs of maternal fecundity.

Shells as Amulets

For this purpose shells also appear to have been used in the Upper Palaeolithic as amulets, judging from their frequent occurrence in graves where they seem to have had a life-giving significance. Thus, in the Grimaldi burials in the Grotte des Enfants four rows of pierced shells were arranged round the head of a youth whose skeleton had been stained red with peroxide of iron. On the arms of the tightly flexed woman buried with him were shell bracelets, and between the skulls lay two pebbles of serpentine, and another against the jaw of the woman.⁸ In the adjoining Grotte du Cavillon were no less than 7,868 marine shells (*Nassa neritae*) of which 875 were pierced, doubtless having belonged to necklaces, 200 of them occurring near the head. On the cranium was a fillet of sea-shells, and twenty-two perforated canine teeth of deer were near the frontal bones.[9] At Barma Grande, the fifth cave of the series, the skeleton of a boy in a grave lined with red ochre was similarly adorned with *Nassa* shells and canine teeth, all perforated, together with ivory pendants, a necklace and two large cowrie shells (*Cyprae millepunctata*), originally apparently a garter.[10] The young woman in this interment had much the same ceremonial equipment, including a collar of shells, teeth and vertebrae. In the sixth cave—Baousso da Torre—a shell collar, a fillet and a grille with shell pendants recurred.

In the rock-shelter known as Crô-Magnon at Les Eyzies, where the first skeletal remains of Upper Palaeolithic man were detected in 1868, 300 sea-shells, mainly *Littorina littorea*, and perforated pendants, were among the bones, while a mile away on the opposite bank of the Vézère at Laugerie-Basse, cowries had been carefully arranged in pairs on a corpse; two pairs on the forehead, one near the humerus, four in the region of the knees and thighs, and two upon each foot.[11] Such a distribution hardly could have been other than for magico-religious purposes connected with the restoration of life to the deceased like the widespread practice of depositing ochreous powder in Palaeolithic interments, with which shells and necklaces are so closely associated as grave-goods. As blood, or its surrogate red ochre, was regarded apparently as a vitalizing agent, so certain shells, such as the cowrie shaped in the form of the portal through which a child enters the world, seem to have been connected with the female principle, and to have been employed as fertility charms.[12] It is not improbable, therefore, that this widespread feature of Upper Palaeolithic mortuary ritual was in the nature of a life-giving rite closely connected with the female figurines and other symbols of what later became the Goddess cult. Indeed, it may have made its way into Europe from the East in association with the Venuses with the rest of the Gravettian culture, and as will be seen as this inquiry is pursued, the worship of the Goddess always was

very closely related to the cult of the dead in its later developments.

The Fertility Dance

It was not, however, only to make the human species fruitful
and replenish the earth, and to revivify the dead, that this type
of ritual was practised in Palaeolithic times. It was also
employed, particularly by the Magdalenians, to stimulate fecundity among the animals on which Early Man mainly depended
for his food-supply. Thus, in the valley of the Beune not very
far from Laussel, proceeding in the direction of Les Eyzies,
lies a long tunnel-like cave, known as Combarelles, containing
quantities of engravings of Pleistocene animals including rein-
deer, bison, mammoth, horses, lions, bears and a rhinoceros,
together with a series of anthropomorphic figures on the wall
of a recess which may perhaps be those of masked dancers
clothed in skins and wearing tails. In one silhouette the shape
of a mammoth's head is suggested with the arms made to
resemble the tusks. Elsewhere there is an obese man apparently
following a woman,[13] interpreted sometimes as having an
erotic significance. But the main purpose of the scenes seems
to have been to depict a fertility ritual dance, doubtless to
render prolific the animals on which man depended for his
subsistence, like the engraving on stag-horn of the three masked
figures masquerading in the skin of a chamois at Abri Mège,
Dordogne, and those with animals' heads in the caves at
Marsoulas, near Salies du Sarlat in the Haute Garonne. On
a schist plaque at Lourdes a man with a long beard, the tail
of a horse, and what may be the antlers of a stag is depicted,
while similar anthropomorphic designs have been detected in
the cave at Altamira and at that of Hornos de la Peña in
Cantabria, near Santander.

That dances were held to promote fecundity is most clearly
shown in the clay models of a female bison followed by a male
placed against a projecting rock in a small chamber at the
end of a long narrow passage in the Tuc d'Audoubert on the
estate of the Count Bégouen in Ariège near St Girons, about

700 metres from the entrance. In a recess near by were pieces of clay in the form of a phallus, and on the soft clay floor of the gallery were impressions of human feet and an incomplete bison 13 centimetres long. To the right were fifty small-sized heel-marks, thought to be those of young dancers engaged perhaps in a fertility dance round the small hillock in the centre in the presence of the clay bison.[14]

Similarly, in the adjoining cave called after the three adventurous sons of the Count, Les Trois Frères, who in 1918 first ventured into it and found there among an immense array of paintings and engravings a mysterious masked figure known as 'the Sorcerer' depicted in black on the wall of a small chamber at the end of a winding corridor in front of a kind of window. Exactly what was the meaning and purpose of this composite figure 75 centimetres high and 50 centimetres wide, 4 metres above the ground, can only be conjectured. The head is full face with round eyes like an owl and between them is a nose. The ears are those of a wolf and the two antlers above the forehead are those of a stag. The claws are those of a lion and the tail of a horse or wolf. The forearms are raised and joined horizontally, ending in two hands. The feet and toes are carefully designed to indicate a movement suggestive of dancing.

Whether or not, as was first supposed, this masked figure represented the chief sorcerer or shaman embodying the attributes and functions of the animals,[15] or, as is now suggested, portrayed the spirit controlling hunting expeditions and the multiplication of game,[16] a cult is indicated in which animals and human beings were brought together in a joint effort to conserve and promote abundance of the species on which man depended for his means of subsistence. The mysterious forces of nutrition and propagation being among the chief centres of emotional interest and concern, a ritual technique was devised to bring them under supernatural control, nature being man's 'living larder', as Malinowski has remarked.[17] To this end a ritual expert arrayed himself in the skin and antlers of a stag, or the feathers of a bird, and imitated the behaviour of the species he personified in the belief that for the time being, and for the prescribed purpose, he was what he represented himself to be. In that capacity he believed he made the copulation of male and female effective in the reproduction of offspring just as he was able, as he supposed, to control the fortunes of the chase by depicting animals wounded by spears and missiles, and uttering incantations over his designs and thereby catching and killing the prey.

The figures of the masked dancers in animal disguises suggest a cult in which the ritual expert impersonated the 'spirits' of the animals he embodied, and represented dramatically in a series of sacred actions what it was earnestly desired should be accomplished. The will to live as a primary emotion was discharged by anticipatory rites as a pre-presentation of either a successful hunt or of the propagation of the species. It was not so much that 'like produces like' as that a ritual which involved a realistic reproduction of a practical activity and a desired result established the *ex post facto* idea of 'sympathetic' causation. The primary function was to give expression to a vital impulse, the urge to act discharging itself on the symbol, the ritual being the vent of pent-up emotions. The purpose of the actions performed and of their representation in visible form was to secure the prey or to effect a successful birth of offspring through the ritual technique, and so to relieve the tension in a precarious situation on which human well-being and survival depended. The symbol was regarded and treated in the same way as the spiritual entity it symbolized by virtue of the supernatural quality it acquired. Hence the efficacy of the mimetic dances and of the amulets, designs and disguises employed to these ends in the cultus.

In a great cavern sanctuary like Les Trois Frères, Niaux, Font-de-Gaume or Lascaux, the ceremonies must have involved an organized effort on the part of the community in a collective attempt to control natural forces and processes by supernatural means directed to the common good. The sacred tradition, be it in relation to the food-supply, the mystery of birth and propagation, or of death, arose and functioned, it would appear, in response to the will to live here and hereafter.

Therefore, it was centred in the critical, arresting and disturbing necessities and occasions of everyday life and experience, and tended to assume a communal character to enable the group to cope with the ever-present perplexities, hazards and extenuating circumstances, the ritual experts exercising their functions in a representative capacity.

The Diffusion of the Cult

As individualized divine beings came to be regarded as ulti-mately responsible for the control of the vital processes, and acquired a recognized status and stylized form, the Mother-goddess, especially in Western Asia and South-eastern Europe, occupied a predominant position by virtue of her life-giving properties *par excellence*. While the Magdalenians in the Palaeo-lithic concentrated upon the maintenance of the vagaries of the chase as the chief source of the food-supply, their Gravettian and Aurignacian predecessors, as has been considered, were interested essentially it would seem in the maternal aspect of the mystery of birth and propagation. Since their cradleland appears to have been in the region of the Caspian Sea, where the Goddess cult subsequently became most prominent, it is in this area that its most probable original home lies. In its westerly extension in Europe it became sufficiently established to become a permanent tradition, especially in the Mediter-ranean phase, where it continued apparently without passing through the Solutrean and Magdalenian stages of Palaeolithic development.[18]

In the Solutrean interlude, centred it would seem in the mountainous country of Northern Hungary, where in its earliest phase it was contemporary with the later Aurignacian culture, there are indications of Gravettian influences not only in some of its blade implements but also in its relief-sculpture (e.g. the animal-frieze on limestone at Le Roc, Charente,)[19] ivory statuettes such as the male figure from Brno, bead collars like that at Předmost, and perforated pebbles at Laugerie-Haute. The Magdalenians perfected the art of carving as well as of cave-painting, which reached its height in the great polychromes at Altamira, Font-de-Gaume and Lascaux. They were confined, however, for the most part to France and Cantabrian Spain with outposts in Bavaria, Belgium and Southern England. Elsewhere the Aurignacian tradition continued to develop independently, as it did where the Solutreans never penetrated—i.e. north and south of an area stretching from Northern Hungary to the Pyrenees, and to North-west France, East Anglia and Southern England.

In France the Magdalenian emerged from a combination of Gravettian and Solutrean influences, but outside this restricted region the Upper Palaeolithic culture remained basically Aurignacian, as is revealed in the Grimaldi caves at Mentone and at Cresswell Crags in Derbyshire. It would seem unlikely, therefore, that there was any definite break in the tradition in which the Venus cult arose and from which in due course it was destined to come to fruition in the worship of the Great Goddess. Moreover, in the Solutrean-Magdalenian interlude in Central and Western Europe it was the same urge to fecundity that found expression in the sacred dances and their associated rites to promote the propagation of the species upon which man depended for his subsistence.

Thus, the famous dancing scene now so faded as to be hardly visible in the rock-shelter adjoining the village of Cogul about twelve miles from Lérida in Catalonia would seem to be connected with the Venus type of fertility cult. As it now appears, nine narrow-waisted women with long pendant breasts, clad in caps and in bell-shaped skirts reaching to the knees, but showing no facial features, are depicted in association with a small naked male figure[20] which, since the penis is not erect, can hardly have a phallic significance, as has been suggested. The scene seems to have been the work of several Palaeolithic artists, perhaps at different times, and the little dark brown male figure may have been added to the earlier black group of the women. Even so, it is difficult to avoid the conclusion that its insertion was connected with a fertility rite in which the women were grouped round a male emblem, perhaps that of a boy, to facilitate the production of life. It is most unlikely, however, that at this early period[21] a male god played any part in the antecedents of the Mother-goddess cult, which throughout this Palaeolithic phase found expression in stylized female figures in clay or paint or bas-relief with hanging breasts, small rudimentary heads, wasp-waists, and sometimes clothed in bell-skirts. Indeed, from its emergence in the Gravettian culture the cult persisted in the various components and derivatives of the Aurignacian in Europe, North Africa and the Middle East, until it acquired a new lease of life under Neolithic conditions.

THE NEOLITHIC CULTUS

With the transition from food-gathering to food-production the female principle continued to predominate the cultus that had grown up around the mysterious processes of birth and generation. Woman being the mother of the race, she was essentially the life-producer and in that capacity she played the essential role in the production of offspring. Nevertheless, as agriculture and herding became the established modes of maintaining the food-supply, the two poles of creative energy, the one female and receptive, the other male and begettive, could hardly fail to be recognized and given their respective symbolic significance. But although phallic emblems became increasingly prominent from Neolithic times onwards, the maternal principle, in due course personified as the Mother-goddess, continued to assume the leading role in the cultus, especially in Western Asia, Crete and the Aegean, where the male god was subordinate to the Goddess. Essential in physiological fact as the conjunction of male and female is in the production of life, it would seem that at first there was some uncertainty about the significance of paternity.[22] Therefore, as the precise function of the male partner in relation to conception and birth was less obvious, and probably less clearly understood, it is hardly surprising that he should be regarded as supplementary rather than as the vital agent in the process. Consequently, the mother and her maternal organs and attributes were the life-giving symbols *par excellence*.

The Arpachiyah Figurines

Thus, in the Mosul district of Northern Iraq, within ten miles of the Tigris and the ancient city of Nineveh, in the Chalco-lithic mound Tell Arpachiyah, the beginnings of which go back before 4000 B.C., numerous headless clay female statuettes have been found of the Venus type. Some have been roughly modelled in the round, others are flat, but in all of them the breasts are pendulous, the navel is prominent, the waist slender and the buttocks are highly developed. Most are represented in a squatting posture suggestive of childbirth, but some would seem to indicate a state of pregnancy. As in the Palaeolithic Venuses, the head seldom is shown and the 'steatopygous' squatting variety exhibit a tendency towards conventionaliza-tion, the body in some cases having been reduced to a peg or cone, though retaining the legs in a sitting position in its simplest form. The painted type with bent head and pendulous breasts, in what is designated as the T.T.6 level of the mound belonging to the height of the Chalcolithic Halafian period, was adorned with a garment in red pigment and braces crossed between the breasts. The truncated fiddle-shaped flat forms in sun-dried clay, either painted or unpainted, have a high peg-shaped head, prominent breasts and navel, and sometimes they are perforated suggesting that they had been worn as amulets. Some of those in terracotta, on the other hand, have hollow bodies, one of which in all probability had been intended to be used as a vase.[23]

This remarkable collection of female figurines is of particular interest because it reveals that these emblems of the Goddess cult, having unmistakable affinities with the Palaeolithic examples, were in common use in a variety of shapes in Northern Iraq, probably in the fifth millennium B.C., long before they appeared in the Eastern Mediterranean. Moreover, they were associated with the double axe and the dove, the bull's head and the serpent, as in Crete and the Aegean.[24] Though often the statuettes are inferior in design and technique they are allied to the Gravettian prototypes and constitute an important link between the Palaeolithic and the later

Chalcolithic and Bronze Age manifestations of the cultus in Anatolia, Crete and the Aegean in the west, and in Persia, Baluchistan and the Indus valley in the east. Sometimes they were so badly modelled, showing only the maternal organs, that they can have been employed merely as charms and amulets to increase fruitfulness and facilitate delivery of the offspring.

Thus, in a much later parallel group of five nude female figurines from an Iron Age Israelite occupation level (Stratum B) at Tell Beit Mirsim in the south of Palestine (probably the Canaanite city Kirjathsepher) 'the process of accouchement' is believed by Dr Albright to have been represented in the exaggerated protrusion of the vulva region in an attempt to suggest the descent of the head of an infant at the moment of birth, doubtless for the purpose of hastening parturition by magical means.[25] It is hardly likely, as he says, that figures of this nature wherever they occurred represented the Goddess herself, being essentially aids to childbirth and fecundity. Nevertheless, they constitute a prominent element in this widely extended cult.

Once the maternal principle had been personified it was either a single Goddess, the Great Mother, with different functions and symbols, or a number of independent and separate deities exercising their several roles in the processes of birth, generation and fertility, in whom the cult was centred. At first it would seem to have been concentrated upon the mystery of birth, including all the major aspects of fecundity and nutrition as the vital concern of man, food and children being the two basic requirements at all times. Therefore, as Dr Mallowan says, there can be little doubt that 'fertility wor-ship connected with a "Mother-goddess" cult must indeed be one of the oldest and longest surviving religions of the ancient world'.[26]

In the Chalcolithic period it became the dominating in-fluence from the Middle Near East to Anatolia, the Aegean and Crete, and to Persia, Baluchistan and India. In the earliest Neolithic sites, however, apart from Tell Arpachiyah it was not very prominent in Western Asia prior to the Halaf period when female figurines became abundant. At Tell Hassuna in North Iraq near Mosul west of the Tigris, in the pre-Halaf stratum a few clay female statuettes have been recovered from level IV resembling those found at Arpachiyah.[27] In level V a squatting woman in red clay poorly preserved and unbaked has an excrescence on the left thigh. The head occurred in five fragments in greenish clay, two of which suggest curved horns with the impression of a reed running through the centre to strengthen it.[28] In the post-Hassuna levels clay statuettes reappear, and in the Halaf deposits they become prevalent everywhere from the Syrian coast to the Zagros mountains where this Halaf culture flourished.

The Halaf and 'Ubaid Periods

Thus, at Tepe Gawra near Nineveh, north-west of Arpachiyah on the caravan route to Iran, they are of common occurrence in the lower levels of the mound and conform to a standardized type. Though male figures predominate on the pottery and in seal designs, they are rare in the form of figurines, which invariably depict women, usually in the squatting posture and holding their breasts. The heads are merely pinched out of the clay, but the facial features sometimes are painted without any attempt at modelling. The eyes are drawn in black paint, and horizontal lines on the shoulders, arms and feet may represent some form of ornamentation, or possibly articles of clothing. Similarly, painted terracotta types recur, as we have seen, at Arpachiyah, and also at Tell Halaf and Chagar Bazar in North Syria, where in addition to details of dress or tattoo marks they are sometimes seated on circular stools as if in parturition, and wearing turbans.[29] At Gawra a highly conventionalized 'fiddle-shaped' torso with prominent breasts was found in level B of area A, in which all details of the lower part of the body are emphasized in contrast to those of the waist and hips. The sexual triangle is marked by incised lines below the navel. The head is merely a short projection while the back is flat. It being at this site an isolated example of this kind of stylization, it may have been introduced specifically to serve the purpose of safe and speedy delivery.[30]

The stratified deposits of the mound have yielded identical figurines painted on the neck and shoulders in brown, red or black, and with the same kind of pinched heads, or with no heads at all. Some are armless, without pointed knees, and having prominent breasts and a painted skirt or kilt suspended from the shoulders by two straps between the breasts. There are also painted strokes on the back and on the shins which may indicate tattoo marks or cicatrices, and horizontal lines on the lower part of the back, possibly representing the spinal column. Fattening of the buttocks, distention of the abdomen or protuberance of the navel do not occur at Gawra. Only one figurine has separate legs, and on this armless and headless specimen the breasts are not marked.[31] Two others from the 'Ubaid period are so stylized that apart from the breasts there is little or nothing to suggest that they are human figures,[32] and it is quite impossible to determine whether they are of the squatting or the erect type. But at Gawra where the posture is shown squatting is the invariable rule, and even in the stylized cones it is usually suggested. The most prominent types are either those of the Halaf pointed knees decorated variety with arms encircling the breasts, pinched and decorated heads and bands across the neck and shoulders; or a later armless type with prominent breasts and a skirt suspended by crossed straps on the shoulders. Instead of pointed knees the laps slope and the legs are very short. Both are common in the lowest levels, but become progressively less numerous, disappearing altogether at the end of the 'Ubaid period in stratum XIII. The only male figure found in the mound has a spot painted at the end of the phallus, and came from near the temple stratum X. In all probability this was a cult object.[33]

In Southern Mesopotamia a series of clay figurines with elongated grotesque heads and reptilian features has been recovered from below the Flood deposits at Ur belonging to the first settlers in the marshes of the Euphrates delta ('Ubaid I and II). The bodies are well modelled with feet together and hands at the waist, or holding a child to the breast, or some/times resting on the hips. Bands and stripes are painted on the nude body to indicate ornaments or tattooing, and the pubes and division between the legs are depicted by linear incision. Some are greenish as a result of overfiring of the clay; others are much lighter in colour. Both represent the slender type painted in black and red with wigs of bitumen applied to the head.[34] A few small clay models survived the Al'Ubaid period and became shapeless grotesques devoid of the skill in technique displayed in the earlier figurines. At Abu Shahrain (Eridu), 14 miles from Ur, the upper part of a similar figure was found by Dr H. R. Hall having a monstrous head with beak/like profile and flattened shoulders. Probably it was that of a male in much the same posture as the Al'Ubaid females, though less skilfully modelled.[35]

The Warka Period

In the mound of Warka which marks Erech, the ancient Uruk in Mesopotamia, the female statuettes resemble those of Ur in form and ornamentation executed in black paint. One has a cylindrical body, a splayed base with the division between the legs marked by incision and wing/like arms. Nude women holding their breasts, with large hips and slender waists, recur on rectangular reliefs, with almond eyes and rounded face. Round the neck are necklaces and incised lines on the wrists indicate bracelets. Sometimes, however, the head is monstrous with a snout and gashes in strips of clay for eyes, and having a peaked head/dress. Others are small and devoid of features except for a large nose. In some of the examples a diagonal band had been painted across the shoulder and under the right arm. The hair is coiled round the head and locks frequently hang down on to the shoulders. Between the C and D levels of the Anu Ziqqurat the upper torso and arms of a very small nude female figure in light translucent stone, excellently modelled with arms bent at the elbow and clenched fists, was used in all probability for amuletic purposes.[36]

In the Early Dynastic Protoliterate period at Khafaje the

upper part of a slab-like human figure from the Sin Temple V has a projecting beaked nose and a prominent occipital region. The eyes were represented by cutting across an applied pellet of clay with a horizontal gash, and the eyebrows by applied strips nicked to show hair. Clay figurines in Jemdet Nasr layers (Sin Temple VIb and layer 12c of the house area), and from Tell Asmar, with a similar facial representation have breasts marked in the form of small pellets and the usual emphasis on sexual features.[37] In Sin Temple IV a small figure, 10 centimetres high, represents a woman in a short skirt and the hands clasped below the breasts. The upper part of the body is nude, the head is bare and the hair hanging to the waist. The rounded face is summarily indicated apart from the carefully modelled hooked nose; the eyes are deep, the eyebrows ridged, and the breasts are prominent, in technique corresponding to the clay figurines of the earlier periods.[38]

Anatolia

In Anatolia the mound Alishar Hüyük, 45 kilometres south-east of Yozgad in the centre of the highland region, first discovered by Dr Osten in 1926,[39] has produced a number of pottery female figurines with pronounced sexual characteristics in stratum II which accumulated during the occupation of the site by an intrusive group of people of different racial type characterized by wheel-made pottery having Cappadocian affinities. With them are three in lead more elaborately constructed, in one of which the upper part is nude and the arms indicate that the hands, though missing, originally held the breasts, below which a dress extends to the feet. In addition to a semicircular head-dress are five necklaces and disk-shaped ornaments. The other two represent males, but one of them shows well-pronounced breasts combined with a phallic elevation,[40] suggesting a divine figure combining male and female attributes. In the clay and pottery types the face is conventionalized with an exaggerated nose and a disk indicating the eye, and in those of women the conical breasts are very prominent and often touched by the hands. The protruding abdomen suggests pregnancy in a few cases, and on one hemispherical breast there is a small depression marking the mammilla.[41] Occasionally the sexual organs are indicated by horizontal dashes with a triangle or with a rectangular incision open below, and the navel by a circular depression.[42]

In the ancient mound Yümük Tepe, about 2 miles to the north-west of the small port of Mersin in Cilicia on the southern Turkish coast, situated on the direct route from east to west, the Neilson expedition under John Garstang brought to light several female figurines which seem to symbolize the cult of the Mother-goddess. One from the Bronze Age level (VIII) is made of stone, and its companion from level IXB of pottery.[43] In the earlier Chalcolithic levels has come an even cruder example[44] among the remains of the village community engaged in agriculture and stock-breeding, and the associated cult practices, going back to a period (*c.* 4000 B.C.) before the time of the Halaf culture when a semi-nomadic mode of life was giving place to that of the settled agriculturist.

Early Iran and Turkestan

In Persia when food-production began to supplement and supplant food-gathering, a quantity of figurines representing a naked goddess have been found on prehistoric Iranian sites. In the Tepe Sialk, however, on the western edge of the arid plateau in North-west Iran, the most ancient statuette was that of a clothed male figure giving no indication of having been a cult object of any kind,[45] just as human figurines are absent in the most ancient level at Tepe Hissar,[46] which cannot be much earlier than the late Uruk period and Sialk III in the beginning of the third millennium B.C. At Tepe Giyan near Nihavend, south of Hamadan, on the other hand, at about the same time nude female figurines occurred with painted hair and eyes but without excessive emphasis on the maternal organs.[47] In short, while in Early Iran there are no traces of the cult in the north-east, it appears to have flourished in the south and south-west.

Thus, at Susa in Elam, where the nearest known material

comparable with that of Giyan V, Sialk III and Hissar I occurs in the earliest settlement (now distinguished as Susa A),[48] figures of women modelled in clay have been recovered with the eyes and breasts rendered by dabs, the nose and brows by thick rolls stuck on the flat slab and on an incised sexual triangle.[49] In the First Elamite period (c. 2800 B.C.) a statuette was found on the Acropolis on which one of the splayed hands is placed on the stomach and the other is shown holding the breast.[50] In another figurine with a cylindrical body the hands are clasped, the head appears to be covered with a turban, the eyes are indicated by incised lines, and two bracelets are shown on each wrist,[51] very much as in a later example, now in the Ashmolean Museum in Oxford, in addition to a turban and bracelets, a necklace of two strings of large beads is shown with a rosette pendant in the middle, and another necklace passing across the chest.[52] In the proto-Elamite period the use of necklaces in this type of figurine was an established feature.[53]

In Russian Turkestan at Anau near Askabad in Trans-caspia on the border of the plateau, in all the fragmentary figurines of naked female forms the breasts, and usually the navel, are clearly marked. A necklace is shown on several torsos, but of the face only the nose is represented by a projection and the eyes by small depressions. The hips are strongly developed and the legs are brought together to a point. In one specimen the region of the vulva is emphasized in a realistic manner by punch-marks.[54] These have come from the middle strata of the South Kurgan in which the culture has some affinities with that of Hissar III. It is also significant that neither at Tepe Hissar nor at Anau have figurines been recorded in the earliest deposits. This, coupled with the marked change in pottery technique in the earlier and later settlements, suggests that an intrusion of a new people occurred in Northern Iran and Turkestan at this time,[55] and that it was they who intro-duced the Goddess cult both among those who settled at Anau and at the adjacent extensive ruins of Old Merv, now called Ghiaur Kala. For there on the Acropolis and on the plateau of the main city naked female torsos have been recovered, sometimes in a sitting posture and painted in red, black and yellow. A robed standing female figure in relief is adorned with neck ornaments though the head is missing. In her right hand she holds a mirror before her breast, and the left hand is placed lower down.[56]

THE BRONZE AGE OF WESTERN INDIA
Baluchistan

Although the course of events in Western India is obscure before 3000 B.C., it would seem that in the secluded mountain valleys in Baluchistan small farming communities were estab
lished in villages, similar to the Early Iranian settlements on the edge of the Persian desert—e.g. Sialk and Giyan—as self
contained peasant societies with a uniform prehistoric culture, but each having its own local distinguishing features. Thus, in the pottery techniques adopted, while in Persia buff ware was characteristic of the south and red ware of the north, black on red predominated in the Zhob valley in the north, and black on buff in the south at Nal, Quetta and Kulli; and at Amri in Sind, where typologically the earliest sherds have occurred.[57]

Now it is in both the Kulli culture in the foothills of Southern Baluchistan, established in Makran before 3000 B.C., and in the Zhob valley culture in the north, that numerous clay figurines of women have been found. Those in the Kulli sites are splayed at the waist in a flat-bottomed pedestal, the arms are bent with hands on the hips, but where the breasts are shown at all they are not unduly exaggerated. This applies to the rest of the maternal organs and features. The faces are grotesque caricatures fashioned in clay with eyes made from pellets, the hair is elaborately dressed and either plaited or kept in place by a fillet. Oval pendants resembling cowrie shells sometimes hang from three rows of necklaces below which are strings of beads reaching to the waist, each having a pendant. Over the ears are conical ornaments, and on the wrists are several bangles, repeated on the left arm at the elbow.

In the cultures to the north and north-east of Quetta grouped

round the Zhob river which flows north-eastwards towards
the Indus plain, a number of identical terracotta figurines have
been found in several sites (e.g. Dabar Kot, Periano Ghundai,
Sur Jangal and Mogul Ghundai) in this red ware province,
although they have not been recorded in the best-known tell,
that of Rana Ghundai, the stratification of which was investigated by Brigadier E. J. Ross between 1935 and 1940.[58]
Elsewhere they belong to the third occupation in the Rana
Ghundai sequence, assignable perhaps to the third millennium
B.C., and consist of clay female figures, ending at the waist in
small pedestals, as in the Kulli series, and adorned with necklaces. But as Professor Piggott points out, the heads are hooded
with a coif or shawl, the foreheads are high and smooth, the
noses are owl-like and beak-shaped, the eye-holes are circular,
the mouths slits, and the breasts are more exaggerated than in
their southern counterparts.[59]

In style and features they are so uniform that Sir Aurel Stein
conjectures that they might have been intended to represent
some tutelary goddess,[60] while Professor Piggott concludes
that they seem to be 'a grim embodiment of the mother-goddess
who is also the guardian of the dead—an underworld deity
concerned alike with the crops and the seed-corn buried beneath
the earth'.[61] That they had a fertility significance is shown by
the representation of a phallus carved in stone at the mound of
Mogul Ghundai nea the left bank of the Zhob river, south-
west of Fort Sandeman, and at the neighbouring mound of
Periano Ghundai on the right bank of the river where a vulva
is depicted with great prominence.[62]

The Indus Valley

In Sind and the Punjab the remarkably homogeneous urban
civilization that flourished there from 2500 to 1500 B.C. which
has been revealed by the excavations in and around the Indus
valley at Harappa, Mohenjo-daro and Chanhu-daro since
1922, the quantity of terracotta female figurines brought to light
suggest that as in Baluchistan, the Goddess cult in some form
was established in what is now generally known as the

'Harappa culture'. The majority of the statuettes are nudes except for a small skirt, sometimes ornamented with medallions, secured by a girdle round the loins, which may have been made of beads like the girdle so constructed found at Mohenjo/ daro.[63] A curious fan/shaped head/dress with pannier/like side projections varying in size are a feature of many of these figurines.[64] Black stains on the panniers, which may have been made by smoke, has led Dr Mackay to surmise that they were used sometimes as small lamps in the practice of a cult con/ nected with the Mother/goddess, of whom the statues, he thinks, were an image.[65]

In support of this conjecture similar head/dresses, as will be considered, recur in Syria and the Eastern Mediterranean in this context, and an abundance of jewellery, including bead necklaces with pendants, ornamental collars with metal rings, armlets and bracelets of spiral wire, finger rings and anklets of beads or embossed metal.[66] Some of the little clay figurines in the higher levels were seated with hands clasped round the knees, roughly modelled and devoid altogether of ornaments.[67] Others were in postures suggesting that they were engaged in a ritual dance such as is shown by the figures on a faience plaque.[68] On one female figure an erection on the top of the head might represent horns, though they could be doves, an important emblem in the Goddess cult.[69] Horned/masks having a magico/religious function have also been dis/ covered.[70]

So far as the facial features are concerned flat pellets of clay slightly oval or of almond/shape serve the purpose of eyes, the pupil being only very rarely incised. The nose was produced by pinching the clay. The mouth is indicated by an incision with or without any attempt to produce lips by the addition of a grooved narrow strip of clay. The elaborate head/dress precluded the fashioning of the ears. Many of the images have been badly damaged, perhaps because only those which had been broken were thrown away, the rest, as a treasured posses/ sion, having been carried off with the domestic equipment when the city was deserted, like the 'household gods' procured and concealed by Rachel in the Jacob story in the book of Genesis.[71] To enhance their life-giving properties most of them were painted over with a red slip or wash, as are many Hindu figurines today; a practice that was current also in Ancient Egypt, Mesopotamia and Malta in prehistoric times.[72]

These sacred images in all probability represented, as Sir John Marshall says, 'a goddess with attributes very similar to those of the great Mother-goddess, "the Lady of Heaven", and a special patroness of women'.[73] Therefore, they may have been kept in the dwellings and streets of Mohenjo-daro and Harappa as a tutelary divinity, very much as the Mother-goddess is still the guardian of the house and village in India presiding over childbirth and daily needs. As household deities they were preserved perhaps in a niche in the wall in almost every house in the ancient Indus valley cities,[74] and held in the same veneration as are their successors today among the illiterate population perennially faced with the perpetual struggle to bring forth and to feed and nurture the ever-increasing family amid all the hazard of outrageous fortune.

Whether or not the goddess or goddesses who presided over the mystery of birth and its concomitants had a male counter-part as a son and partner cannot be determined from the available evidence. In the Harappa culture male gods, frequently horned, recur,[75] but they do not appear to have been prevalent and seldom are brought into conjunction with goddesses in the iconography, as is also the case in respect of the village goddesses in modern India.[76] On pottery they are also rare, and unlike the skirted female statuettes are entirely nude, though on one of the male figures red lines on the arms and neck may represent bangles and a scarf necklace.[77] Usually they are bare-headed or have merely a simple fillet round the forehead to keep the hair in place.[78] No attempt has been made to conceal the sexual organs.

That at least some of these male figures represent a deity is suggested by their adornment. In the well-known carved seal from Mohenjo-daro showing a three-faced male god sitting in what has been interpreted as the *yoga* posture, heels together

and arms outstretched, is covered with bangles. On the chest
are triangular necklaces or torques resembling the figurines
from Kulli and Zhob in Baluchistan, and on the arms a
number of bracelets. A pair of horns crowns the head with a
tall head-dress between them, and at the end of the waistband
a projection which might be the phallus. The figure has three
faces, one in front and two in profile, and on either side are
four animals; an elephant and tiger on his right, and a rhinoceros and buffalo on his left. Below the dais on which it is
seated are two deer.[79] Both the form and symbolism indicate
that here is portrayed a prototype of the Hindu god Shiva in
his aspect as Pasupati, Lord of the Beasts and Prince of *Yoga*.
Moreover, on several other seals a similar nude figure occurs
associated with the *pipal*-tree (i.e. the sacred fig-tree) and cult
animals.[80] One of them has three faces, and all have bangles
and head-dresses and horns. The flowers or leaves rising from
the head between the horns suggest a fertility motif.

On another seal a horned goddess is represented in the midst
of a *pipal*-tree before which a horned figure is kneeling. Behind
is a goat with a human face, and a row of seven females, each
wearing a sprig on the head and a long pigtail behind, but
without horns.[81] Since the *pipal* is still regarded as a life-giving
sacred tree to which offerings are made by women to secure
male offspring, the practice may have been derived from the
Harappa culture, where it seems to have been firmly established
as one of the aspects of the cult, to which these scenes bear
witness and in which male and female generative organs, often
in association with the *pipal*, have such a prominent place.

In addition to these seal-amulets and figurines a number of
limestone conical *lingas* have been found at Harappa comparable to the phallic emblems from Mogul Ghundai, and still in
use in India among the Saivites for life-bestowing purposes. In
the light of the Shiva figure from Mohenjo-daro that these cones
were cult objects employed as fertility charms and amulets is
by no means improbable,[82] though it is possible that some of
the smooth worn large stones at Mohenjo-daro in dwellings,
and some of the beautifully fashioned cones in chalcedony

carnelian, lapis lazuli, alabaster, faience and limestone, could have been 'chessmen' used in board-games. But the more realistically modelled examples[83] unquestionably are phalli, just as certain large undulating stone rings represent their female counterpart (i.e. *yoni* or vulva),[84] sometimes brought into conjunction to indicate the union of the two organs, as, for example, in the *yoni* bases of *linga*. Thus, a conventionalized *linga* in yellow sandstone at Harappa with finely cut coils and necklaces may have had a *yoni* base, and six occurred in an earthenware jar with some small pieces of shell, a unicorn seal, stone pestles and a stone palette. Some miniature conical baetyls have a sort of ring round the body which has been regarded as a possible *yoni*.[85]

It would seem, therefore, that the widespread veneration of the *linga* in the worship of Shiva in Hindu India is very deeply laid in the prehistoric substratum of the Harappa culture, going back to the third millennium B.C. in the form of large and small cone-shaped *linga* and *yoni* rings like their Hindu counter-parts. Behind this phallic cult lay the mystery of birth and the predominance of the female statuettes over male figures in the earliest levels of all the cultures in which they occur in the Ancient East, from the Indus valley to the Mediterranean, suggests that attention at first was concentrated on the feminine and maternal aspects of the process of generation, whether or not its divine personification (when it occurred) was a virgin or mother-goddess or goddesses. Generally speaking, when deities of this nature emerged, in their earliest representations they were not accompanied with a consort or male figure of any kind, young or mature. Their primary function was to promote fecundity in its several aspects and attributes, to guard the sacred portal through which life entered the world, and not infrequently to play their part in the care and revivification of the dead, though in the Harappa culture they do not appear to have assumed this role. There, as in Baluchistan, they were connected essentially with household shrines and the well-being of home and family life, sometimes it would seem presiding over the village or city as the cult developed.

EGYPT AND THE EASTERN MEDITERRANEAN

In the Nile valley three small figures of women have been found in graves of the Badarian Age. One is very narrow waisted and somewhat steatopygous, the breasts are small and pointed, the arms folded in front and a wide sexual triangle has horizontal lines. The second has little waist, no steatopygy, the breasts are long and pendulous, the triangle is narrow with some vertical lines, and the nipples are clearly marked, as are the nose and eyes. The third figure is very crudely fashioned without arms and legs, and the pendulous breasts are broken. The triangle is wide and shallow, having diagonal lines, the waist is defined, the buttocks are steatopygous, the head is small with a string of beads in front of the neck, and there are three chevrons in the centre of the back, resembling in several of these respects similar Amratian statuettes.[86]

These figurines of the so-called steatopygous type are all female, and Petrie links them with the Palaeolithic Brassempouy examples.[87] They are almost all from the Early Period (SD. 31–34), and do not recur until Protodynastic times when they are plentiful at Hierakonpolis and Abydos.[88] Pendant breasts are more common than thickening of the buttocks, and the resemblances are most marked among the pottery and clay figures where the sexual triangle and narrow waists are recurrent features. Whether or not the steatopygous group belong to an earlier race, as Petrie contends,[89] they fall into line with those of the Venus tradition, and are combined with a slim variety as elsewhere.

Thus, in Cyprus, which from Mycenaean times became the easternmost outpost of Aegean culture,[90] while fiddle-shaped squatting and flat figurines in stone have been found in the Chalcolithic city at Khirokitia (between 4000 and 3500 B.C.) with practically no indication of sex,[91] in the Erimi culture at the transition from the Chalcolithic to the Early Bronze Age, the genitalia are pronounced, sometimes with painted ornamentation in the terracotta female statuettes. As at Arpachiyah in Northern Iraq, they were discovered in the neighbourhood of the tholoi and in association with fertility amulets and

ornaments, which include a model of a goddess on a pendant.[92]
They are true to type and may have been introduced as a result
of culture contact with Western Asia, where, as we have
seen, the cult was so firmly established in the Chalcolithic
period.[93]

In the first city of Troy (*c.* 3000 or 2750 B.C.), occupying a
key position on the Hellespont as the meeting point of trade
routes by land and sea from Mesopotamia to the Aegean across
the Anatolian plateau and up the Straits, a relatively large
figure of the Goddess type, roughly heart shaped, has been
found carved in low relief on a stele flanking the gateway,
accentuated by the arrangement of the hair, represented by a
series of holes on either side of the head. The nose is rather
long, and the left eye and mouth are marked giving an owl like
appearance. To the left is what seems to be the shaft of a staff
or sceptre, with a spherical knob. Below the face to the right
further carving can be detected, possibly an arm or hand.[94] In
the second city (*c.* 2600 B.C.) jars with similar figures having
Anatolian and Sumerian affinities recur,[95] while in the first
four of the superimposed ancient towns of Thermi in Lesbos,
which are parallel to the first city of Troy, there are links with
the Troad, Southern and Central Anatolia and Mesopotamia;
also with the Cyclades and Thessaly.

The stone statuettes are highly conventionalized in the low
(i.e. earlier) Thermi towns, the fiddle type predominating.
Later they were replaced by terracotta figurines in clay, badly
fired and often fragmentary. Some are dressed and ornamented,
though the head and arms often may be missing. Straps often
are crossed across the breasts, and meet low down at the back.
The punctured dots on the chest and shoulders may represent
a necklace. Sometimes when the sex is indicated the nose and
breasts are rendered plastically, but generally the generative
organs are emphasized if shown at all. The hips may be
angular or curved, and the legs divided with the arms folded
on the breasts. At the neck and below the waist are fringes or
lines of embroidery, perhaps a belt or collar to the dress.
Pendants also have been made anthropomorphic by the

addition of breasts and perforated for suspension at the top. The fiddle-shaped examples sometimes were punctured with holes, apparently for the insertion of some form of ornamentation.[96]

In the Cyclades, where the culture reached its height in the third millennium B.C., very crude fiddle figurines in marble occur in the poorer prehistoric graves at Antiparos, but the technique improves in those from the cemetery to the south-east. The sexual triangle is invariably represented on the female statuettes, and in one case the sitting posture is indicated. From Amorgos came a female torso with the arm of another person round her back, and in some of the graves were single marble legs. The head invariably was pointed, resembling the blade of a stone implement, and everywhere there was an excess of female statuettes over male, suggesting, it has been concluded, that a Goddess cult was practised.[97]

On the mainland, except in the case of a stone head from a mound at the village of Topuslar in North-eastern Greece, where the features were indicated plastically, the Thessalian stone figurines bear little or no resemblance to those in the Cyclades. This also applies to the fiddle-shaped variety where the neck is much larger than in the Cycladic types and the features are not represented plastically.[98] The majority of the terracotta examples are female and fragmentary. Those belonging to the First and Second Neolithic periods are either standing steatopygous figures with long necks and hands touching the breasts, or seated with the thighs and buttocks rather less highly developed, and the hands sometimes placed on the knees instead of on the breasts. In one instance the woman is shown seated on a four-legged stool nursing a baby. They are all well made and polished, care having been given to detail in the rendering of the hair and other features in contrast to the shapeless degenerate type at the end of the Second (Neolithic B) period, and in the Third or Chalcolithic period, until they come to an end in the Bronze Age. In technique the terracotta figurines recovered from the site at Dimini near the Gulf of Volo, which flourished from the Second to the Fourth Thessalian prehistoric periods, are inferior to those from Sesklo, Tsangli and the other deposits where the First period was represented.[99]

Since the affinities of these Neolithic Thessalian figurines are with Thrace and the north rather than with the metal-users in the Troad, Anatolia, the Aegean basin and Crete, it is possible that they represent an independent phase in the development and diffusion of the cult from the Near East when generations of peaceful farming communities lived in relative isolation from their warlike neighbours until they were invaded by the people who fortified Dimini and the associated sites, some of whom may have come from Vinča on the loess bank of the Danube and the surrounding district between Belgrade and Nis in what is now Yugoslavia. Here too female figurines in clay and stone abounded crudely modelled with the genital organs emphasized. The older solid statuettes are steatopygous, standing or else seated, sometimes on a throne. The face is triangular and in the more developed varieties the nose and eyes are indicated by incised lines or painting, except in the decadent examples where it is bird-shaped with a monstrous nose. The upper part of the body is nude with or without ornamentation, and two square-cut loincloths hanging from a belt. The connexions in type and technique are with the Aegean, the Cyclades and the Morava and Vardar valleys with Anatolian and the Vinča-Koros region.[100]

Minoan Crete

It was, however, in Minoan Crete that the cult found its fullest expression in the Eastern Mediterranean. There in the earliest Neolithic stratum at Knossos all the principal types of clay figurines in South-eastern Europe, the Aegean basin, Anatolia and Western Asia are represented, though it is mainly to the squatting and sitting varieties that the majority belong.[101] Invariably the head has been broken off or is a protuberance until in the succeeding period in Central Crete attempts were made to reproduce facial features. In a sub-Neolithic marble specimen steatopygy is indicated by means of an expanded contour suggesting the shortened legs of the crouching type, and showing affinities with the Western Asiatic types, notably those of Northern Syria and North Iraq.

Since it was from Asia Minor that the earliest Neolithic influences were felt in Crete about 4000 B.C., there can be no reasonable doubt that it was from these centres that the Goddess emblems were introduced together with the double axe and the dove, both of which, as we have seen, occurred in this context among the Arpachiyahians and elsewhere in the Ancient Middle East in the Chalcolithic period, a thousand years before the cult was established in the Eastern Mediterranean. When this was accomplished, however, Crete became virtually its cradleland in the west, and later it was represented as the original home of the Phrygian mysteries of Cybele (e.g. Rhea).[102] Here the Minoan Goddess was depicted in clay and porcelain as the Earth/mother, the Mountain/mother, the Mistress of trees and the Lady of wild beasts with outstretched or uplifted arms, often holding or encircled by snakes, and clad in a skirt with flounces, wearing a high crown. Sometimes she was accom/panied by a priestess or a facsimile of herself, together with the double axe, horns of consecration and votive garments.[103] On some of the seals and signets she is represented as seated beneath her tree receiving offerings of the first/fruits of her bounty, or in later Minoan scenes (*c.* 1500 B.C.) as the hunting goddess accompanied by lions and with a spear in her hand, or replaced by a pillar or mountain standing between rampant lions.[104]

But these Minoan figures belong to a stage in the develop/ment of the cult when the Mother/goddess had emerged as a clearly defined personification of the female principle in a manner not portrayed in the Neolithic 'idols' or the Palaeo/lithic Venuses. That they all stand in the same tradition is suggested by their technological affinities, their distribution and magico/religious significance and functions. Moreover, as Evans has pointed out, it can scarcely be a mere coincidence that all the various centres from the Aegean to Elam in which they occur became 'the later scenes of the cult, under varying names and attributes, of a series of Great Goddesses, who often combined ideas of motherhood and virginity'. Furthermore, he maintained that 'in Crete itself it is impossible to dissociate these primitive images from those that appear in the shrines and sanctuaries of the Great Minoan Goddess'.[105]

It may be that originally they were symbolic of the maternal attributes and functions of womanhood without any very specific personification in an all-embracing Goddess of fecundity, or in that of a series of separate and independent fertility divinities. Nevertheless, they represent the antecedents of the Goddess cult giving expression to the deeply rooted mystery of birth and generation, of fertility and regeneration. With the development of conceptual thought and of technical skill the special attributes and functions associated with the Mother-goddess became deified, differentiated and personalized in a being or beings constituting the major aspects of the generative process in its manifold forms and phases, with its various symbols and emblems. The mode of portrayal necessarily has been conditioned to some extent by the medium employed (e.g. bas-reliefs, cylinder seals and signets, terracotta votive offerings, clay figurines, potsherds and sarcophagi) as well as by the purposes for which they were designed.

WESTERN EUROPE
Malta

On the sacred island of Malta, which from the third millennium B.C. appears to have been the meeting-place of a number of streams of culture from Western Asia, Egypt, the Eastern Mediterranean, the Balkans and Italy,[106] an obese female statue of Western Asiatic type was of immense proportions. It stood in the main court of the temple at Hal Tarxien, over 7 feet high, arrayed in a fluted skirt, with thick pear-shaped legs. In spite of its fragmentary condition it obviously closely resembled the naked steatopygous headless figurines which have been found in considerable numbers at Hagar Qim and at the great rock-cut Hypogeum at Hal Saflieni. In attendance apparently were priests dressed in long skirts and short wigs like Chaldean officials, offering before the statue burnt sacrifices on the near-by altar. Blood would seem to have been poured into a cylindrical stone vessel with a hollow base, decorated with pit marks on the outside and a deep cavity at the top to receive it, while incense was burnt in the cup-shaped cylindrical tops of pillars.[107]

The Maltese Neolithic megalithic 'temples', like the tholoi at Arpachiyah, appear to have been primarily sanctuaries before they were ossuaries, judging from their structure, decoration and cult objects. Thus, in the vast Hypogeum of Hal Saflieni with its subterranean domed vaults decorated with spirals, caves and chambers with huge trilithons in front of them, contained in addition to some 7,000 interments, shell necklaces, amulets, clay and alabaster figurines of the naked steatopygous type, comparable to those found at Haġar Qim and in the Tarxien group, together with a well-baked clay model of a woman lying asleep on a couch with the head resting on her arm supported by a pillow.[108] This may indicate, as Zammit suggests, that it was used for the practice of incubation in the consultation of oracles, with cubicles for devotees who slept there to have their dreams interpreted by the priests in the service of the Goddess, since emblems of her cult abound in the sanctuary. The breasts of the sleeping figure are large and prominent, the abdomen is transversely grooved and the hips are enormous. Above the flounced skirt the body is naked, and conforms in all essentials to the Tarxien and Haġar Qim type. With it was a similar terracotta model, very fat, naked to the waist and showing the remains of red pigment. It lies on its face, and although the head is missing the pillow remains.[109]

It would seem, therefore, that in these great shrines with their Western Asiatic affinities, a complex and composite cultus was practised centred in the worship of the Goddess, so deeply laid, as we have seen, in the Tell Halaf and associated cultures. The Neolithic pottery in the sites, which conforms to a Near Eastern Anatolian and Cretan tradition rather than to that of the Eastern Mediterranean and the Aegean,[110] supports the conclusion that the cult connexions were with Western Asia by way of the hinterland of South-west Asia Minor and Thessaly, though there are indications also of Neolithic Cretan,

Cycladic and Siculan influences having been felt before it reached the sacred isle (Malta) about 3000 B.C., prior to the introduction of metal of which there is no trace in the Maltese temples.

The Iberian Peninsula

Passing westwards it spread to the Iberian Peninsula, where in Almeria it produced vast quantities of female figurines, many of which have been recovered from the megalithic tombs and huts at Los Millares on the Andarax river. So numerous, in fact, were they that in addition to their prominence in the cult of the dead they would seem to have found a place in the regular sacred domestic equipment of every household, as at Mohenjo-daro in the Indus valley. Here, however, it is the Aegean type of stone statuette that occurs together with schist plaques without faces, bone or ivory cylinders and bovine phalanges decorated with 'owl-eyes'. Often they are stylized almost beyond recognition, and they are never as excessively corpulent as the Maltese figures. At El Garcel on the high ground near the Mediterranean coast of South-east Spain, in a district rich in copper and silver and lead, a small fiddle-shaped 'idol' characteristic of the Eastern Mediterranean tradi-tion suggests that the first Neolithic settlers on the mainland of Western Europe (*c.* 2700 B.C.) were familiar with the cult which doubtless they brought with them from the Eastern Mediterranean islands and the Fertile Crescent, their cultural affinities being with those of the Badarians, the Merimdians and the Fayum. Similar examples have recurred at El Castillo near Pavia and Alemtejo in Portugal.[111]

From El Garcel the cult spread to the south-west of the Iberian Peninsula where marble cylindrical idols with incised face and eyes became a characteristic feature distinct from the Almerian phalange-bones with 'owl-eyes'. The Aegean type of stone figurine simplified into a flat plaque-figure of schist common in Almeria[112] recurs in collective tombs on the plateau of Granada in the neighbourhood of Guardix, Gor and Gorafe.[113] Similar designs are incised on croziers and plaque-idols in the Palmella graves in Portugal in addition to phalange and Almerian statuettes. On the Portuguese high lands schist and marble figurines are among the funerary furni-ture in the slab-cists,[114] and on the north-eastern Spanish coast phalanges recur sporadically in Catalonia.[115] But like the mega-lithic monuments with which the cult was intimately associated in the Iberian Peninsula, in the hinterland and the north, the more conventionalized and degenerate does it become.

North-west Europe

That in its diffusion along the Atlantic littoral and from the Pyrenees to the Seine–Oise–Marne (S.O.M.) region in France the worship of the Mother-goddess was an integral element in the megalithic culture is shown by the recurrence of its symbolism in the form of statue-menhirs and similar designs in Brittany, the Paris Basin, the Marne and the Channel Islands. Thus, the female figures with breasts and U-shaped necklaces in Aveyron, the Tarn and Gard, and in Guernsey conform to the Goddess tradition, while the Abbé Breuil has detected what he believes to be the face and features of the Goddess in highly conventionalized 'buckler' and 'octapus' patterns on the slabs of a tomb on the island of Gavr'inis in Southern Morbihan.[116] The centre of the cult in this region was the Seine and Oise valleys, where it was a characteristic feature of the S.O.M. culture, introduced from the south of France, Sardinia and the Balearic Isles, spreading up the Rhône valley to the Paris Basin and the chalk Downs of Champagne. Having acquired a funerary significance, thence it reached the Amorican Peninsula as the great pilgrimage centre with its Iberian contacts and extensions to the Channel Islands and the mouth of the Loire.

In its northerly diffusion it made its way across the English Channel to Britain, where it has been detected on the chalk Downs and uplands from Wessex to Devon. At Maiden Castle in Dorset a conventionalized headless torso has been found with two holes at the base for the insertion of legs, and from Windmill Hill near Avebury in Wiltshire (the site that has given its name to the Neolithic A culture in Britain) a female statuette together with phalli carved in the chalk have been recovered.[117] A carved object in bone from the Neolithic occupation level at Trundle above the Goodwood race-course in Sussex resembles a phallus,[118] and in a long barrow on Thickthorn Down, Cranbourne Chase, Dorset, a more convincing well-carved example has been discovered in association with the Windmill Hill culture.[119] Similar finds have been recorded at Whitehawk Camp on the Brighton race-course with its causewayed camp typical of the Windmill Hill Neolithic A culture, and in flint-mines at Blackpatch on the Sussex Downs.

In the flint-mines at Grimes Graves in Norfolk an obese figure of a pregnant woman carved in chalk was brought to light in 1939 in Pit 15 with a phallus below her, also carved in the chalk on the left side. In front was an erection composed of blocks of flint in the form of a triangle with a chalk cup at the base opposite the female figure, and seven deer antler picks on the 'altar', perhaps as a votive offering. This remarkable ritual deposit has been interpreted as a shrine of an Earth-goddess placed in a sterile shaft to restore its productivity, or to make the mine as a whole a rich flint-bed,[120] thereby extending the idea of the earth's abundance to its mineral content. The affinity of this statuette, however, is with the Palaeolithic Venuses rather than with the Iberian technique, while its associated phallic symbolism suggests Anatolian and Minoan influences in contradistinction to those of the Mediterranean littoral and Western Europe, where the mystery of birth and generation, and of fertility in all its forms and phases, found expression primarily in the various antecedents of the Goddess cult and its tradition.

CHAPTER II

The Goddess Cult
in Mesopotamia and Egypt

WHETHER or not the very ancient cult centred in the mystery of birth and fecundity in its Palaeolithic and Neolithic modes of expression can be rightly described as that of a single goddess or of several goddesses personifying and controlling all the processes of generation and fertility, it can be safely asserted that it was in this context that with the rise of agriculture and the keeping of flocks and herds in the Ancient Near East that the figure of such a divine being or beings emerged and became clearly defined. In the first instance it seems to have been as the unmarried Goddess that she became the dominant influence from India to the Mediterranean. Thus, in Mesopotamia, as Langdon pointed out, whereas 'the intensity of the worship of other gods depended somewhat upon the political importance of the cities where their chief cult existed, before the orders of the gods of nature arose, before the complex theology of emana-tions supplied the religion with a vast pantheon, in which the masculine element predominated, the productive powers of the earth had supplied in prehistoric times a divinity in which the female element predominated'.[1]

THE MESOPOTAMIAN MOTHER-GODDESS

With the establishment of husbandry and domestication, how-ever, as the function of the male in the process of generation became more apparent and was recognized to be a vital element in the situation, the life-producing Mother, be it as Mother-earth or in any other capacity, was assigned a spouse to play his essential role as the begetter, even though, as in Mesopotamia, he remained the servant or son of the Goddess, the producer of all life. Moreover, when the birth cult was brought into relation with the seasonal cycle and its vegetation ritual in agricultural communities, such as those of the Tigris-Euphrates valley, the Earth-goddess was conceived as the generative power in nature as a whole and so she became responsible for the periodic renewal of life in the spring after the blight of the winter or the summer drought. Therefore, she assumed the form of a many-sided goddess, both mother and bride, destined to be known by many names and epithets such as Ninhursaga, Mah, Ninmah, Inanna-Ishtar, Nintu or Aruru. Thus, in Sumerian mythology the Goddess Ninhursaga, 'the mother of the land', was Ninsikil-la, 'the pure lady', until she was approached by Enki, the Water-god of wisdom, and gave birth to a number of deities. Then she became Nintu ama Kalamma, 'the lady who gives birth, the mother of the land'. When she had accepted him she was Dam-gal-nunna, 'the great spouse of the prince' (i.e. Enki), and having conceived as the fertile soil and given birth to vegetation, she was Nin-hur-sag-ga, 'the lady of the mountain', where nature manifested its powers of fecundity in the spring on its lush slopes.[2]

Inanna-Ishtar and Dumuzi-Tammuz

Similarly, Inanna, although as a marriageable girl she was represented as having accepted the divine farmer Enkidu for her husband and rejected the advances of the divine shepherd Dumuzi,[3] nevertheless, as the Sumerian counterpart of Ishtar, her nuptials with Dumuzi-Tammuz were celebrated annually at the spring festival in Isin to awaken the vital forces in nature. Whatever may be the interpretation of the relative merits of the shepherd and the farmer as her respective wooers in the mythopoeic tradition, the ritual situation required the union of the goddess who incarnated fertility in general with the god who incarnated the creative powers of spring in order to reawaken the dormant earth and the process of fecundity at this season. Therefore, it was her marriage with Dumuzi that gave expression to the vegetation cycle. As 'the faithful son of the waters that came forth from the earth' he was essentially the youthful suffering god who was dependent upon his spouse-mother, the Goddess Inanna-Ishtar. Annually he died in the normal rotation of the seasons and passed into the land of darkness and death from which there was no return for ordinary mortals. Inanna, however, as queen of heaven (being among her many matrimonial alliances the wife of Anu, the Mesopotamian god of the sky), had determined to visit the nether regions in order to rescue her lover-son.

Arraying herself in all her regalia, and equipped with the appropriate divine decrees, she set forth on her perilous quest instructing her messenger Ninshubur to raise the alarm in the assembly hall of the gods and in their principal cities on earth should she not return within three days. Arriving at the gate of the grim abode, she gained admittance on false pretences, but, having been recognized, she was led through its seven gates, losing at each of them part of her robes and jewels until on reaching the lapis lazuli temple of Ereshkigal, queen of the underworld, she was stark naked and promptly turned into a corpse by 'the look of death' that was fastened upon her. On the fourth day Ninshubur followed his instructions, and Enki, the Water-god of wisdom, devised a plan to restore her to life. Fashioning two sexless creatures, he sent them to the nether regions with the 'food of life' and the 'water of life' to sprinkle them on her corpse. This they did and she revived. Accom-panied by some of its shades, bogies and harpies, she left the land of the dead and ascended to the earth, where with her ghostly companions she wandered from city to city in Sumer.[4]

Here the Sumerian version of the myth breaks off, but as it follows so closely the Semitic 'Descent of Ishtar to the Nether Regions' inscribed on Akkadian tablets dating from the first millennium B.C., of which clearly it is the prototype, there can be little doubt that the sequel was not very different from that in the later story. Thus, some new material now indicates that Inanna did bring with her the shepherd-god Dumuzi on her return, but because he did not show any signs of mourning for her descent to rescue him, 'seating himself on a high-seat', she handed him over to the demons, presumably to carry him back whence he had come. But here, again, the text breaks off at the crucial point.[5] Nevertheless, it is clear that Inanna was essentially the Sumerian counterpart of the Akkadian Ishtar, and in this capacity she stood in much the same relation to Dumuzi as did Ishtar to Tammuz, the embodiment of the creative powers of spring and the personification of the autumnal decline in the seasonal cycle. In the Semitic myth, however, although the precise purpose for which Ishtar visited her sister Ereshkigal in the nether regions is not specified, it would appear to have been to rescue the shepherd-god Tammuz, since it seems that it was their joint return that restored the blight that had fallen on the land during her absence.[6]

Thus, in the Tammuz liturgies, and subsequently in the Annual Festival when Marduk had assumed a Tammuz role on replacing Enlil as head of the pantheon after the city of Babylon had become the capital (*c.* 1728 B.C.), this theme of the suffering god and the sorrowing goddess was enacted, accompanied with bitter wailing and the singing of dirges over the effigy of the dead god, for the scorched earth of summer seemed to threaten a return of the desolation when Ishtar wandered in barren fields and empty sheepfolds while her lover-son was in the underworld.[7] In the laments of the priests and people the cry of the suffering youthful god was echoed until he was released by the Goddess and restored to the upper world as her 'resurrected child'. Then sorrow was turned into joy and defeat into victory which at the Annual Festival was celebrated by a dramatic re-enactment of the primeval cosmic battle between the beneficent powers led by Marduk and the hosts of chaos under Tiamat, the imprisonment of Marduk in a mountain (i.e. the land of the dead), his subsequent release and reunion with the Goddess.

The Sacred Marriage of the Goddess and the King

In this recreative ritual Sumerian rulers played the part of Dumuzi-Tammuz, incarnating the life-giving forces of spring through union with Inanna-Ishtar, the source of all life, by engaging in a sacred marriage with the queen or a priestess to restore fecundity in nature. Thus, in a hymn to Ishtar as the planet Venus written for the cult of the deified king of Isin-Dagan as Tammuz, the third king of the Amorite dynasty (*c.* 2258–2237 B.C.), there are references to his enjoying the amours of the Mother-goddess at the season of her return from the land of the dead, bringing Tammuz with her. Images of the king and the Goddess lay side by side on a marble bed in the sanctuary, and when the union had been consummated the king became the symbol of life and death, having thereby acquired the status of the dying and reviving god.[8] But throughout the Goddess is represented as taking the initiative. It was to her 'far-famed temple' that the king went, bringing to her cakes 'to set the table for the feast', and it was she who embraced her beloved husband who was subservient to her will and enjoyed the favours she was pleased to bestow upon him.

The prosperity of the New Year and the bounty of the sacred marriage were vouchsafed by the Goddess, her consort being merely the instrument she employed to bestow her gifts. This has led Frankfort to conclude that it was only those kings were deified who had been commanded by a goddess to share her couch.[9] But whether or not this rule was universally or widely observed, unquestionably the sacred marriage of a local ruler to a goddess was of fundamental importance in the Sumerian New Year celebrations as a ritual observance to secure the revival of nature in the spring.

In Mesopotamia 'mother earth' was the inexhaustible source of new life. Therefore, the divine power manifest in fertility in all its manifold forms was personified in the Goddess who was regarded as the incarnation of the reproductive forces in nature and the mother of the gods and of mankind. It was she who renewed vegetation, promoted the growth of the crops and the propagation of man and beast. In her Inanna-Ishtar guise her marriage with the shepherd-god Dumuzi or Tammuz, who incarnated the creative powers of spring, was held to symbolize and effect the renewal of life at the turn of the year, delivering the earth from the blight of sterility. But this union was only achieved and consummated after the perennial struggle between the two opposed forces in nature, those of fecundity and barren-ness, had been successfully accomplished and Tammuz had been rescued from the land of the dead in the fullness of his virile manhood. It was upon this restoration of the 'resurrected child' of the Goddess that the revival of the new life springing forth from the parched ground depended.

The Akitu *Festival at Babylon*

When Babylon became the capital and Marduk replaced Tammuz as the central male deity in the Annual Festival, known in Akkadian as the *Akitu*, held in spring during the first eleven days of the month of Nisan, the king played the leading role. This involved in addition to an elaborate series of purificatory rites and the recitation of the story of creation (*Enuma elish*), his abdication and reinstallation on the fifth day in the shrine of Marduk. There before the statue of the god he was stripped of his royal insignia and diverted of all his regalia, struck on the cheek by the high-priest and forced to his knees and made to declare that he had not been negligent regarding the divinity of 'the lord of the lands', or of having destroyed Babylon. He was then re-established in his office, having made a negative confession ('I have not been negligent', etc.), just as on the sixth or seventh day Marduk, his divine counterpart, was released by his son Nabu from the mountain (i.e. the underworld) in which he had been imprisoned. Thus, on seals of the Sargonic Age in the middle of the third millen-nium B.C. fighting groups are shown which may refer to the battle waged during the Festival to free the god. Similarly, the Goddess seated on a mountain from which the head, arms and legs of the imprisoned deity project, seems to depict Inanna-Ishtar seeking and leading forth Tammuz-Marduk from his mountain-grave.[10] The god miraculously revived is shown emerging from the ground, assisted by the Goddess, while another god pulls up and destroys the vegetation upon the mountain, personifying the sun whose rays in summer are inimical to all life.

In the *Akitu* celebration after the release of Marduk and the reinstatement of the king, the statues of the various gods taking part in the Festival were assembled in the Chamber of Destinies on the eighth day to confer upon their leader (Marduk) their combined strength for the conquest of the forces of death and to determine the 'destinies' during the forthcoming year. The resuscitated sovereign, having received a fresh outpouring of divine vitality, conducted the statue of Marduk in a triumphal procession to the Festival House (*Bit akitu*) outside the city. At this point the statements in the liturgical texts and the inscriptions of the Neo-Babylonia kings are confused, but it is not improbable that it was in the Festival House that the primeval battle was enacted between Marduk and Tiamat, depicted by Sennacherib on its copper doors, the king himself personifying the 'victorious prince' who had conquered the powers of evil at the turn of the year. Thus, at the conclusion of the rites in the *bit akitu* a banquet appears to have been held to celebrate the victory, and after the return to the Esagila on the 11th of Nisan a sacred marriage between the king and a priestess, probably of the royal blood, was consummated.[11] For this purpose a shrine containing a sacred bridal chamber or chapel, called *gigunu*, was erected, apparently on one of the stages of the ziqqurat, and decorated with greenery.[12] In it the connubium was accomplished for the purpose of restoring the fertility of the fields, of the flocks and of mankind, through the intercourse of the human embodiments of the god and the goddess upon whom fecundity depended. But in this union, although the king in the capacity of Tammuz personified the generative force in nature as the husband-son of Ishtar, the Goddess was the active partner who summoned him to her couch and thereby gave him a divine but subservient status in the creative process. Thus, Lipit-Ishtar was deified as a prelude to his sacred marriage with Ishtar by being fused with a fertility god Urash after he had been appointed king of Isin by Anu, the god of the sky; and the Isin texts leave no doubt that the initiative was ascribed to the Goddess.[13]

THE GODDESS IN THE NILE VALLEY

The Egyptian Monarchy and the Goddess

In Egypt, on the other hand, it was the Pharaoh rather than the Goddess who was predominant because since he was the incarnation of the Sun-god and the living son of Osiris, from the Fifth Dynasty (*c.* 2580 B.C.) when the solar theology was established by the Heliopolitan priesthood, he exercised his life-giving functions in his own right by virtue of his divine origin and office. In all the converging traditions and mytho- logies handed down from remote prehistoric times, his divinity became so firmly established that he was the epitome of all that was divine in the Nile valley. Before the beginning of the dynastic period (*c.* 3200 B.C.) the country was divided into a number of administrative nomes ruled by local gods from whom the nomarchs (i.e. the chiefs of the clans) derived their authority. When the nome became a kingdom and the nomarch a king he was regarded as the son of the god who exercised his rule and functions by virtue of his divine status.

During the first Protodynastic civilization a group of Asiatic people arrived in the Nile valley who were worshippers of Horus, a sky deity of the falcon clan. From the neighbourhood of Koptos they made their way to the Western Delta and set up a single line of kings with a centralized administration, making Hierakonpolis in the third nome the predynastic centre of this worship. Other falcon-gods were identified with Horus, and King 'Scorpion', who probably preceded the traditional founder of the dynasty, Menes, claimed to be the incarnation of Horus. Upper Egypt, the Eastern Delta, and the desert regions, however, remained under the dominion of Seth, the indigenous god, until his worshippers were driven south by the Horus conquerors who made Edfu (Behdet) their cult centre. Henceforth Horus became known as the Behdetite, 'He of Behdet', and with the union of the 'Two Lands' (i.e. Upper and Lower Egypt) as a single nation he became the pre- eminent figure in the kingship represented as the last of the Protodynastic kings in visible form and henceforth embodied in the person of the Pharaoh upon whom he bestowed their

Horus-name. Moreover, the Falcon-god Horus is represented in the Pyramid texts as the source of life and death, of rain and of celestial fire, thereby connecting the reigning king with an ancient predynastic Sky- and Weather-god before he had been replaced by the Sun-god.

In the Eastern Delta at Busiris (Per-Usire, or Djedu), the capital of the ninth nome, the cult of Osiris, another ancient ruler who was thought to have been a deified human king, was established at an early date. This death and resurrection cultus also seems to have entered the Nile valley from the East and to have had very close affinities with that of Tammuz in Western Asia. In both the divine hero personified vegetation and water, and stood in a very intimate relationship with the Goddess associated with birth and fertility and with the king-ship. Nevertheless, the relation of Osiris to his sister-spouse Isis was very different from that of Tammuz to Ishtar, as, indeed, it was to the reigning monarch in Egypt who occupied the throne as Horus, the living son of Osiris, as against the Mesopotamian conception of the king as the instrument and servant of the Goddess. Exactly how and under what circum-stances Horus the Elder became identified with the son of Osiris is still a matter of debate. It is possible that originally Osiris was the chief and leader of the second wave of immi-grants from Western Asia who subsequently was deified after he had introduced agriculture among the indigenous people in the northern part of the Delta. At first they may have regarded him as a brother of their own god Seth and of their goddess Isis of Sebennytes, who eventually became the deified throne —the 'throne woman' who gave birth to the prototype of the living king in his Horus capacity.[14]

The Heliopolitan Ennead

In the meantime during the Second Predynastic civilization another group of intruders, coming probably from the Eastern Mediterranean, penetrated the Delta and settled at Heliopolis. As they were worshippers of Re, the Sun-god, this city which they established at the head of the Delta became the centre of

their solar theology, destined to exercise a very profound influence on the subsequent course of development of Egyptian
civilization. It was there in the Fifth Dynasty (*c.* 2580 B.C.)
that its priesthood equated the solar line of kings with their god
Atum-Re and then associated him with Osiris in the elabora-
tion of their Ennead in which the gods were grouped in pairs
derived ultimately from Atum-Re, the head of the solar
pantheon. Atum having emerged from Nun, the waters of
Chaos, at the creation and become an aspect of Re, the
personification of the sun, appearing in the form of a phoenix
on the top of the primordial 'sandhill'. This became the centre
of the earth, and on it 'the House of the Obelisk' was erected
as the great solar temple. Atum-Re then mated with himself
and produced Shu, the god of the atmosphere, and his consort
Tefnut, the goddess of moisture, from whom were born Geb,
the Earth-god, and Nut, the Sky-goddess, the parents of Osiris
and Isis and of Seth and Nephthys.

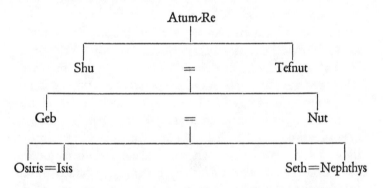

When after the unification of Upper and Lower Egypt Re
became the head of this Great Ennead of Heliopolis he combined in himself all the creative forces in nature and was
absolute in his control of his government in the Nile valley.
Therefore, in the Pyramid Age he was equated with Atum,
the original Sun-god who created out of himself the rest of the
gods standing on the Primeval Hill in the midst of the waters
of Chaos (Nun), and so Re was also accredited with begetting

the rest of the Heliopolitan Ennead. Consequently, he became the self-created Creator, the source of life and increase and the father of the gods as well as the personification of the sun and its manifold aspects.[15] Thus, he assumed the role elsewhere played by the Mother-goddess, and like her he had many names. As the begetter of the gods he was addressed as 'Creator' and 'Body' of Atum, since from him had proceeded the remaining eight gods of the Ennead, including Horus, Khepri (the rising sun) and Re-Harakhte, the youthful god of the eastern horizon, until eventually in the Eighteenth Dynasty he was worshipped with great magnificence at Karnak and Luxor as Amon-Re, 'the king of the gods', supreme in heaven and on earth.[16]

Re and Horus the Elder, however, were essentially royal celestial gods associated primarily with the throne and its stability. Osiris, on the other hand, was the god of the people who had bestowed his beneficent gifts on mankind, and after himself falling a victim of the malice of his brother Seth, he was restored to life by the aid and intervention of Isis his devoted sister-spouse, Anubis the funerary physician, and Horus his posthumous son, and so became the judge of the dead. Behind this mythology may lie the peaceful penetration of the nomadic Asiatic people who, after having settled in the eastern section of the Delta and adopted an agricultural mode of life, welded the Horus and Re groups into a confederacy with themselves and so produced a united kingdom of Lower Egypt. This accomplished, the extension of the domain of the Osiris clans to Abydos raised the hostility of the Seth group, who drove them back to the Eastern Delta and slew Osiris at Busiris, where a portion of his dismembered body was said to have been buried. The traditional mortal combat of Horus, the son of Osiris, with his uncle Seth may be a reminiscence of the predynastic tribal conflicts which resulted in the conquest of Upper Egypt by the Horus kings and the union of the 'Two Lands' in a single monarchy consolidated on the basis of a combination of the solar and Osirian theologies. This found expression in the Great Ennead in which Atum-Re continued to reign supreme, but the ancient Sky-god Horus was Osirian-ized as 'the seed of Geb' and transformed into the posthumous son of Osiris by Isis born to avenge the murder of his father. Moreover, the celestial gods and goddesses of the solar cycle were brought into relation with the earth and chthonic divinities of the Osirian tradition, and with the cult of the dead.

It was this Heliopolitan Ennead, formulated before the Pyramid texts were preserved from the Fifth Dynasty, which became the pattern followed by other towns and districts in their genealogical pantheons (e.g. those of Memphis, Hermo-polis and Thebes). Therefore, it determined the way in which the cosmic order was envisaged in Dynastic Egypt. Unlike Mesopotamia, Western Asia and the Aegean, in the Nile valley the earth was not conceived in terms of the Goddess, 'Mother-earth'. On the contrary, the earth was represented as a male god, Geb, or in the Memphite Theology as hatched from an egg fashioned by Ptah, the Supreme Creator, who in the Ennead of Memphis was elevated above Atum.[17] Simi-larly, from the dawn of Egyptian civilization it was the male god Min of Koptos who personified the generative force in nature as the bestower of procreative power, 'opening the clouds', and so giving life to vegetation.[18]

Nut and Re

It was Heaven that was regarded as a woman deified as the Goddess Nut whom, as the Goddess of the West, the Sun enters in his daily course to be reborn by her in the sky. He makes his entrance by impregnating her and his coming is greeted by her as that of 'the Bull of Heaven'—the dominating male and embodiment of virile fertility.[19] 'O Re, impregnate the body of Nut with the seed of that spirit that must be in her.'[20] Similarly, Geb, the Earth-god, was called the Bull of the Sky-goddess Nut,[21] the sky like the queen-mother was described as 'the cow who bore the bull'; the rising sun being the calf born of her each morning.[22]

Being the celestial counterpart of Nun, Nut was 'the Lady of Heaven' who gave birth to the gods, and also 'Mistress of the

Two Lands' on earth and proprietress of the dead in the under-world.[23] Like Isis, she was depicted usually with cow's horns and often in the form of a great cow with stars on her body and her legs corresponding to the four pillars at the cardinal points of the compass. The stars were her children while the souls of the dead could be seen at night on her body as stars. She was the 'one with a thousand souls' (*Kha-bewes*), but she was too remote to be an object of worship. Therefore, she had no temples though in the 'Osireion' at Abydos there were sculp-tured representations of her on the roof of a chamber behind the temple of Seti I belonging to the Nineteenth Dynasty. In course of time she absorbed the attributes of many goddesses as her various titles indicate. In one myth she was the Sky-mother who produced the Sun-god, and sometimes Re was shown seated on her back. At Denderah she was identified with Hathor, the Mother-goddess *par excellence* whose name means 'the House of Horus'; the designation of that part of the sky which is called Qebhu.[24]

Hathor and Horus

Worshipped in the form of a cow, Hathor became the mother of Horus the Elder, and later one of his many wives when all the great goddesses became one of her forms and attributes worshipped under different names.[25] She was not, however, exclusively the husband of Horus, as Junker has contended,[26] since originally she was his mother, just as Ishtar was the mother of Tammuz. She was never, however, the spouse of Osiris or the mother of his son Horus, the posthumous off-spring born of Isis. It was not until all reproductive goddesses became identified with Hathor that Isis was equated with her and adopted her horns, when as the 'throne woman' it was she (Isis) who was said to give birth to the prototype of the living king in his Horus capacity. 'Thou art Horus, son of Osiris, the eldest god, son of Hathor',[27] notwithstanding the assertion that the son of Hathor was the celestial Horus. Since both goddesses exercised maternal functions and were associated with the composite deity Horus, who was so intimately connected with the kingship, it is not surprising that a good deal of confusion arose in the complex myth and ritual that grew up around them.

The Great Goddess Neith

Thus, in the Eighteenth Dynasty the very ancient goddess Neith of Sais in the Western Delta was identified with Isis and Hathor, and so became at once the wife of Osiris, the mother of Horus and 'the great cow which gave birth to Re'. Indeed, she was 'the great goddess, the mother of all the gods', and two of the queens of the First Dynasty (e.g. Neit-Hotep and Meryt-Neit) adopted her name, and sixteen out of seventy of the *stelae* round the tomb of Zer bore names compounded with Neith.[28] Eventually, in the late Dynastic times, she was regarded merely as a form of Hathor, and represented various aspects of mother-hood as a Cow-goddess, though originally she seems to have been a personification of the primeval watery chaos like Nut, with whom she may have been identified if her name Neith or Net was akin in meaning to Nut, as Brugsch has suggested. But her oldest symbols (i.e. arrows or a shield) connect her with hunting or war before she became a personification of the pre-cosmic waters and of the sky. In any case she combined a number of goddesses and their respective functions which eventually were brought together in a composite figure identified with Isis and Hathor.[29]

As early as the Fourth Dynasty she was regarded as at once the mother and the daughter of Re, and possessed also the power to conceive and give birth to the new Sun-god daily. Since she was called 'the opener of the ways' she was a kind of female counterpart of Anubis and protectress of the dead, giving rebirth to the deceased in the after-life.[30] It was as Isis that she first gave birth to a god, and as Hathor she produced Re.[31] As 'the Lady of Heaven' and 'Mistress of all the gods' she occupied a position in the pantheon comparable to that of Re or Ptah, or of Hathor, as the supreme Goddess, and in the Twenty-sixth Dynasty she rose to a position of pre-eminence when the Pharaohs of Sais were at the height of their power, from which exalted status she declined after the fall of the Dynasty (663–525 B.C.). Till then she was the divine being *par excellence*, the creative and ruling power of heaven, earth and the underworld, and of every creature and thing in them.[32] She was eternal and self-produced, personifying from very early times the female principle, self-existent, self-sustaining and all-pervading. Thus, without the aid of a male partner she was believed to have brought forth the transcendent Sun-god Re very much as in the Memphite Theology Ptah created all things virtually *ex nihilo*, by thinking as the 'heart' and commanding as the 'tongue'. In her character of the universal mother she 'made the germ of gods and men, the mother of Re, who raised up Atum in primeval times, who existed when nothing else had being and who created that which exists after she had come into being'.[33]

Isis of Many Names

The most popular and important of all the maternal goddesses, however, was Isis, the prototype of motherhood and the embodiment of wifely love and fidelity. Around her myths and legends have accumulated, together with a mystery cultus which have given her a unique position in the Goddess cult, notwithstanding the fact that she was not herself a Mother-goddess comparable to Inanna-Ishtar, or Nut, or Hathor and Neith. In addition to being the daughter of Geb and Nut and the sister-spouse of Osiris and the mother of his son Horus, in the Heliopolitan Ennead, she was also the daughter of Neith, according to *The Contendings of Horus and Set* in the Chester Beatty Papyrus, while Plutarch represented her as the daughter of Thoth. Originally, as we have seen, she was a predynastic goddess of the Twelfth Nome of Lower Egypt, Sebennytos, and in all probability it was there that she was first incorporated in the Osiris tradition which came from Djedu, the capital of the Ninth Nome, Per-Usire, the 'house of Osiris'. Since her name means 'seat' or 'throne' it is very probable that originally she was the deified throne, as we have seen, and since enthronement has long been an essential element in royal installation, 'the throne which made the king' readily would become the Great Mother charged with the mysterious power of kingship.[34]

Depicted in female form with a vulture head-dress, the horns of Hathor and the solar disk with two plumes surmounted by the hieroglyphic symbol of her name (i.e. the throne), and sometimes wearing the double crowns of Upper and Lower Egypt, adorned with the feather of truth (*maat*) and holding in her hands a papyrus sceptre and the *crux ansata* (sign of life) with the uraeus over her forehead showing her divine origin, she was unquestionably the greatest and most beneficent goddess in Egypt, personifying all that was most vital in the maternal principle, its attributes, functions and duties. Often she has been represented with her son Horus on her lap, like the Virgin and Child in Christian iconography, and in the Book of the Dead and on a stele from a Nineteenth Dynasty tomb at Saqqara she is shown standing behind Osiris in the Judgment Hall. In the later examples often she is crowned with either the crescent moon or lotus flowers, and holds in one hand a sistrum and in the other the horn of plenty. A long veil covers her head, and she is clad in a tunic with fringe reaching to her feet.

In her various capacities not only was she identified in some way with almost every goddess in Egypt, as 'the Goddess of many names', but eventually in spite of her subservience to Osiris she was equated with the Great Mother of Western Asia, Greece and Rome, as well as with the great indigenous goddesses of the Nile valley (e.g. Hathor, Neith, Bast of Bubastis). Thus, as will be considered later, her search for the mortal remains of her murdered husband (Osiris) at Byblos in the Delta, as described in the classical literature,[35] was identical with that of Demeter for her daughter Kore (Persephone) at Eleusis, while in association with the Memphite cult of Serapis at Alexandria, the worship of Isis spread rapidly in the Hellenistic period until it became a predominant element in the welter of religions in the Roman Empire before and after the beginning of the Christian era. In its sanctuaries in the Campus Martius in Rome, at Pompeii, at Tithorea and Philae,

to mention but a few of the cult centres, the syncretistic veneration of the composite goddess attracted more and more votaries
during the first century B.C., when in spite of official opposition
it had spread throughout the Empire from Athens, the Aegean
and the adjacent islands. In the process, however, it lost much
of its original character and absorbed so many of the features
of the Greek and Asiatic cults that it is very difficult to determine to what extent these later Byblite versions in the classical
sources can be regarded as representative of uncontaminated
Egyptian worship of Isis and Osiris.

   All the goddesses, however, were concerned with motherhood as their principal function, giving birth to gods, suckling
kings and conferring upon them their divinity and immortality.
But although Isis stands in this tradition and the Pharaohs
reigned as her son Horus, as regards their divine potency they
were Horus the son of Hathor. Isis provided the royal descent
which gave the occupant of the throne his right of succession
through the instrumentality of his human mother the queen,
who was the vehicle of his incarnation,[36] though his divinity
came from Hathor and the royal god Horus. Nevertheless, in
practice all the motherhood goddesses were treated as more or
less synonymous divine figures so that Hathor and Isis and Nut
and Neith were never clearly differentiated, especially in respect
of the royal sacred marriage myth and ritual.

The Marriage of Hathor and Horus

This becomes apparent in the Hellenistic period when on the
18th day of the tenth month (Payni) the image of Hathor
was taken by ship by her priests from her temple at Denderah
on the western bank of the Nile, about 40 miles north of
Thebes, to Edfu (Behdet) to visit her husband Horus, with
whom she consorted for a fortnight.[37] On the eve of the festival
in honour of the victory of Horus over Seth, Horus of Edfu
and his retinue went forth in procession to meet the Goddess
and Horus of El-Kab and embarked on her ship to make a
triumphal entry into Edfu, pausing *en route* to sacrifice to Geb,
the wife of the Earth-god Nut. Arriving at their destination,

the various gods and their followers passed the night near the temple at Edfu and then proceeded to an 'upper temple' on the desert level. There they performed the prescribed rites to celebrate the victory of Horus in his combat to the satisfaction of Isis, who rejoiced 'because he (i.e. Horus) has undertaken this charge with a glad heart'.

When 'all that had been commanded has been accom-plished' the procession broke up and went to the halls of the school to offer a goat and an ox as a burnt offering. After reading 'The veneration of Horus, whose inheritance is made sure', and four other books, offerings were made to Re, who was called upon 'in all his names'. Loaves, jugs of beer, dates, milk, geese and wine were brought to him. Then the priests pro-claimed, 'Praise to thee, Re; praise to thee, Khepre, in all these thy beautiful names. Thou comest hither strong and mighty and hast ascended beautiful, and hast overthrown the dragon (Apophis). Incline thy beautiful countenance to the king.' Four geese were then released to fly to the four winds to inform the gods that 'King Horus of Edfu, the great god, the lord of heaven, had taken the white crown and had added the red crown thereto'. Four arrows were shot to the four quarters of heaven to slay the enemies of the gods. An ox was killed and its right leg thrown to a man called Horus, and a number of ceremonies were performed for the purpose of destroying the enemies of the gods and the king. This accomplished, the ritual of the day ended and the evening was spent in revelry, 'drinking before the god' (i.e. Horus of Edfu).[38]

Since it was 'to consummate the beauteous embrace with her Horus' that Hathor sailed from Denderah to Edfu,[39] a ritual marriage must have occurred during the course of the festival. Thus, on the fourth day the young Horus is said to have been conceived to be born on the 28th of the eighth month (Phar-muthi). This is confirmed by a similar marriage festival at Luxor in the latter half of the second month (Paophi), depicted on reliefs in the walls of the court of Amenhotep III in which is shown the image of Amon and his consort Mut and their son Khonsu being conveyed by river in barges escorted by the king and queen, the priests, musicians and nobles, from the temple at Karnak to his *harîm* at Luxor.[40] As the embodiment of Hathor, the queen as 'the God's Wife' and the musician-priestesses as his concubines under her rule, exercised their functions in the 'Southern *Harîm* of Amon' (i.e. the temple at Luxor), and there the union of the god and the queen was supposed to take place when at the Theban festival of Opet he visited the sanctuary in all his magnificence for this purpose.[41] Therefore, it was on these reliefs that the conception and birth of the Pharaoh were depicted,[42] just as in the temple of Hatshepsut at Deir el Bahari the presentation of the infant-queen to her heavenly father Amon and the presiding goddesses is shown in the birth scenes.[43]

Queen Hatshepsut, Daughter of Amon-Re

The anomalous position of Queen Hatshepsut, the only surviving child of Thutmose I by his half-sister, reigning as Pharaoh in her own right in a country where women were excluded from accession to the throne, required special regularization. Therefore, in the reliefs in her temple, Amon-Re is shown taking the form of Thutmose I in order to have intercourse with his queen, a princess directly descended from Ahmose I and of the same name. Having in this way become a wife of the royal blood, as the text explains, Amon then 'went to her immediately; then he had intercourse with her', and declared, 'now Khenemet-Amon-Hatshepsut is the name of my daughter whom I have placed in thy body. . . . She is to exercise beneficent kingship in this entire land.'[44] As 'the daughter of his loins whom he loved, the royal image', living for ever on the throne of Horus, she was shown, acknowledged and worshipped by the gods, surrounded with their protection of life and well-being, fashioned by Khnum, the ram-headed god, upon his potter's wheel at the express command of Amon.[45] But because she claimed to reign as king, not as queen, she was represented as a boy, presumably as a concession to the tradition of succession in the male line.

After her birth amid celestial jubilation, and her presentation to the gods and the nobles, she was depicted at the time of her accession visiting the ancient shrines in great pomp in every part of Egypt, 'beautiful to look upon' and 'like unto a god'. On her arrival at Heliopolis she was crowned by the king, Thutmose I, and set upon his throne before Amon-Re in the presence of the nobles and State officials, who did homage to her. Entering the sanctuary, she is shown having the white crown of Lower Egypt placed on her head by the priests in the guise of Horus and Seth, and then the red crown of Upper Egypt. Wearing the double crown she appears seated on a throne between the two gods of the south and the north (i.e. Horus and Seth), who tie together under her feet flowers and branches of papyrus, the emblems of Lower and Upper Egypt, to symbolize the union of the Two Lands. Finally, arrayed in her crown and mantle and holding in her hands the scourge and flail of Osiris, her procession round the walls of the sanctuary is represented to indicate her taking possession of the domains of Horus and Seth which henceforth she will protect. The scenes conclude with her being led to the shrine of Amon to be embraced by her celestial father as his daughter, duly installed by him in the throne of Horus.[46]

Although the special circumstances under which Hatshepsut acceded to the throne led to her divine status with the approval of the gods being given particular emphasis in the reliefs in her temple at Deir el Bahari, this was only to bring her into line with her predecessors as a god incarnate; the living Horus conceived and born in a sacred marriage in which the Pharaoh in the guise of the Sun-god had sexual relations with the queen as the wife of the god in order to beget an heir to the throne. In the case of Hatshepsut every aspect of the process of generation was associated with the divine intervention of her heavenly father Amon-Re to make it quite clear that in fact she was his offspring designed by him to reign as his daughter. But this was only because for a woman to assume the royal status required official interpretation and justification as a divine decree. It was, however, only the ancient belief and practice concerning the monarchy that was applied to her in spite of her sex, the procedure being the normal method of maintaining the royal succession.

Theban Queens as 'The God's Wife'

Therefore, in Egypt instead of the king being invited to share the nuptial couch of the Mother-goddess as in Mesopotamia, he cohabited with the queen in his divine status as the incarnation of the Sun-god. As the 'Bull of Heaven'[47] he was the dominant male, the embodiment of virile fertility, and in this capacity he impregnated the queen, called 'the cow who bore the bull', as Re impregnated the body of Nut 'with the seed of that spirit that must be in her'.[48] Thus, the consort of the ancient king of Heliopolis was the wife of the Sun-god on earth, and so was identified with Hathor his celestial spouse to enable him to become the physical father of the Pharaoh. Since her husband was the high-priest of Re, from the Fifth Dynasty in theory his wife was the high-priestess, and eventually Ahhotep, the mother of Ahmose I, the founder of the Eighteenth Dynasty, was described as 'the God's Wife'.[49] The title 'Divine Wife' was assumed, it is true, by Queen Neferu in the Eleventh Dynasty, but it was not until the Eighteenth Dynasty that 'God's Wife' became the designation of the queens as the chief-priestesses of Amon-Re.

From then onwards royal heiresses became increasingly prominent in Egypt. Hereditary queens bore the titles 'The Royal Daughter', 'Royal Sister', 'Great Royal Wife', 'Hereditary Princess', 'Lady of the Two Lands', as well as the priestess designation 'God's Wife'. They were not confined, however, to a queen-consort, and could be extended to priestesses of Hathor and those who stood in the Goddess tradition by virtue of their office. But the Divine Wives of Amon and the Mothers of the god Khonsu (who at Thebes became the son of Amon and Mut) were of royal rank, while the title of 'Divine Worshipper' (*Neter tuat*) carried with it virtual independence of the throne of Thebes. Indeed, in the Twenty-second Dynasty the God's Wife overshadowed the throne and the Amonite priesthood, and it only remained for Asurbani-palto conquer Thebes in 663 to reduce Amon-Re to the rank of a local god. With the establishment of the Saitic line (*c.* 663–525 B.C.) a succession of five 'God's Wives', who were no longer the wives of the Pharaohs, became the governors, and beside whom in the State the high-priests were little more than figure-heads.[50] The practice of sister-marriages still prevailed, and the high-priestess succession continued to follow in the female line with the title 'Mistress of Egypt' assigned to the Theban priestess.

In the temple of Osiris at Karnak a life-sized alabaster statue of the Queen Amenertas, the daughter of Kashta, presumably by his wife Shepenapt II, the Theban priestess-sovereign who shared the crown with her two brothers, has the following inscription: 'This is an offering for the Theban Amon-Re of Apt, to the god Mentu-Re, the Lord of Thebes. May he grant everything that is good and pure, by which the divine (nature) lives, all that the heaven bestows and the earth brings forth, to the princess the most pleasant, the most gracious, the kindest and the most amiable queen of Upper and Lower Egypt, the sister of the king, the ever-living daughter of the deceased king, the wife of the divine one—Amenertas—may she live.'

'I was the wife of the divine one, a benefactress of her city (Thebes), a bounteous giver of her land. I gave food to the hungry, drink to the thirsty, clothes to the naked.'[51]

For many years Queen Amenertas had dominion over Thebes as the princess-priestess, and when the Ethiopian Dynasty came to an end about 663 B.C. its sovereign rights were carried over to the new Saitic rulers by Shepenart III, the Royal Daughter of Pankhy II and Amenertas, from whom she had inherited the Theban principality.[52] Thus, at the accession of the Saitic king Psammetichus I (663–609) his daughter Nitaqert was made the legal heiress of Shepenart, the former queen,[53] in an attempt to transmit metaphorically the solar succession through the line of priestesses of Amon's harem, very much as Hatshepsut's position had been regularized by the intervention of Amon. So the fiction was maintained long after the earthly embodiments of the gods and goddesses they incarnated had ceased to be the dynamic centre of the united nation consolidated in their divine sovereignty.

CHAPTER III

Palestine and Anatolia

THE CULT IN PALESTINE

IN Palestine the Goddess cult is less clearly defined in the available documentary and archaeological sources than in those of Ancient Egypt and Mesopotamia. Nevertheless, as we have seen, an abundance of female figurines, amulets and 'Astarte' plaques have been recovered from almost every important excavation in the country from the Chalcolithic and Bronze Age to the Early Iron Age,[1] though the identification of the figures depicted with particular goddesses often is more con-jectural than elsewhere in Western Asia. Some of them, how-ever, are closely allied in their form and features to the Egyptian examples showing nude females wearing a Hathor head-dress, and sometimes the sexual triangle.[2] A lotus blossom or a papyrus sceptre may be held in an outstretched hand,[3] as in many Egyptian Hathor figures of the Twelfth Dynasty and onwards,[4] while on others a feather head-dress occurs familiar in the Kassite period in Mesopotamia. In Syria and Palestine it would seem these various features were brought together in the Goddess cult in the Late Bronze Age, and subsequently in Egypt in the Nineteenth Dynasty as a goddess called Qadesh.

Baal and Anat in the Ugaritic Texts

So far as Palestine is concerned, the principal goddesses whose names recur in the literary sources most frequently and con-tinuously are those of Anat, Asherah, Astarte and Ashtaroth, all of whom have much in common with each other and with the iconic representations in the female figurines in their several forms and adornments, as well as in their cultic context. Thus, in the Ugaritic texts first discovered in 1929 at Ras Shamra (the ancient Ugarit) by C. F. A. Schaeffer on the north coast of Syria and deciphered by H. Bauer and E. Dhorme, there are unmistakable indications of the Goddess cult as an integral element in the great Baal-Anat epic. From these clay tablets written in alphabetic cuneiform in an archaic Canaanite dialect akin to ancient Hebrew and Phoenician, which date mainly from the fourteenth century B.C., though going back in origin to a much earlier age, it has become apparent that early Canaanite myth and ritual had much in common with that of the rest of Western Asia. Like the Babylonian tablets, these Ugaritic texts appear to be part of the archives of the local temple and, therefore, originally to have been compiled prior to the middle of the second millennium B.C. Variant examples of the same alphabetic script have been found at Beth Shemesh and Mount Tabor, but as it was suitable only for use on clay tablets, which were never the normal medium of writing in Palestine, it was a Canaanite-Hurrian dialectal adaptation of cuneiform of short duration. Nevertheless, the very considerable number of large and small fragments of mythological texts shows that while it lasted the literature was prolific, and in it the leading roles were played by Aleyan-Baal and the Goddess Anat, his consort and sister, who is also called 'the Lady of the Mountain'.[5]

As elsewhere in the Near East and the Aegean, she was the principal patroness of the Storm- and Weather-god designated in the Ras Shamra texts Aleyan-Baal, who full of strength and vigour rose to pre-eminence in the Ugaritic mythology after he had eclipsed El, the remote and shadowy Supreme Deity, the progenitor of the gods and of mankind. Thus, Baal occupied a position similar to that of Marduk in Babylonia when as the younger god he replaced Anu and Enlil at the head of the pantheon—a recurrence in both regions of the Older and Younger god themes. Once he was established as the personification of the storm, the wind and the clouds, and the controller of the rainfall and the growth of the crops, Baal became the counterpart of Tammuz as the fertility-god of vegetation whose descent into the nether regions caused the languishing of the earth, though in a modified guise peculiar to this complex and still very fragmentary mythology.

In the Baal-Anat cycle, in which the glorification of Baal as the hero is the central theme, it appears that he was installed in a royal palace in the heavens after he had engaged in a victorious struggle with the dragon, Yam or Nahar. At first he refused to have any windows in it, perhaps as a precautionary measure lest one of his several enemies (e.g. Yam, lord of the Sea, or Mot, the ruler of the underworld) should attack him through them. When these misgivings were dispelled he ordered the lattice to be made, presumably to allow the rain to fall on the earth when it was opened.[6] Dr Gaster, in fact, suggests that the episode is a mythological interpretation of a rain-making ceremony during the autumnal festival when the windows in the temple at Ras Shamra were opened to simulate the opening of the 'windows of heaven' through which the rain was released.[7] Schaeffer has made the ingenious suggestion that the rain, which was to begin to fall at the decree of Baal, was perhaps intended to descend through the skylight in the roof of the temple on the face of the god represented on a stele which stood in the sanctuary.[8]

Be this as it may, Baal was the giver of fertility nourished by the vitalizing rain over which he exercised control. He was 'the Rider of the Clouds', and in Syria rain was the primary source of fertility, not a river like the Nile in Egypt or the Euphrates in Mesopotamia. Therefore, because he was equated with the rainfall which gave life to the earth he was 'lord over the furrows of the field' and 'Prince, lord of the Earth'.[9] When somehow his adversary Mot, the god of sterility and death, contrived to cause him to descend to the nether regions where he was killed, all vegetation languished and fecundity ceased amid universal lamentation.[10] To remedy this devastating state of affairs his sister-consort Anat, with the help of the Sun-goddess Shapesh, went in search of Baal, hunting every mountain in the land, lamenting as bitterly as Demeter or Adonis grieved for Kore and Attis, 'desiring him as doth a cow her calf or a ewe her lamb'.[11]

For what reasons he descended to the nether regions and was killed cannot be determined from the fragmentary state of the texts at this point. It appears, however, that he was found dead in the pastures of Shlmmt, and although El was thereby rid of his rival, even he joined in sorrowing and mourning for his loss, and under the name of Ltpn, god of mercy, he went down from his exalted throne in heaven and sat on the earth in sackcloth and ashes, lacerating himself and crying 'Baal is dead'—a refrain repeated by Anat when she found his body.[12] Taking his mortal remains to the heights of Sapan, his former abode,[13] she performed the prescribed mortuary ritual and buried him.[14] This duly accomplished, Anat, knowing that her rival Asherah, the consort of El, would try to get one of her sons (i.e. Attar) appointed to the vacant throne of Baal, she poured out her complaint to the Supreme God, El, taunting Asherah and her brood with rejoicing at the demise of the fertility-god (Baal). A violent discussion ensued and Attar recognized his incapacity to succeed to the throne.[15]

In the meantime Anat had continued her search for Mot, whom she knew to have been responsible for her lover's death. Having at length found him, she seized him, ripped his garments, and demanded her brother-spouse. He admitted that he had killed him, 'making him like a lamb in his mouth and crushing him in his jaw like a kid'. Thereupon Anat clave Mot with a *harpé* (ritual sickle), winnowed him in a sieve, scorched him, ground him in a mill, scattered his flesh over the fields, like the dismembered body of Osiris, and gave him to the birds to eat.[16] In short, she treated him as the reaped grain, which is an anomaly in view of Mot being represented as the god of death and sterility whose abode was the underworld. But consistency is not a characteristic feature of mythological traditions of this nature, and in seasonal folk-lore the corn-spirit often has been treated as was Mot and equated with death.[17]

Although Mot played a number of roles in the Ugaritic texts,[18] nevertheless he was essentially the antithesis of Baal in the vegetation theme. As Baal was the god of rain and fertility, so his adversary (Mot) was the god of aridity and drought, 'wandering over every mountain to the heart of the earth, every hill to the earth's very bowels', turning them into desolation by robbing all living things of the breath of life.[19] When he was treated by Anat as the harvested grain it was as the slain corn-spirit dying at the in-gathering of harvest that he was repre-sented, ushering in the season of sterility until life was restored and renewed with the release of Baal from the nether regions, the land of death, whither he had taken the rain-producing clouds. Then 'the heavens rain oil and the wadies run with honey'.[20]

Since the theme was the perennial struggle between life and death in nature, be it of annual or septennial recurrence, neither of the contending forces could be ultimately destroyed. There-fore, notwithstanding Anat's drastic treatment of Mot, he survived to continue the combat when Baal returned to life. At their first encounter Baal had been completely paralysed with fear, and returned to his house weeping at the approach of his enemy, ready to become his slave without resistance.[21] This loss of vigour typified the decline in vitality and the dying vegetation in the dry season, even though summer fruits may still ripen. With the return of the rains the renewal of the urge of life in its full strength found mythological expression in the energetic battle waged by Baal against Mot with the aid of the Sun-goddess, Shapesh; Baal attacking with all his might and resources. They bit like serpents, gored each other like wild bulls and kicked like chargers. Neither yielded, until at length the Sun-goddess intervened, urging Mot to give up the fight since he was vanquished, and return to the underworld because the season of his reign had come to an end. Now it was the turn of Baal to bring life out of the earth, and so to continue the struggle was useless.[22] Therefore, El 'overturned Mot's throne' and 'broke the sceptre of his dominion', thereby forcing him to surrender and acknowledge the kingship of Baal. The drought then ended and fertility was re-established on earth.[23] Thus, the efforts of Anat on behalf of her brother-husband ultimately prevailed.

Indeed, throughout his varied and tumultuous career she was

always at his side in her dual capacity as his sister and consort. She did not hesitate to threaten to use against her father El, the head of the pantheon, all the violence in which she delighted if he did not comply with her wishes on behalf of Baal.[24] In the Aqht text she and Baal are represented as taking opposite sides, it is true, but otherwise they always fought together, Anat being the goddess of war and slaughter, wallowing in blood, though she never ceased to be primarily concerned with love and fertility. In the Ras Shamra texts this aspect of her character to some extent has been overshadowed by Aleyan-Baal having assumed the role of the giver of life *par excellence*. As his consort she was his helper, but she never occupied the predominant position of Inanna-Ishtar in Mesopotamia. With her Baal has passionate marital intercourse described in a manner suggesting that originally it may have been connected with the sacred marriage in the Annual Festival cultus,[25] if the texts were in fact cult rituals recited dramatically, as has been suggested with some plausibility.

For example, in the 'Gracious Gods' texts (52), first published by Virolleaud in 1933,[26] which Dr Gaster maintains were the libretto of a sacred drama addressed to certain 'Gracious and Beautiful Gods' described as 'princes' and 'high ones', and performed at the Canaanite Spring Festival of the first-fruits, there is an erotic scene between two girls who may be identified with Anat and Asherah, both of whom are characterized as at once the daughters and wives of El.[27] The aged supreme god, having duly impressed his admirers by his agility in drawing and carrying water for cooking, and by his marksmanship in securing a bird for the pot, incidents which seem to be capable of interpretation in terms of sexual symbolism, he then kissed and seduced them, with the result that they conceived and bore two sons, Shahru, the Dawn, and Shalma, the Sunset.[28] The birth was duly announced to El, and they were called 'Gracious Gods' who 'suckled the breast of Mistress Lady Queen' (Asherah).[29]

The crude episode would seem to have been connected with the *hieros gamos*, probably during the New Year Festival when El was the principal deity in the fertility cultus before he had been replaced by Baal. In all probability it represents the climax of a sacred dance in a ritual marriage between the priests of El and the temple priestesses in order to produce symbolically the birth of certain gods (e.g. Shahru and Shalma) and the promotion of fertility, very likely to secure abundance of bread and wine when the gathering of the first-fruits was celebrated at the beginning of summer, or possibly as a septennial obser-vance at the end of every seven-year cycle.[30] But whatever may have been the precise occasion of the ritual, there is every indication that the sacred marriage in its customary setting was an essential element in the underlying theme of the drama.

In the sexual symbolism, however, El's impotence is indi-cated. Therefore, it is not surprising that Anat also became the wife of the virile younger god Baal, the Rider on the Clouds,[31] their union being represented as that of a bull and a cow.[32] Consequently, when Baal was said to love a heifer[33] this was merely a mythological expression of his union with Anat. Nevertheless, since she, with Asherah, is alleged to have had sexual relations with El in his old age,[34] it is not improbable that originally she was his consort when he was head of the pantheon before Baal became the dominant figure and the most potent force in nature.[35] When the older god El became subservient to, or was eclipsed by, the younger divinity Baal, Anat assumed the status of his (Baal's) wife and sister while El was regarded as her father. But notwithstanding her promi-nence in the *A.B.* texts, although she took her place by the side of Baal as the goddess of birth, and fought his battles as a warrior goddess, in some measure she receded into the back-ground. It was Baal who was the supreme figure dwarfing all the other divinities, male and female alike, but in the beginning in all probability it was El and Anat who together dominated the scene. Although the original character of Anat is very obscure, she was principally concerned with sex and war, sensuous and perennially fruitful, yet without losing her virginity.[36]

Asherah, El and Baal

Her rival and arch enemy Asherah seems to have occupied much the same position as Anat as the consort and daughter of El, who bore to him a brood of seventy gods and goddesses, thereby earning her epithet 'Creatress of the gods', 'lady of the Sea'.[37] Her relations with Baal, however, are by no means clear. On the one hand she is represented as his mother and his bitter antagonist, even apparently to the extent of conceiving and giving birth to the 'Devourers' for the purpose of destroying him at the command of El,[38] if this is the correct rendering of the very defective tablet entitled 'Les chasses de Baal', published by Virolleaud in 1935.[39] In any case, as we have seen, Anat chided Asherah and her sons with rejoicing at the death of Baal, and it was one of her (Asherah's) offspring who was made king in his stead.[40] Yet Anat and Baal joined forces in seeking the help of Asherah in the creation of his palace,[41] and while she had to be bribed with silver and gold to intervene with El on his behalf, she seems to have recognized Baal's claims to pre-eminence, since she refers to him as 'our king', 'our judge', asserting that 'none is above him'.[42]

The situation is involved, but it may be that the change of attitude is to be explained as a result of Baal's ascendancy over El as the leading god controlling the weather and the storms as the Rider on the Clouds, and as virile as the bull he symbolized in the promotion of fertility and setting the seasons. Then Asherah was content to be the daughter of El[43] and to champion the cause of the young god, now supreme in power, as described in the texts, which doubtless come from the Baal priesthood of rather later date after his temple was complete.[44] The precise relationship of Asherah to him in this capacity cannot be determined. Sometimes it seems that she is his mother, but in the list of sacrifices reference is made to an 'ox for Baal and Asherah' as though she was connected with him in much the same way as formerly she had been the consort of El. It is not improbable, therefore, that although Baal had his own wife Anat, he may have annexed Asherah when he obtained absolute sovereignty, as under these conditions the chief god in the pantheon invariably consorted with the chief goddess, often in the capacity of spouse and sister.

In Syria the emphasis was on the warlike as well as on the erotic aspects of these patronesses of the forces of reproduction and sexuality. Consequently, the goddesses in competition with each other strove against their rival to become the consort of the leader of the pantheon and to dominate the natural processes on which the well-being of mankind depended.[45] Thus, both Anat and Asherah appear as allies in the building of Baal's palace. This may be the result of the two tablets representing different accounts of the same event told by different narrators and written by different scribes, as Obermann has suggested.[46] But probably behind the saga lay the conflict between the two goddesses to attain the status of the wife of Baal. In this struggle, however, neither seems to have been victorious since both Anat and Asherah remained in joint possession of one and the same office in which fertility and war were combined without ever merging completely into the 'Goddess of many names'.

Anta

In Egypt, Anat was fused with Astarte, the Semitic Ashtaroth, a goddess of war and the counterpart of the Syrian Asherah. Thus, in the New Kingdom in Egypt, when the Semitic influences were strongly felt, especially at Memphis, she became the composite deity Anta, 'the Mistress of the sky', 'Lady of the gods', the daughter of Ptah, or of Re, 'the master of the universe'. In the magical texts she was described as the goddess who 'conceives but never brings forth', and in the treaty with the Hittites she with Astarte was represented as the national goddess of the Syrian Kheta. In addition to being 'mistress of horses, lady of chariots', and 'shield of the king against his enemies', she was the goddess of love—'the foreign Aphrodite'. In many syncretisms she was identified with Isis and Hathor as a mother-goddess, with Sekhmet, the wife of Ptah, and Rameses III called his favourite daughter *Bent anta*, 'daughter of Anta'. But although the attributes and functions of Anat and

Astarte were virtually indistinguishable, the two foreign god﹣ desses actually were almost distinct in Egypt as were Anat and Asherah in Syria. Indeed, while they normally exist together, in the fifth﹣century Aramaic Elephantine papyri Anat is compounded with Yahu as the consort of Yahweh.[47]

ISRAEL

Ashtaroth and the Baalim in Israel

In Israel, Asherah (i.e. Ashtaroth) was coupled with Baal,[48] but the word 'asherah' has a wider significance in the Old Testament as it is frequently applied to the wooden posts symbolizing the mother﹣goddess which stood beside the altars or mazzebôth (i.e. menhirs) in the sanctuaries and sacred groves where vegetation rites were performed.[49] No doubt when the Biblical narratives were drawn up before and after the Exile, Asherah as the name of the goddess had become confused with anything connected with her cult, so it was employed in a generic sense, just as all vegetation gods and their cultus were called 'Baal'. But at an earlier period the deities were clearly defined as is shown by the tradition con﹣ cerning the grim struggle between Elijah, the *Nabi* of Yahweh, and Ahab's queen, Jezebel, an ardent devotee of the Tyrian Baal (later known as the chthonic Melkart) and his wife or mother Asherah. That Mount Carmel was a sanctuary of the Canaanite deity Aleyan﹣Baal is by no means improbable,[50] and the conflict alleged to have been enacted thereon may represent a struggle between Yahwism and the Baal﹣Asherah cult at this important centre of the cultus in Northern Palestine, served, it is asserted, by some four hundred and fifty priests of Baal and four hundred priestesses of Asherah.[51] That Asherah was the chief goddess of Tyre is indicated in the Ugaritic Keret text,[52] where the hero Keret is said to have visited 'the shrine of Asherah of Tyre and Elath (the goddess of Sidon)' in order to make a vow to them on his way to obtain the daughter of King Pabel for his bride.[53] Therefore, as one of the votaries of Baal, Jezebel doubtless regarded Carmel as a vantage﹣point in the conflict between the two rival cults, and it may well have

been there that the ritual battle between Baal-Asherah and
Yahweh took place.

Yahweh and Baalism

Although Elijah is represented as having triumphed in the
conflict, while Yahweh henceforth may have been the dominant deity in Israel, Baalism continued to flourish. Indeed,
according to the narrative, in view of the bitter lamentation of
Elijah at Horeb concerning the throwing down of the altars of
Yahweh and the wholesale slaying of the Yahwistic prophets,
there was a violent reaction, so, as he imagined, he alone
remained and went in terror of his life.[54] The term Baal, it is
true, was the designation of foreign gods in general, and it was
incorporated in the names of Israelites (e.g. Jerubba'al, Meri-
baal), Yahweh himself being worshipped as a Baal in the guise
of a young bull.[55] But as the central figure of a highly organized
fertility and sexual cultus, the Canaanite Baal and his worship
became the object of strenuous opposition in the monarchy in
and after the ninth century when the Yahwistic prophetic
movement began to make its influence felt, however exaggerated this may be in the literature that was compiled after the
conflict had reached its climax.

In fact, such was the strength of the Canaanite cult that
Yahweh from being a desert god was transformed virtually into
a vegetation deity. From the days of the Judges when the
loosely consolidated tribes were struggling to gain a foothold
in Palestine and to control the fertile plains, the indigenous
religion had been assimilated so that the fertile aspects of Baal
and his associates were predominant. Even Gideon, who is
represented as the Manassite protagonist of Yahweh, was named
Jerubba'al, 'Baal fights', and his father Joash, notwithstanding
his designation (Yo=Yahweh), was the custodian of an altar
to the Canaanite god and its asherah (i.e. sacred pole). The
two cults, therefore, would seem to have been interchangeable,
though always liable to come in conflict, as apparently
on this occasion, if the very ancient tribal story bears any
relation to what actually occurred before it was reinterpreted

by a later Yahwistic narrator.[56] Bull worship with its fertility
significance continued to flourish at the northern shrines (e.g.
Shechem, Shiloh, Gilgal, Bethel, etc.),[57] and absorbed many
of the attributes of the Canaanite fertility cultus centres in the
Storm⁄ and Weather⁄god Aleyan⁄Baal and his consorts.

The Astarte figurines recovered from Gezer with their
horned head⁄dress,[58] and a similar representation of the goddess
on a stele at Beth⁄Shan dedicated to Ashtoreth⁄Karnaim,[59]
together with numerous Astarte plaques and fragmentary
female figurines in clay and stone from Late Bronze Age and
Early Iron Age deposits elsewhere (e.g. Tell Beit Mirsim,
Shechem, Megiddo and Gerar) show that the cult was firmly
established in Palestine except at Gibeah, Tell en⁄Nasbeh and
Shiloh, and in the Early Israelite levels in the central region.[60]
There can be little doubt that Anat was as much at home at
Beth⁄Shan or Gezer as at Ugarit or Beth⁄Anat or Denderah,[61]
as was Astarte everywhere.

On the wall at Mizpeh (Tell en⁄Nasbeh) temples of
Asherah and Yahweh appear to have stood side by side in the
ninth century B.C., and to have survived until the city was
destroyed. In the centre of what is thought to have been a
temple of Yahweh, resting on the Canaanite city wall, was
the base of an altar, and on either side was a smaller room with
a storage bin containing two flint knives but no female
statuettes. To the east stood the Astarte temple constructed in
the same manner, and in it was a clay dove, a fragment of a
female figurine painted red, and a 'saucer lamp' in the three⁄
branch fork of a tree, both in terracotta. Near by were a number
of similar figurines and a conical mazzebah.[62] This equipment
suggests that it was a centre of the Goddess cult where Astarte
was worshipped, probably in later times alongside of Yahweh
at the neighbouring shrine, possibly as his consort. If this were
so, the goddesses under Canaanite names (e.g. Anath⁄Yahu
comparable to Yo⁄Elat in the Ugaritic texts) assigned to
Yahweh in the Jewish community at Elephantine after the
Exile[63] can hardly have been an innovation.

In spite of the repeated attempts at drastic reformation by the

pre-exilic mono-Yahwists in the northern and southern kingdoms of Israel and Judah, so deeply ingrained was the Goddess
cult that it still flourished in the last days of the monarchy after
the death of Josiah (*c.* 609 B.C.). Thus, it is recorded that
Jeremiah to his dismay encountered children gathering wood
in the streets of Jerusalem and in the cities of Judah for the fires
to be kindled by their fathers for the worship of the Queen of
Heaven, while the women kneaded the dough to make the
sacrificial cakes on which her image was inscribed.[64] When
he remonstrated with them after the Exile, they declared that
they would continue to burn incense and pour out drink
offerings to her as their kings and princes had done always, for
then there was food in abundance and the people were well
and knew no evil.[65] Since the cult had been suppressed
by Josiah nothing but misfortune had befallen them, they
declared—Jehoahaz had been deported to Egypt, Jehoiachin
and the cream of the nation had been carried away into
captivity in Mesopotamia, Jerusalem had been captured,
Zedekiah had had his eyes put out, and after the murder of
Gedaliah the remnant left in the capital had had to flee into
Egypt to escape the retaliation of the Chaldaeans. Confronted
with such a succession of catastrophes attributed to the neglect
of the Queen of Heaven, all the prophet could reply was that
in fact they were reaping the due reward of their apostasy from
Yahwism, and to heap upon them curses for their back-
slidings.[66]

Ritual Prostitution

Similarly in the Northern Kingdom Amos and Hosea were
no less scathing in their denunciations of the cultus at the local
shrines (Bethel, Gilgal, Beersheba) in their day,[67] and in all
probability it was refugees from Bethel who played an important part in the development of the syncretistic cult at Elephantine in the sixth and fifth centuries B.C.[68] At Shiloh at the
beginning of the monarchy priestesses appear to have been
attached to the temple there with whom the sons of Eli had
intercourse,[69] and Amos inveighed against those who profaned

the name of Yahweh by having congress with the *zonah* (i.e.
ritual prostitute) at a sacrificial meal, 'drinking the wine of the
raped',[70] just as Jeremiah later chided the people of Jerusalem
for assembling themselves by troops in the sanctuaries of sacred
prostitutes whose blandishments he described.[71] As in Mesopotamia the king was invited to share the couch of the
Goddess, so these Palestinian shrines were equipped with
'beds of love' for the priestesses and their lovers[72] who assumed
the same role as the Babylonian king and queen in the
dramatization of the sacred marriage.[73]

It is not improbable that the prophet Isaiah of Jerusalem
resorted to one of these shrines to obtain a second child by a
professional prophetess (i.e. a *zonah*) for ritual purposes,[74] and
in the Northern Kingdom, as Hosea makes abundantly clear
(750–735 B.C.), the priestesses exercised their functions with
undiminished vigour in his day in spite of all the efforts of the
reformers like Asa to drive the *zonah* and *qedeshîm* (Sodomites)
out of the land.[75] The Deuteronomic Law in the south in the
next century, which endeavoured to suppress both male and
female hierodouloi,[76] was equally unsuccessful. As in the case
of other aspects of the Goddess cult, the practice was too deeply
laid in the Palestinian cultus to be eradicated by denunciation
and Deuteronomic legislation, going back as an established
institution to protohistoric times, as the Patriarchal tradition
suggests,[77] in spite of the gloss over the cultic terms *zonah* and
qedeshah by later narrators who represented them as common
harlots rather than sacred prostitutes in the service of the
Mother-goddess. Behind the story of the Gileadite hero
Jephthah, himself the son of a *zonah*,[78] lay the ritual bewailing
of their virginity by the maidens of Gilead, and although the
cultic function of sacred women in general became confused,
the cult, as we have seen, persisted until after the Exile, notwithstanding the drastic action of Josiah who destroyed the
houses of the Sodomites and of those of the sacred prostitutes who wove hangings for Asherah and practised her
rites in the temple at Jerusalem.[79] If the hire of a harlot
could not be accepted by the sanctuary, the proceeds gained

by the ritual prostitutes were intended for the worship of Yahweh.[80]

To eliminate from Yahwism these very ancient crude practices Hosea endeavoured to give a loftier interpretation to the conception of the marriage of Israel with its god in a manner that was in accord with the agricultural tradition of the popular religion, looking forward to the time when the nation would be purged of its corruptions and be remarried to Yahweh. Then the soil would be again cultivated and yield bountiful harvests, and the people would recognize that it was Yahweh and not the Baalim who had given the increase in the fruitfulness of the land.[81] Since the country was his and he was the true husband of Israel, in consorting with other gods (i.e. the Baalim) and keeping lovers the people had been unfaithful to him and their fertility rites were likened to fornication and adultery. This is expressed in terms of the prophet's own unhappy domestic life, married as he is alleged to have been to an unfaithful wife, Gomer, who may have been originally a sacred prostitute.[82] Anyway, the symbolism employed is that of the Goddess ritual, and the underlying theme is that of the cultus reinterpreted in relation to the Yahwist conception of the covenant with Yahweh in which no place is allowed for alien deities and their worship, including the sacred prostitution which almost invariably was a concomitant of the Goddess cult in Syria, Phoenicia and Palestine.

The fall of Samaria in 721 B.C. before the Assyrian forces, followed by the destruction of the cities of Phoenicia in the next century (677–673), gave a fresh impetus to Mesopotamian influences in the Aramaic culture that developed in the neo-Assyrian Canaanite province. Moreover, in Judah it stimulated the pagan reaction under Ahaz (c. 735–715 B.C.) and Manasseh (c. 687–642). But although Assyria now became dominant as the focus of influence, the resulting product was a Syro-Mesopotamian syncretism in which the worship of Baal and Asherah was combined with that of 'Molech', whatever this obscure term may imply,[83] and Adrammelech, a form of the Syrian god Hadah, and the Sumerian Anu, which included child-sacrifice.[84] That the Goddess cult was among the prominent elements is clear from the references to the *qedeshim* and *zonah* in the temple at Jerusalem as votaries of Asherah, and to women weeping for Tammuz, the consort of Ishtar, and their Canaanite counterparts. Thus, having become firmly rooted in the Aramaean culture on Palestinian soil it survived the break-up of the Israelite communities in 721 and 571 B.C. until in the post-exilic period Yahwism was re-established purged of most of its Canaanite and Mesopotamian accretions.

ANATOLIA
The Hittite Goddess
Closely related both geographically and culturally to Syria and Palestine, 'the Land of Hatti' to the north-east of the Anatolian plateau of Asia Minor, within the circuit of the Hals river (Kizil Irmak), the Hittite Empire flourished in the second millennium B.C. In the Middle Bronze Age the pre-Hittite Anatolian princes had established a stable civilization in this mountain stronghold, and recent excavations in 1954 to 1956 at Kultepe (Kanesh) near Kayseri have brought to light an inscription on a bronze spear-head bearing the words 'Palace of Anittas, the King', whose name occurs on three tablets in cuneiform Hittite as a historical character who apparently controlled the greater part of the plateau himself, residing at Kussara. From him the royal Hittite line may have descended, though in fact it was from the ancient ruler Labarnas that the Hittite kings traced their lineage.[85] By about 1380 B.C. the kingdom had been established by Suppiluliumas, king of Hatti, who conquered and incorporated into his empire the Mesopotamian kingdoms of Mitanni and the Hussilands, and sent armies into Syria and Palestine making Lebanon his frontier (*c.* 1370). Therefore, the references to the Hittites in the Old Testament narratives as one of the Palestinian tribes whom the Hebrews encountered and with whom they had relations during their occupation of Canaan[86] are misleading

since they place this great ancient civilization on a level with the Perizzites, Rephaims, Girgashites and Hivites. It was not until the time of the monarchy that its importance seems to have been recognized.[87]

It has only been in recent years, however, that the full significance of the Hittite culture and religion has become apparent as a result of the recovery and decipherment of the inscriptions and texts written in this particular form of cuneiform script from about 1900 to 1100 B.C. Hrozny led the way by publishing the first attempt at a grammar and gradually, in spite of many set-backs, it has become possible to translate a number of tablets that are now available, and so to gain a considerable knowledge of the life and beliefs of this highly syncretistic civilization occupying a key position in Asia Minor.

Thus, so far as our present inquiry is concerned, it now appears that the Hittite city-states were welded as a group under the rule of the 'Great King', who in addition to being the head of the army and the supreme judge was also the chief priest of the gods and 'held by the hand' of the Goddess. Although he was never regarded as divine during his lifetime, he was believed to be endowed with supernatural powers, and it is in his priestly capacity in relation to the Weather-god that he has been usually depicted on the monuments. At the death of the queen-mother the reigning queen became the *tavanna*, the priestess of the Mother-goddess, and she could then act as regent during his absence. Indeed, it was through her probably that the sovereign was brought into relation with the Goddess by means of a sacred marriage. Here, however, the evidence is obscure and its interpretation can be only conjectural, based as it is mainly on the iconography of Yazilikaya.

The Yazilikaya Reliefs

In this great rock-sanctuary about two miles from the village of Boghazköy where the oldest Hittite settlement at Hattusas occurs, there are bas-reliefs of two converging processions of gods and goddesses which meet in the centre at the end wall of the chamber, opposite the entrance. On the right side, except

for two males, all the figures are those of robed females, while
on the left side they are males with two females, together with
winged mythological beings. The weathering of the rocks
makes it extremely difficult to identify any of the divinities
depicted in the absence of the specification of the gods by their
names with the exception of that of the goddess designated in
the hieroglyphic script Hepatu (i.e. Hebat, or Hepit, the chief
goddess in the Hurrian pantheon, the consort of Teshub the
Weather-god). She is represented standing on a panther or
lioness and clad in a full-sleeved robe with pleated skirt. Her
hair is braided and on her head she wears a tiara. In her left
hand she holds a long staff, and with her right hand stretched
out to greet the male figure approaching her she proffers her
gifts in the form of symbolic or hieroglyphic signs.

Behind her in the procession, also mounted on a lioness or
panther, is a smaller figure of a beardless youth with a pigtail,
wearing a short tunic, upturned shoes and a conical fluted hat.
He too clasps a staff with his outstretched right hand, and in his
left hand he holds a double axe. His symbol, a pair of human
legs, suggests that he may depict the youthful son of the
Goddess whose name in Hurrian was Sharma or Sharruma,
and who appears again on the large scale in the small gallery
beside the main shrine holding King Tudhaliya IV in his
embrace. Behind him follow two goddesses vested like Hapatu
(Hebat) at the head of the procession, making the same gestures
but standing on a single double-headed eagle with outspread
wings. They may represent Mazzulla, the daughter of the Sun-
goddess of Arinna, and Zintulu, her granddaughter. The
divinity in the background, wearing a horned mitre, clad in
a kilt and carrying a mace or club and a sword, may be the
Storm- and Weather-god (Teshub), who leads the males in the
procession on the left walls just as the females on the right are led
by the Sun-goddess of Arinna; both groups moving towards
the god and goddess, followed by priests and priestesses.[88]

In the smaller chamber, the entrance to which is guarded by
two winged figures, a colossal erect figure of the 'dirk-god' is
curiously carved to represent a youthful deity with a human

head, wearing a conical cap, and the body composed of four crouching lions, two facing downwards and two upwards, back to back. Below the knees the legs taper to the point of a sword. To the right are two figures, the larger similarly clad, resembling the youth on the panther in the outer sanctuary, has his left arm round the neck of the smaller figure, a beardless priest/king in a cloak from which the hilt of a sword projects. His right wrist is grasped by the god's left hand, and a staff (*lituus*) is held in his right hand, as in the representation of the priest in the outer sanctuary. In the palace of Ala Hüyük (Euyuk), some twenty miles to the north/east of Boghazköy, a similar figure is followed by a priestess, each with one hand raised, approaching the image of a bull on a pedestal with an altar before it. On another relief the priest followed by a priestess is shown moving towards a seated goddess pouring a libation at her feet.[89]

Of the various uses and purposes of the great sanctuary known as Yazilikaya it is highly probable that the outer recess was a shrine of the Mother/goddess and the inner chamber a shrine of her son, the Young God, to which the king had access by virtue of his office as high/priest. Since the reliefs on its walls seem to give symbolic expression to the sacred marriage of the Goddess with the Hattic Weather/god, it is by no means unlikely that the reigning king and queen repaired to Yazili/kaya at the spring festival to perform the renewal rites so widely practised in Western Asia.[90] If this conjecture is correct, it is probable that the sacred marriage between the Sun/goddess of Arinna and the Weather/god of Hatti was enacted in the main hall in the presence of Sharma, the Young God. Garstang, in fact, suggests that it may have been the scene of the union of the Hurrian Teshub with the Mother/goddess Hebat of Kizzu/watna (the Cataonia of the Roman period), accompanied by their retinues on the occasion of the marriage of Hattusilis III to the high/priestess of the Sun/goddess of Arinna, Puduhepa, the daughter of the priest of Ishtar of Lawazantiya.[91] There is nothing in the texts to confirm this interesting conjecture, but in the Egyptian version of the treaty between Hattusilis and

Rameses II the Hittite queen Puduhepa appears on the royal seal embracing the Sun-goddess of Arinna.[92] The converging processions suggest perambulations in the New Year ritual closely connected with the sacred marriage, and since the bull is the animal of the Weather-god with whom originally he was equated in his fertility functions, the presence of the bull-man in them doubtless had the same significance.

Throughout Anatolia and Northern Mesopotamia the bucranium recurs from the Early Bronze Age, as, for instance, on the seals and on Tell Halaf painted pottery, and in graves at Aladjahüyük,[93] while in Hurrian mythology and icono-graphy Teshub is associated with two bulls, probably Seri and Hurri, 'Day and Night', who are attached to his chariot. Sometimes he is represented standing on a bull and holding a thunderbolt in his hand, thunder like rain being among his fertility aspects as the Storm- and Weather-god, just as the tempest and the rain were in the hands of Baal, the 'energizer' and 'Rider on the Clouds' in Syria. Thus, the bull being the embodiment or symbol of vital force so intimately connected with the Goddess and the cow, its appearance round the legs of the Weather-god and his consort at Yazilikaya leaves little room for doubt concerning the nature of the ritual at this great sanctuary.

The Sun-goddess of Arinna

The position of the Sun-goddess of Arinna is more difficult to determine. She was the consort of the Weather-god of Hatti, who, as we have seen, was connected with the bull,[94] and was the chief Hittite deity of the principal religious centre (i.e. Arinna). In the State religion she was 'the Queen of the Land of Hatti, Heaven and Earth, Mistress of the kings and queens of the Land of Hatti, directing the government of the King and Queen of Hatti', but unlike the Hurrian Hebat she was essen-tially a solar deity.[95] Her relationship, however, with the male Sun-god was never clearly established. Originally the principal goddess at Arinna was called Wurusemu, and Arimitti,[96] whose consort was subordinate to her just as in the State the

Sun-goddess of Arinna became the supreme goddess. Her husband, however, was the Weather-god of Hatti, not the Sun-god, and although he was a war-god like his spouse, it was she who fought his battles.

When the Hittite Empire came under Hurrian influence its goddess Hebat was identified with the Sun-goddess of Arinna,[97] and it is not improbable that the Hurrian Teshub then was equated with the Weather-god of Hatti and his son Sharma with his opposite number, the Weather-god of Nerik and Zippalanda.[98] Similarly, in this process of syncretism Shaushka, the Hurrian goddess of love, sexuality and warfare, the sister of Teshub, was identified with the great Babylonian goddess Ishtar, and worshipped in South-east Anatolia at Samuha and elsewhere in the Hurrian region.[99] Among her female attendants were the goddesses Ninatta and Kulitta, and there were also a number of local 'Ishtars' who must have been known originally under Anatolian names.

At Kummanni (i.e. Comana Cappadociae) in the Taurus area, where some of the oldest Hittite sanctuaries were situated, the Goddess Hebat, eventually known as Ma, became possessed of the essential attributes of the Sun-goddess of Arinna, and, like Ishtar and Anat, developed martial characteristics so that she was identified by the Romans with Ma-Bellona, thereby following the familiar transformation of the fertility-goddess into a war-goddess; a feature absent from the Hittite texts. Her alliance with Teshub in the Hurrian pantheon led to their being worshipped together at Aleppo, Samuha (? Malatya), Huma and Apzisna, as well as at Comana. At Yazilikaya, however, the youthful Weather-god, her son and lover, like Tammuz in relation to Ishtar, occupied a subordinate position before he was exalted as 'Lord of Heaven' and became the husband of the Sun-goddess of Arinna.

Here the Sun-god does not seem to have been conspicuous, despite the fact that the chief deity was the Sun-goddess. It may be that he was not indigenous in the Hittite pantheon and that it was only after he had been introduced into Anatolia that he acquired a definite status *vis-à-vis* the Sun-goddess.[100] But once he was celestialized as the ruler of the skies he could hardly fail to be identified with the Sun, even though in the official theology the husband of the Sun-goddess of Arinna was the Weather-god of Hatti, who appropriately became the Weather-god of Heaven, since his function was the fertilization of the earth. Similarly, the Anatolian goddesses were primarily Earth-mothers, and the Sun-goddess of Arinna originally was no exception to the rule apparently as she was so intimately connected with the indigenous fertility tradition and its divinities. She was 'Lady of the Land' and of 'the king and queens of Hatti'; indeed, 'the father and mother of every land' and the patroness of kingship.[101] She was, however, essentially a solar deity,[102] and with her the kingship was inextricably linked in which the queen exercised an independent cultic role, especially at the New Year Festival in the winter when, as it would seem, the nuptials of the Goddess and her spouse were celebrated in the manner customary in the Ancient Near East.

The Telipinu Myth

Nevertheless, although the Sun-goddess of Arinna was the supreme Goddess with whom the life and cultus of the State were bound up, and through a process of syncretization she had absorbed most of the characteristic features of the local goddesses and the sun-gods of a similar type, largely as a result of political fusion it was Hannahanna, the 'Grandmother', whose name was written with the ideogram of the Sumerian Mother-goddess Nintud. In the Telipinu myth it was she who was consulted by the Weather-god and took the initiative when a drought had brought all life to a standstill on the earth as a result of his son Telipinu, the Hittite Dumuzi-Tammuz, having disappeared in a rage and taken the grain with him. So the cattle, sheep and mankind no longer bred, and those with young could not bring forth. The vegetation dried up and the trees were unable to produce fresh shoots. Thus, a famine arose which threatened the life of the gods as well as of the human race, since they were dependent upon mankind for their sustenance. In this devastating state of affairs the Sun-god arranged a great feast to which he invited the thousand gods. They ate, however, but were not satisfied; they drank but their thirst was not quenched. Then the Weather-god remembered that his son Telipinu was not in the land and these disasters must have arisen because of his withdrawal in high dudgeon. Consequently, a diligent search for him was made in the high mountains, the deep valleys and the watery abyss, but nowhere could he be found. Realizing that if something were not done at once all would die of starvation, the Weather-god sought the advice of the Goddess Hannahanna, being herself so largely responsible for fertility. Thereupon she urged him to go himself to the city of Telipinu, but without success. The goddess then sent forth a bee, who finding him asleep near the town of Lihzina stung him on his hands and feet. This only made him more furious and determined to destroy all life upon the earth. At this point there is a break in the text, but eventually his malice was exorcized by the goddess of healing, Kamrusepas, who made him return on the wings of an eagle. Then 'the sheep went to the fold, the cattle to the pen, the mother tended her child, the ewe her lamb, the cow her calf'. An account follows of the ritual performed to assuage the wrath of Telipinu and restore fertility culminating in his 'tending the king and queen and providing them with enduring life and vigour'. An evergreen was set up in the temple and from it the fleece was suspended in which the fat of sheep was placed, and offerings of corn and wine, oxen and sheep were made to Telipinu.[103]

In this very incomplete version of the Telipinu myth in the form of a ritual commentary intended to be used in a fertility cult, the Tammuz theme was latent, though it differed consider-ably in its details from the Babylonian story. The cause of the wrath of the son of the Weather-god is missing, but the effects of his disappearance were the same as those produced by the descent of Tammuz into the underworld. Again, it was the Mother-goddess who intervened to secure his return, but there are no indications that Telipinu had died and was restored from the nether regions. Moreover, Hannahanna is not repre-sented as his consort or mother. His return, however, brought about a renewal of vegetation and fecundity in general, and of the life and vigour of the king and queen in particular, which doubtless constituted the purpose of the ritual ceremony in section C of the text appended to the narrative.

Although the episode is not connected with a seasonal rite, the theme and its ritual suggest that the myth was associated with the vegetation cult drama. Closely connected with it is a combat story recited at the *Purulli* festival that may have been held in the spring,[104] in which the Weather-god slays a dragon, Illuyankas, personifying the forces of evil in their various aspects with the help of a goddess Inaras. In the cycle of cult legends grouped round the Weather-god and his consorts the principal figures—the vegetation deity, the Mother-goddess, the king and the queen—assume their customary roles with local peculiarities and differentiations, while in the background are the Sumero-Babylonian cosmic struggles among the gods, as, for example, in the Hurrian Song of Ullikummi.[105] The predominant theme centres in a blight that descended upon the land because of a conflict between the Weather-god and a malign supernatural being in which the Goddess, with whom he stood in an intimate relationship, championed his cause. But although the texts cannot be explicitly connected with a particular seasonal celebration, their contents give every indication of having been cult legends, recited either at the critical junctures at the turn of the year, or whenever occasion required, for the purpose of restoring and maintaining the right ordering of the cosmic forces and reinvigorating the process of vegetation in the seasonal sequence.

CHAPTER IV

Iran and India

IRAN

In the welter of religions which characterized Western Asia in the third and second millennia B.C. the Iranian plateau by virtue of its geographical position was destined to become the connecting link between the west and the east in the develop﹍ment of a composite myth and ritual, as well as in other respects of a complex culture in which many streams met. To the south and south﹍east lay Mesopotamia, the Arabian Sea and the Persian Gulf. Northward to the east of the Caspian Sea, Turkestan extended as a broad lowland, and to the east the plain of the Indus valley, with the hill﹍villages of Afghanistan and Baluchistan, Makran and Sind, to the west of the Punjab, forming another line of communication with India. So placed in the very heart of the cradleland of the agricultural civilization of Western Asia, the Iranian plateau hardly could fail to make its contribution to the development and diffusion of the God﹍dess cult, which was firmly established in the peripheral regions of ancient Persia.

The Elamite Goddess

Thus, as has been considered,[1] on the plains of Elam in the protohistoric and in the First Elamite period (c. 2800 B.C.) rude female figurines holding the breast, often adorned with bracelets, pendants and necklaces, were prevalent. On a bas﹍relief on a rock at the entrance to the village of Sar﹍i﹍Pul, on the ancient highway from Baghdad to Teheran, Annubanimi king of Lullubi is depicted with the Goddess Ninni in a fringed *kaunakes* with a tall mitre on her head, leading on a cord two captives and stretching out her hand to the king. The accompanying Akkadian inscription invoking various gods against the enemy shows that strong Babylonian influences

were exercised in Elam in the first half of the third millennium
B.C. when the scene was inscribed and erected. In the second
millennium B.C., however, the Goddess Shala and her consort,
Inshushinak, were invoked rather than their Babylonian
counterparts. At Susa the fertility-goddess was worshipped
under the name of Kiririsha, who on Luristan votive disks
was represented in her characteristic attitudes, holding her
breasts and squatting in the posture of childbirth.[2] So deeply
laid was the cult, extending from Asia Minor to Susa, that it
survived the break-up of the Elamite power in 640 B.C., and
under the name of Nanaia the Mother-goddess continued to
exercise her customary functions down to the Parthian period
(*c.* 250 B.C.–A.D. 229).

Anahita

By a similar process of syncretism she became the Avestan
goddess of fertility and water, Anahita, who in the Yashts
personified the mystical life-giving river 'in the shape of a maid,
fair of body, most strong, tall-formed, high-girded, pure, nobly
born of a glorious race'.[3] As the goddess of the waters let down
from heaven to fructify the earth and bring increase to flocks
and herds and mankind, easy labour to women and abundant
milk, she was endowed with the form of Ishtar, depicted in the
statues erected at Susa, Ecbatana, Damascus, Babylon, Bactria,
and elsewhere by Artaxerxes II, with prominent breasts, a
crown of gold, a golden embroidered cloak, ear-rings, a necklace and a girdle. As such she was worshipped as 'the Great
Goddess whose name is Lady', the 'all-powerful immaculate
one', purifying 'the seed of males and the womb and the milk
of females'.[4] Like most fertility-goddesses, she was also regarded
as engaged in warfare, riding in a chariot drawn by four white
horses in which are wind, rain, cloud and hail. She was, in
fact, the Iranian counterpart of the Syrian Anat, the Babylonian
Inanna-Ishtar, the Hittite goddess of Comana, and the Greek
Aphrodite,[5] and as a member of the triad, Ahura Mazda-
Mithra-Anahita in the Mazdaean pantheon, she appears in
Achaemenian cuneiform inscriptions in association with

Mithra as the Young God and victorious hero liberating life by the sacrifice of the primeval bull.[6]

Although Artaxerxes II (414–361 B.C.) is said to have been the first to erect images of Anahita in various parts of his dominion,[7] the popular appeal of the cult is to be explained by the long history that lay behind it in Iran and the surrounding countries. In Egypt as the goddess of Kheta she was represented seated on a throne or on a horse, holding a spear and shield and brandishing a halbert.[8] In Cappadocia and Cilicia she was identified with the Mother-goddess Ma and equipped with a retinue of priestesses engaged in sacred prostitution.[9] Her very close resemblances to Ishtar reveal Mesopotamian influences, but while Herodotus may have been justified in regarding her as a foreigner in Persia, identifying her with an Assyrian goddess called Mylitta whom he confused with Mithras,[10] she stands in the same tradition as the Elamite Kiririsha and Nanaia, so that the cult has a continuous history in Iran down to the Parthian period (*c.* 250 B.C.–A.D. 229) when it became preponderant. The cult centres established throughout the empire by Artaxerxes II and the other Achaemenian kings were further extended, so that all the temples mentioned in the texts of the Parthian period were sacred to her. At Ecbatana, the summer royal residence, it is stated that 'they sacrifice always to her'; at Arsak, where Tiridales I was crowned, she had another shrine; and at Kengavar she was worshipped as the 'Persian Artemis', the 'Mistress of the Beasts', fulfilling the role of the Hellenic Artemis and Gaia as the mother of all creatures from whom they derived their sustenance and protection over all the earth.

Similarly, in Elymais two sanctuaries dedicated to Artemis and Athene were associated with her, very much as at Susa she was worshipped as Nanaia. At Istakhr there was a fire-temple of Anahita in the Sasanian period (*c.* A.D. 229–651). In a rock-relief at Naqsh-i-Rustam an investiture scene depicts King Narseh (A.D. 293–302) receiving his insignia from Anahita,[11] just as in a high relief on the walls of the huge grotto at Taq-i-Bustan near Kermanshah Chosroes II (A.D. 590–628) is shown being presented with the symbols of his office by Anahita and Ormuzd (i.e. Ahura Mazda).[12] In Northern Iran in the district of Shiz, Azerbaijan, the tradi/ tional home of Zarathustra, the chief fire-temple was dedicated to her, and she was held in great veneration by the very ancient Magian community there, who maintained the traditional Goddess cult in conjunction with Zoroastrianism in a highly complex syncretistic cultus.

Outside Iran it was especially prominent not only in Lydia, Pontus and Cappadocia, but particularly in Armenia. There 'the great Lady' was 'the glory and life-giver of the nation', the daughter of Ahura Mazda, and the benefactress of all man/ kind.[13] She was not, however, equated with water and the planet Venus as in the Avestan *Yasht*. Although she was called by Tiridates 'the mother of all sobriety', she also had a sexual and possibly an orgiastic side. According to Strabo ritual prostitution was a prominent feature, as in Cappadocia, 'the most illustrious men of the nation' giving their virgin daughters to the Goddess for a considerable period before their marriage.[14] Indeed, Anahita is said to have had male as well as female 'servants' (hierodules) consecrated to her service at her temple at Akilisene as at Castabala in Cilicia and Zela in Pontus, as well as in her Cappadocian sanctuaries.[15] In Lydia she was syncretized with her Greek and Phrygian counterparts, including Kybele, and in this guise eventually she emerged as the Magna Mater, as will be considered later.

Mithras and Anahita

Her association with Mithra and Ahura Mazda in the inscrip/ tion from Hamadan (the ancient Ecbatana), now in the British Museum,[16] shows that when the ancient Iranian nature religion was restored by Artaxerxes II under Magian influence, it remained true to type. The Goddess cult, as we have seen, was established in the second millennium B.C. when the nomadic pastoral Indo-European tribes began to enter the plateau in a succession of waves, some of whom settled permanently in Iran, bringing with them their own Vedic pantheon of nature gods.[17] In the resulting process of fusion Mitra became Mithras, the Lord of the Heavenly Light (not the physical sun), ever alert, and being light he was the giver of life and increase; 'the Lord of wide pastures' and of fecundity, as well as the antagonist of all the forces of darkness and evil. It was he who gave abundance, making the fertile soil to produce its fruits and the herds their progeny.

In India, Mitra was associated with Varuna, the allencompassing sky who supported heaven, earth and the air, like the Greek Ouranos (sky) with whom his name is equated in Sanskrit.[18] He was also the bestower of rain and in his celestial realms he lived in a golden abode. This connected him with Mitra as the light proceeding from the sun. Therefore, the two gods, Varuna and Mitra, were regarded as the great Twin Brothers representing two aspects of celestial light. Behind them lay the ancient Indo-European Sky- and Weather-god, Dyaus Pitar, who personified the heavens, the prototype of the Greek Zeus and the Roman Juppiter. As the source of the fertilizing rain in his procreative capacity he was united with Prithivi, the earth, but in the Rig-veda he was only very vaguely conceived, having been replaced by Varuna, Mitra and the Vedic nature gods and goddesses. In Iran the *devas* ('shining ones') were transformed into *daevas* ('evil spirits'), and the demons (*asuras*) were made the *ahura* ('lords' and 'masters') with Asura Varuna proclaimed by Zarathustra as Ahura Mazda, 'the Wise Lord', the sole supreme Deity. To him all other divine beings were subordinated in the Zoroastrian reform as his attributes, modalities of his action. Therefore, Mitra (now called Mithra) ceased to be his Twin Brother, and in the Avestan Gathas he is not even mentioned.

Nevertheless, in the perennial struggle between good and evil, light and darkness, the Sky-god Varuna had been brought into conjunction with the celestial Mitra under the guise of Ahura Mazda, and raised to the level of a genuine ethical monotheistic deity. Both the ancient gods who lie behind the All-wise Lord of the Avesta were heavenly beings representing

the all-encompassing sky in its complementary aspects, nocturnal and diurnal. Although Mithra was not the sun,[19] his
celestial origins and connexions with the light opened the way
for him to acquire solar attributes and functions until in the
Mithraic Mystery eventually the identification became complete.
In the later Avestan literature, however, as we have seen,
Mithra reappeared in association with Ahura, who was represented on the Achaemenian tombs and monuments at Persa-
polis by a winged disk out of which the head and shoulders
of the Wise Lord arose, symbolizing his reign in the sky and
his protection of the earth. Often he was surrounded with
divine assistants who originally were the ancient nature gods,
and the equation of Mithra and Anahita in the Mazdaean
triad shows the high position these two divinities held in
relation to Ahura Mazda in later Zoroastrian theology, and
how closely they were connected with each other.

In order to fulfil the needs of mankind the beneficence of the
celestial realms had to be made accessible on earth, providing
fruitful seasons, destroying the forces of evil and giving immortality to the dead. Therefore, the Sky cult had to be brought
into conjunction with that of the Earth-gods and goddesses. In
this syncretism the heavenly god as the Sky-father usually has
been the Supreme Being responsible for sending rain and giving
fertility to the soil, but he has been regarded as fulfilling his
functions in union with the Earth-mother. It is not surprising,
therefore, that in Achaemenian Iran the worship of the Lord
of fecundity was fused with that of the Goddess of the waters,
representing together the Father and the Mother aspects of
nature—Ahura-Mithras and Anahita—an assimilation that
may have been fostered largely under Anatolian influence
where the Goddess cult was so very prominent. Moreover, it
was with Kybele and the worship of the Magna Mater that
Mithraism eventually was allied (e.g. in the Taurobolium).[20]
But Mithraism was essentially a male cult, and although the
alliances were made with female divinities Anahita failed to
retain a permanent place in the Mystery as the companion of
Mithras.

INDIA

Indo-Iranian Relations

The same combination of Western Asiatic and Indo-European traditions manifest in Iran recurred in North-west India in the second millennium B.C. In both these regions a firmly established cultus in which the Mother-goddess played an important part was overlaid by an influx of Indo-European divinities when the tall, light-skinned Aryan-speaking intruders made their way from the Eurasian plains of Southern Russia into Sind and the Punjab between 1500 and 1200 B.C. In their earlier habitat they must have been very closely associated in language and culture with the rest of the undifferentiated Indo-Iranians even though they may not have been in actual contact with each other in their cradleland east of the Caspian Sea. This common home is reflected in the Iranian mythology, but it does not occur in the earliest Vedic texts (i.e. the Rig-veda) in the latter half of the second millennium B.C., notwithstanding the recurrence of Iranian names in India and implied references to Persia in the Vedic literature,[21] perhaps because the two groups had long been in a state of hostility. They were both, however, part of the eastern branch, commonly known as Indo-Iranians. One section crossed the Caucasus in an eastern direction and made their way to Northern Mesopotamia and the Zagros mountains (e.g. the Mitanni and Kassites) whose rulers bear Indo-European names.[22] Another group entered the Iranian plateau and settled there as the *Ariana*, while a third later moved gradually towards India through Transoxiana, the Oxus (Amu-Daria) and Bactria to the Hindu Kush passes, carrying with them their pantheon, even though they regarded their *devas* as beneficent and the *asura* as malign, thereby reversing the earlier Iranian differentiation.

There can be little doubt that it was they who encountered the Harappa civilization which had flourished as a highly organized urban culture from about 2500 to 1500 B.C.,[23] and apparently was brought to an end summarily by barbarian invaders from the west who sacked Harappa on the Ravi rivers and Mohenjo-daro and Chandhu-daro in the Lower

Indus valley, and burnt the Baluchi villages. To what extent, if at all, the Aryans were involved in this destruction is difficult to say, but they may have settled in the ruins of the ancient cities. In any case, to the south of the citadel of Harappa a post-Harappan cemetery (known as 'cemetery H') contains the skeletal remains of what appears to have been an alien population, though its ethnological affinities have yet to be established. The pottery is distinctive, and on one of the burial urns a symbolic scene in the frieze has been related to Vedic conceptions of the transmigration of souls.[24] But the pre-Aryan culture with its myths, legends and cultus was by no means obliterated. On the contrary, the emergent product was a composite creation, the warp of its original texture being Harappan (i.e. probably Dravidian), and the weft Indo-European (Aryan).

As the Indo-European immigrants were Aryan-speaking, so in all probability the builders of the ancient cities in Sind and the Southern Punjab were of Dravidian speech. This is almost certainly the oldest language in India, brought into the continent by invaders from the north-west in the third millennium B.C. before it passed to the south. Thus, the oldest form of the word *Tamil* or *Dravida* was apparently *Dramila*, or *Dramiza*, and had affinities with Asia Minor and the Eastern Mediterranean. Moreover, many traits of a pre-Aryan culture have been detected in Old Tamil.[25] Again, that the movement was from north to south is indicated by the existence of a Dravidian-speaking tribe, the Brahni, in Baluchistan, and throughout its distribution in India it gives the appearance of having been an intrusive cultural element overlaying the aboriginal pre-Dravidian substratum that survived in the Veddas and Todas and the hill tribes. Ethnologically it represented a mixture of types, and after the advent of the Aryans the two main linguistic and cultural streams coalesced in spite of subsequent attempts in the second half of the first millennium B.C. to keep them apart by the Caste-system imposed by the dominant Aryans, based originally on a colour bar; *varna*, the Hindu term for 'caste', meaning 'colour'.

There is no indication, however, of any division of this kind in the sacred literature of the early Vedic period, and it was not until about the fifth century B.C. that Caste began to make its appearance in the Ganges valley in districts ruled by Aryan hereditary rajahs, and under the powerful influence of Brahmanism to spread rapidly throughout the country, interpreted as an ordinance of divine appointment. By then, however, the syncretism had become permanently established, Hinduism in practice being a combination of preAryan (Dravidian) and Vedic Aryan elements inextricably fused into a composite system of belief and practice in which the Goddess cult played an essential role.

Throughout the distribution of the Dravidian people the Earthmother and her male counterpart were recurrent figures of fundamental importance in the religious, social and economic life of the community. The Aryans, it is true, were familiar with the Skygod, Dyaus Pitar, usually coupled with Prithivi Mata, the Earthgoddess, as the universal parents. But they were vaguely conceived as father and mother and their anthropomorphism was never clearly defined. Dyaus Pitar was overshadowed by Varuna, and Prithivi, like other Vedic goddesses except the Ushas, was not much more than a faint reflection of her husband, though as 'the earth' she had a status of her own. But it was the material heavens and the earth that they personified respectively, whereas the Dravidian conception was that of the fundamental forces of fertility and fecundity upon which all life depended.

Shiva and His Consorts

Shiva was the god of many names who became identified with the Vedic Stormgod Rudra and with Agni, the Lord of fire and sacrifice, while on his orgiastic side he was Bhairava, a Bacchic figure and the centre of a licentious cultus revealing traces of the Mothergoddess tradition going back to the Harappa civilization. The union of a god with a goddess typified the sources of reproduction in which male and female were united and became symbols of a single divine power with

male and female aspects so that Shiva 'the auspicious' was
regarded as the androgynous Creator who produced his own
consort from the female side of his nature. But when a deity
had a dual nature, one quiescent and the other active, his female
energy (*sakti*) usually was personified as his wife, inseparable
from him and joining with him in creation, sustaining and
destroying the phenomenal universe. Thus, the worship of the
Mother-goddesses received Brahmanical sanction by interpreting them as manifestations of *sakti* personified in the consort of
Shiva, 'combining in one shape life and death'. At a higher
level *sakti* was interpreted as the eternal reproductive principle
(*prakriti*) united with the eternal male principle (*purusha*) in the
generation of the gods and the universe, and Shiva became pure
spirit assuming a body to render himself perceptible.

Since the principal emblem of Shiva always has been the
linga, a phallic symbol typifying the male generative organ,
which at Mohenjo-daro and Harappa was associated with
yoni rings representing the vulva, there can be little doubt that
he was essentially a fertility-god. This is confirmed by the bull,
known as Nandi, being his constant attendant. Therefore, his
living representative, the white bull, has been allowed to
wander in complete freedom everywhere, and his image has
been depicted in stone in all Saivite temples as the guardian of
the shrine. To this day at Benares holy inviolable cattle roam
about the narrow streets of the sacred city as well as in the
courtyards of the temples, unmolested and receiving quasi
divine honours. There Shiva is worshipped as Visvesvara, the
Lord of All, the divine Ruler of Benares, and a *linga* of
supreme sanctity is there venerated by his votaries. Therefore,
this aspect of his nature has survived throughout the ages, and
when gradually his character as the regenerator of nature and
the destroyer of evil was transferred from the physical to the
moral sphere, he became the purifier of the soul and the
guardian of mankind. But the *linga* and the bull have remained
the principal symbols of the cult, together with an undisciplined
sexualism in its popular practice, even though from being
a phallic symbol the *linga* stands for a Supreme Being as

the Ultimate Reality of the evolution and involution of the universe.[26] It is true that neither the iconography nor the ritual is priapic, and many of its devotees may be quite oblivious of the original significance of the objects portrayed and the sacred actions performed. The natural functions of procreation quite reasonably are not regarded as obscene *per se*, and so there seems to be nothing improper in personifying male and female energy (*sakti*) in religious worship and divine relationships, or in erotic mythology, interpreted as allegories embodying spiritual realities, though among the unsophisticated it has too often degenerated into sordid license.[27]

But however the cult may have been transformed and interpreted mystically, metaphysically and symbolically, its original character and significance are apparent. The phallic element unquestionably goes back to the prehistoric substratum of the Goddess cult, and, as Sir John Marshall has pointed out, the religion of the Indus peoples is 'so characteristically Indian as hardly to be distinguishable from still living Hinduism, or at least from that aspect of it which is bound up with animism and the cults of Siva and the Mother-goddess—still the two most potent forces in popular worship'.[28] From this source it was introduced into Vedic worship as an intrusive element, but because it answered to certain fundamental human needs it found a ready response and acquired deeper and more philosophic traits which were given expression in the syncretistic figures of Shiva and his consort without destroying their original personalities as vegetation deities. The 'Great God' was 'in the fall of the leaf', yet he was primarily concerned with the renewal of nature, the death and decay of vegetation being but the prelude to its revival in the spring. As the symbol of life he was identified with the processes of reproduction in all their forms and aspects as creative energy in the cycles of birth and death and rebirth.[29]

Thus, Uma ('light'), the wife of Shiva, was a syncretistic goddess of nature and fertility in the beginning, as foreign to the Vedic tradition as her husband. In course of development she evolved into his female counterpart becoming the feminine side of his character. In her northern cradleland she was a Mountain-goddess, Parvati, and there she acquired the wild and furious attributes of a similar mountain-goddess, Vindhyava-sini, who also became a wife of Shiva, just as Uma was identified with the wife of Rudra, and as Kali or Mahakati ('the black') she was at once helpful, sinister and terrible. In course of time a number of goddesses beneficent and malevolent were combined into one Great Goddess, the spouse of Shiva personifying his *sakti*, often bearing the name of Devi or Durga, one of the common epithets of Uma, especially in her terrific character, at the end of the Vedic period.

Some of the goddesses she absorbed and fused in the one consort of Shiva-Rudra may have been connected with moun-tains and with the element of fire which was personified in its sacrificial aspects as Agni the mediator between heaven and earth and the sustainer of the universe, destructive yet expiating evil. Consequently, sometimes she was regarded in the Sanskrit literature as the daughter of Agni, or of the sun,[30] and in this capacity she again was connected with new birth, since the function of the god of fire was that of purifying, cleansing, protecting and giving new life and vigour, light and wisdom. He consecrated marriage, was a spiritual husband of maidens and brother of men, as well as priest and mediator between the gods and mankind. When the fire-altar was erected by the Brahmins in seven layers in the form of a falcon, representing the structure of the universe which was described as the body of Agni who became Prajapati, the Lord of generation, they were thought to repeat the process of creation. Since Agni was 'yonder sun', when he was born anew every morning the sacred flame kindled by the fire-sticks of the priests re-created the life that pervaded the universe and sustained it.[31]

Thus, the equation of Uma with Agni brought her into relation with the Brahmanic fire-altar symbolism which was the Vedic counterpart of the renewal rites of the Ancient Near East. The Brahmins as gods played the same role as the divine king in the seasonal drama of regeneration to ensure the con-tinuance of the cosmic order and the prosperity of the community.

'The universe is the Brahmin's', says the Code of Manu, 'for the Brahmin is entitled to the universe by his superiority and his birth.'[32] Therefore, the priesthood in Vedic India usurped the position previously held by the sacral kingship in the supreme control of the fortunes of heaven and earth, of the gods and men, and of the State. As masters of the all-sustaining sacrifice they were able to bring within their sphere of absolute jurisdiction every aspect of creative supernatural power. This was facilitated by the conception of a single cosmic divine principle, *rta*, beyond the gods governing alike the mundane and transcendental orders and associated particularly with Varuna, the King of Heaven, and subsequently with Shiva and his consorts and with Agni, the Lord of sacrifice. Consequently, it only required this fundamental principle (*rta*) to be made subject to the control of the Brahmanic ritual technique as the 'womb of *rta*'[33] to establish the complete supremacy of the priestly offering and all that this implied. Every part of the altar was identified with some part of the universe and the god who was responsible for it. The sacrificer in becoming the sacrifice was united with the universe in all its parts resolved into a unity and sustained by a cosmic offering in which the body of the Creator in his several forms and attributes was broken anew and restored for the conservation of the world.

By making Uma, whose name signifies 'light', the daughter of Agni she was brought into the closest relationship with the god (Agni) whose abode was in the eternal light and who was the first principle of all things.[34] Like him, she too made women to conceive and all the fruits of the earth to spring up and grow.[35] Therefore, when she first appeared in the last period of the Brahmana texts and in the later Puranas, she had become the feminine expression of the character both of Agni and Shiva, creative and destructive. She was the author and giver of life seated in her temple on the summit of a mountain adored by Shiva, Agni, Vishnu, Brahma and Indra, with the sun (Surya) and the moon (Candra) in their chariots above her.[36] But she was equally potent as the terrible foe of the demons, attacking the Daityas with her three heads and twenty

arms, slaying them in enormous numbers. Even in the Vaishnavite Mahabharata she is represented sitting enthroned beside
her husband (Shiva), while Ambika, 'the good mother', is
identified with her in the familiar role of the sister of the God of
fertility. Uma, in short, is the exact counterpart of Shiva, with
her many names and forms and functions as the Goddess of life
and death.

Vishnu and Lakshmi

The wife of Vishnu was Lakshmi or Sri, who originally was
an Aryan deity, the Indian counterpart of the Latin Ceres,
and, therefore, connected with the harvest or corn, as well as
with beauty, pleasure, wealth, wellbeing and victory. But in
her association with Vishnu she too appears to have been
indigenous and preAryan;[37] Vishnu, in fact, like Shiva, was
himself a composite figure, being a combination of the
Dravidian Skygod and the Aryan Sungod.[38] In the Rigveda he is only mentioned in six hymns, but in the Brahmanas
he comes into greater prominence by being identified with
sacrifice and all that this involved and implied in the control
of the vital processes in heaven and on earth.[39] By the fourth
century B.C., at the end of the Vedic period the name Narayana
('moving in the waters') had been applied to him, and the
god Vasudeva, the celestial father of Krishna, originally probably a nonAryan divinity in the northwest,[40] was regarded
as his incarnation, together with the 'Manlion' Narasimha.
Nevertheless, he did not rival Shiva in the Brahmanas, and it
was not until the great Mahabharata epic was composed in its
present form from the second century B.C. to the second
century A.D. that the Vaishnavite cultus became a central
feature in the Bhakti devotional movement and Vishnu the
most popular Hindu deity. The Mahabharata, it is true, may
go back at least to 400 B.C. in its earliest forms, but it was not
until the beginning of the second century B.C. that Krishna
became like Rama, one of his *avatars*, or 'descents', and assumed
the status of an *isvara*, occupying an intermediate position
between the Absolute and his projected *avatar*, who was

virtually a divine king (i.e. a man-god) concerned with the renewal of the world and its processes and with the material and spiritual well-being of mankind. Thus, Krishna was almost indistinguishable from a 'personal saviour', while Vishnu was the 'preserver' of all things.[41]

In popular belief Vishnu is thought to sleep for four months, from the eleventh to the bright half of the month Asark (June–July) until the corresponding period in the month Karttik (October–November). During this time demons are abroad and vegetation is in a state of decline. To contract marriages in this season of the year is inauspicious, being liable to become devoid of issue and to attacks by the rampant forces of evil. At the commencement of the sugar-cane harvest in the north figures of Vishnu and his wife Lakshmi are painted on a wooden board on which offerings are placed. A fire-sacrifice is offered and five sugar-canes are tied together at the top of a board. The mill is then marked with red paint and lamps are lighted upon it. Vishnu is thereupon awakened with an incantation and called upon to arise because 'the clouds are dispersed, the full moon will soon appear in perfect brightness'. Fresh fruits of the season are offered to him and the harvest begins with mirth, revelry and dancing.[42] Thus, the Vaishnavite cultus is brought into line with the seasonal vegetation ritual.

The consort of Vishnu, Lakshmi, who according to the Ramayana came forth at the churning of the primeval ocean, or was born from a lotus on the forehead of Vishnu, unlike Uma and Kali, had only a vague and shadowy personality, being little more than a reflex of her husband. Originally, however, she appears to have been an independent goddess who was subsequently made over to Vishnu. She was also the wife of Prajapati and of Dharma, the son of the Sun-god Kam. Indeed, she appeared in as many guises as her spouse chose to assume, so that when he was reborn as Rama she was Sita; when he was incarnated in Krishna she was Rukmini. She appeared as divine when he took a celestial form and as a mortal when he became mortal.[43]

When, like Aphrodite, she rose glorious from a sea of milk churned up by gods and demons, she was greeted by a heavenly choir and nymphs danced before her; the Ganges and other sacred rivers followed her, and the heavenly elephants poured the waters upon her. The sea of milk presented her with a wreath of unfolding flowers and the gods adorned her with ornaments. Thus arrayed, she cast herself on the breast of Vishnu and reclining there as his wife she gazed upon the gods who were enraptured with her. Having become the beloved of her spouse and removed a curse that had been placed on Indra, the sun shone with a new splendour.[44]

A nature myth of clouds and storms would seem to lie in the background of this curious story with gods and demons engaged in a mortal combat found all over the world, before it was allegorized in terms of the liberation of the soul through the practice of asceticism. That Lakshmi was the source of life which was coveted alike by the gods and the demons is suggested in the *Satapatha Brahmana*, where they are represented as seeking the permission of Prajapati to kill her. Instead he advised them to take her gifts without depriving her of her life. Therefore, 'Agni took her food; Soma, kingly authority; Varuna, imperial authority; Mitra, martial energy; Indra, force; Brihaspati, priestly glory; Savitri, dominion; Pushan, splendour; Sarasvati, nourishment'.[45]

But she remained the model of constancy and wifely devotion, and when Vishnu was incarnated as Rama of her own will she sprang from the furrow as Sita, the paragon of the most faithful of wives. Nevertheless, she was essentially 'the mother of the world, eternal, imperishable'. As Vishnu was 'all-pervading', so she was omnipresent. 'He is meaning, she is speech; he is polity, she prudence. He understanding, and she intellect; he righteousness and she devotion. In a word Vishnu is all that is called male and Lakshmi all that is termed female; there is nothing else than they.'[46] Her first birth was as the daughter of Bhrigu and Khyati. It was at a subsequent period that she was produced from the sea at the churning of the ocean by the demons and the gods.[47] But while the cult of the female counterpart of Shiva in its various manifestations has predominated in Saivism, in Vaishnavism Vishnu has retained his supremacy. Lakshmi, notwithstanding her charm and beauty of character in her various guises, has been so accom- modating to her husband that she has never fulfilled the role of the active and virile Goddess to the same extent as the Saivite Sakti of a thousand names, the mother of the universe, the reproducer, the destructress; mild and benevolent, fierce and cruel—Uma and Parvati, Durga and Kali.

Brahma and Sarasvati

Similarly, Sarasvati, the wife of the first of the three great Hindu deities, Brahma the supreme pre-existent Creator who as Prajapati became the Lord of production and the source of light and life,[48] was subordinate to her husband, though she was renowned as the Goddess of wisdom and was known as the 'Mother of the Vedas'. In the Rig-veda, however, she is represented as a river-goddess, though she is invoked for fruit- fulness in other characters, and once she is associated with a river-god, Sarasvat.[49] Later she became the patroness of learning and literary accomplishment, represented sitting on a lotus, graceful in form and appearance and adorned with a crescent on her brow. But her name signifies 'the watery one', and in ancient Hindu tradition she was assigned to a river[50] which now survives only as the dried bed of Hakra in Rajpu- tana where a number of prehistoric sites have been discovered by Sir Aurel Stein. In the Vedic Age it was the holy stream *par excellence*, and its disappearance is mentioned in the *Panchavimsa Brahmana*.[51] Consequently, the goddess whose name it bore must have been of considerable antiquity, and its sacred waters instinct with the divinity she conferred upon them were to the early Hindus what the Ganges has become to their descendants.[52] Thus, in the Rig-veda they were said to 'purify with butter', to 'bear away defile- ment' so that those who bathe therein 'come out of them pure and cleansed'. Indeed, they were declared to 'possess excellent power and immortality: ye are the mistresses of wealth and progeny; may Sarasvati bestow this vitality on her worshipper'.[53]

That she was primarily a river-goddess is clear from the numerous references to her in this capacity in the Vedic hymns and the Brahmanas in connexion with the sacrifices offered on the banks of the river, and with her reputation for sanctity throughout the region westward of the Jumna river.[54] It was she who was regarded as the patroness of the ceremonies celebrated at the holy stream, and who was identified with the hymns sung at them as an essential part of the 'uttered rite'. In the later mythology she became the daughter of Brahma and under various names his spouse, like most Mother-goddesses, the One Being dividing himself into a duality of male and female, husband and wife.[55] Among the Vaishnavas of Bengal she was also one of the wives of Vishnu, but when they disagreed he transferred her to Brahma and Ma Ganga to Shiva, contenting himself with Lakshmi as his sole spouse. But in the main tradition she was originally betrothed to Brahma and was a goddess of wisdom and eloquence invoked as a Muse. In the Mahabharata she is described as the 'mother of the Vedas',[56] and in the Brahmanas as the wife of Indra, containing in himself all worlds.[57]

Brahma also is accredited with a second wife Gayatri in the *Skanda Purana* as a result of the refusal of Sarasvati to assist at the offering of a sacrifice at Pushkara, apparently for the purpose of obtaining rain. Her presence being essential for the due performance of the rite, Brahma in anger and despair commanded Indra to procure him a wife from somewhere. Seeing a young and beautiful milkmaid, Gayatri, carrying a jar of butter, he brought her to the assembled gods and holy sages to espouse her to Brahma. When the maid had been adorned with costly ornaments and seated in the bower of the bride while the priests offered the sacrifice, Sarasvati arrived, accompanied by the wives of Vishnu, Rudra and of the other gods. Loudly she protested against the 'shameful act' whereby she had been rejected as the wedded wife of the Supreme God and cursed all concerned in the betrayal. Brahma should never be worshipped in a temple except on one day in the year, she decreed; Indra should be bound in chains and confined to a strange country; Vishnu, who gave Gayatri in marriage to Brahma, should be born amongst men as the humble keeper of cattle; Rudra should be deprived of his manhood; Agni should be a devourer of all things; while the priests and Brahmins henceforth should perform sacrifice solely to obtain gifts. Gayatri then modified the curses, promising blessings and the final absorption into Brahma to all his worshippers. Vishnu and Lakshmi, however, induced Sarasvati to return and at her own request both she and Gayatri were to be attached to Brahma as his joint wives.

According to the later *Padma Purana*, to this union Gayatri agreed, declaring 'thy orders will I always obey, and esteem thy friendship precious as my life. Thy daughter am I, O God-dess! Deign to protect me!' Hence in its mythological guise the title Sarasvati Gayatri was applied to the consort of Brahma. But before she acquired her later creative qualities of learning, language and invention as the patroness of the arts, rhetoric and knowledge—the Goddess of speech and wisdom—she was primarily a river deity, the personification of the fertilizing waters of the stream that bore her name, brought into nuptial relation with the Creator of the universe, Brahma. When eventually he became the one impersonal self-existent Being (i.e. the neuter Brahman) out of which all things, including the Creator and his consorts, were evolved, the personal Brahma (masculine) was the producer and instigator of the phenomenal order, united in the Hindu Tri-murti with their female counterparts.

Dyaus Pitar and Prithivi

Thus, besides the three great gods the oldest and chief among the Vedic deities, Dyaus Pitar, the Sky-father, going back to the Indo-European period and identical with the Greek Zeus and the Latin Juppiter, has been paired with Prithivi, the Earth-mother, in the compound Dyavaprithivi, the universal parents of the gods and mankind.[58] Among the gods he is represented as the father of Ushas, the Goddess of Dawn, who rises perpetually in the east clad in a garment of light and exhibits her youthful graces. Night is her sister, and the sun her lover, though because she precedes him she is also said to be his mother. She is never, however, described as married to the Sun-god, though he always continues to pursue her. In the Rig-veda the original divine pair, Dyaus Pitar (Sky) and Prithivi (Earth), were fashioned from the primeval cosmic waters, apparently by the god Tvashtri, the Hindu Vulcan, and from them Indra was born.[59] Gradually he superseded his father as the champion of the gods against Vritra and his consorts, and forcing heaven and earth apart he released the cosmic waters and gave birth to the sun. The demons were then relegated to the nether regions.[60]

Nevertheless, although Dyaus faded into the background he and his consort Prithivi continued to be represented in the Vedas as the progenitors of the gods and the beneficent Father and the mighty Mother of all creatures.[61] Their functions, however, did not advance beyond the idea of paternity and maternity—Dyaus being the bull fertilizing the earth (Prithivi) in the manner commonly adopted by male and female deities in the Ancient East. Therefore, it was the marriage of Heaven and Earth rather than their personifications that was empha-sized in the texts, irrespective of the particular divine beings concerned in the union. It sufficed that 'the gods brought the two, Heaven and Earth, together and performed a wedding of the gods'.[62] But while the original pair, Dyaus and Prithivi, were superseded by Indra when he was said to have produced heaven and earth,[63] not to mention the venerable Varuna as the all-encompassing heavens, they were invoked at the festivals with offerings as the prolific parents who made all creatures, and through whose favours immortality has been conferred on their offspring.[64]

It is not improbable that Indra came to occupy a position in the tradition of the more ancient Indo-European divinity, Dyaus, and that as his consort Prithivi retained many of the attributes and functions of the Earth-mother, it was she rather than her husband who was the chief object of devotion in the cultus. Dyaus is not mentioned in all the hymns celebrating Heaven and Earth,[65] and often Heaven and Earth are called the 'two mothers', even when Dyaus is one of them. Thus, the Earth is besought to be 'kindly, full of dwellings and painless', and to give protection.[66] The dead are exhorted to 'go into kindly mother earth who will be "wool-soft like a maiden"'.[67] Similarly, Aditi, the mother of Varuna, is also an ancient Vedic deity akin to the Mother-goddess who in the Rig-veda is supplicated for blessings on children and cattle,[68] and sometimes equated with Prithivi as the protectress of the earth.[69] But the Earth being regarded as the common womb of all existences the goddess who personifies it cannot be contained in a single figure. She is 'what has been born, and what will be born',[70] very much as the various manifestations of water in the form of rivers, streams, springs, clouds and rain have been conceived as the substratum of life and fecundity with which fertility vegetation goddesses have tended to be identified.

The Village Goddesses

Therefore, the worship of the Earth and its fertilizing waters has assumed many forms, the cult having become universal in India. It is not surprising that its principal personification, Prithivi, should have been made the consort of the most ancient Sky-god Dyaus Pitar, and though she and her husband were eclipsed by the more popular and intimate sectarian figures—Shiva and Uma; Parvati, Durga and Kali; Vishnu and Lakshmi; Rama and Sita; and even Brahma and Sarasvati—the sanctity of the Earth has remained a fundamental belief throughout India for all time, and around it the Goddess cult has found its several modes of expression. Thus, in every village the Mother-goddess is represented as the tutelary deity (*grama devata*) under various names, such as Mata, Amba, Amma, Kali, Rati and so on; sometimes dreaded, sometimes protective, warding off evil influences and imparting fertility by virtue of her life-giving energies (*sakti*). Usually a male partner is associated with her, but as his functions on the whole are less

onerous he tends to play a more passive role, relegating to his
female counterparts (i.e. the female half of his nature) the
control of natural forces and potentialities in relation to the
supernatural order. Therefore, in spite of the fact that in
Brahmanism where the highest condition of self-existent Being
(Brahma) is quiescent inactivity, goddesses inevitably are at a
discount except as the personification of abstract qualities of
maternal energy, in Saktism (notably in Saivism) and in the
popular village cultus the female principle is worshipped not
only symbolically but in the person of a goddess and her human
embodiments.

Thus, the cult of the divine Matris or Mothers is one of the
most outstanding features of Hindu rural communities; in the
north under the name of Mata or Amba, in the south under
that of Amma or Ankamma. Each village has its own local
goddess, and practically all the people except the Brahmins
join actively in the sacrifices and the attendant rites held in her
honour and to secure her good offices, particularly when
cholera, smallpox and other scourges are rampant. Being at
once propitious and malevolent she can either protect or
destroy, and so it behoves those who live within her 'sphere of
influence' not to neglect her worship or offend her in any way,
lest instead of securing their well-being she brings upon them
disease and death, drought and sterility, and all the ills to
which flesh is heir. Indeed, 'the Mothers' are more dreaded
than loved, though some of them are primarily beneficent, as,
for example, Dhartri Mai who sustains all life and represents
a continuation of the Vedic worship of the Earth-mother,
Prithivi and Ma Ganga.

Shashthi, the 'Sixth Mother', is the guardian of the home in
the United Provinces presiding over childbirth, protecting
infants and married women in their various avocations.
Therefore, she is worshipped by mothers arrayed in their best
attire with all their ornaments at least six times a year, and
every month when they have a lost child. To the small stone
which is her emblem in the shrine under a banyan-tree they
bring their offerings. These are blessed by the officiating priest,

and after they have been presented to the goddess they are then given either to him or to women desiring a child who eagerly receive them, vowing to make similar offerings every year if the goddess bestows this blessing upon them. On the sixth day after birth, when an infant is especially liable to contract lock-jaw, figures of the goddess are drawn on the wall and the father performs the appointed rites at the shrine. On the twenty-first day, when the danger is over, if all has been well the mother makes a thank-offering, placing garlands on the stone. Should she be unable to visit the shrine a branch of the banyan-tree is taken to her house and the ceremonies are performed there before it.

As a village goddess Mother-earth is generally aniconic and her shrine often is in charge of women, or of a non-Brahminic priest drawn from one of the pre-Aryan tribes. In this capacity as Mother-earth she is regarded as beneficent, being the upholder of human, animal and vegetable life omnipresent in the ground with which she is equated, as in the Rig-veda where she is the personified 'furrow', and later a godling of the ploughed field. In the Ramayana Sita is a manifestation of Mother-earth having risen from the furrow which her adopted father Janaka was ploughing. Similarly, Balarama, 'Rama the strong', the *avatar* of the chthonic serpent Sesha or Ananta, appears to have been an ancient agricultural deity who presided over the tillage of the soil and the harvest.[71] His weapon is the ploughshare with which he cuts down his wife to suit his stature, very much as Anat treated Mot as the reaped grain in the Ugaritic myth.[72] Therefore, like the Goddess, he had his sinister side, annihilating his enemies by the glances of his eye when he was filled with wine.

The village 'Mothers', in fact, invariably assume a malignant character and are very far from maternal in their ways and works. Thus, in Gujerat among the 140 Grama-devata worshipped from time immemorial all are said to delight in blood and to be the cause of sickness and death when it is not presented to them by the sacrifice of goats, swine and cocks. One requires no less than three or four thousand kids annually to keep her from her mischievous attacks on the villagers. The outbreak of cholera or smallpox is attributed to an angry Mother, as is whooping-cough and the various symptoms of demoniacal possession, such as epilepsy, hysteria, delirium, convulsions and fever.[73] Smallpox, in fact, is assigned to a special divine Mother under different names all over India. In the Northern Provinces she is called Sitala Devi, 'she who makes cool', a euphemistic title based on the high fever that is the customary symptom of the disease. Among her other names (e.g. Mata, 'Mother'; Mataji, 'Honourable Mother'; Maha Mai, 'the Great Mother') 'mata' meaning 'Mother', and smallpox is usually included, since she is the goddess who at one and the same time prevents, produces and personifies the disease.

The Pods regard her as their chief deity, and in the Central Provinces she is worshipped under the form of indented stones placed beneath a medicinal Nim-tree, alleged to have the power of curing lepers. In the Punjab her abode is a Kikar-tree, the roots of which are watered by women to cool those who are suffering from smallpox. In the Maratha districts an image of the goddess is bathed in water mixed with Nim leaves, and sprinkled on the patient. On his or her recovery rice and curds are offered to her, and chicken and goats are sacrificed. Costly silver images sometimes are among the votive offerings to Sitala to secure recovery without loss of sight or disfigurement.[74] Little respect is paid to her by men, however, except during epidemics.

In Southern India in the Tamil country she is known as Mari Amma, 'the destroying Mother', and in the Telugu region as Poleramma. Her shrines of mud and stones usually are outside the village, often on the side of a reservoir, and contain merely an upright stone as the image of the Goddess. When smallpox occurs cactus is placed outside the house of the victim in the hope that the Goddess will think the place is uninhabited. Then a sheep or buffalo is tied to the bed on which the sick man is lying and subsequently sacrificed outside the village. On the decapitated head of the animal pots of food are left outside the boundaries to keep Poleramma at bay. If this does not prove to be efficacious and the disease becomes an epidemic a more elaborate rite (*jatara*) is performed after food and buttermilk have been collected from each house in the village, and the legend of Poleramma recited describing her powers and the need to placate her. The fourth of an anna, some turmeric, charcoal and rice are placed in a new pot which is carried in procession through the village on the first day of the festival to the accompaniment of the beating of drums. Offerings of food are made at the house of the dead man of the shepherd caste. The various vows to the Goddess are then publicly announced and more food is collected from the houses. The procession goes to the temple of Poleramma outside the village, where the image of the Mother is bathed and before it are placed the pot of food and other offerings. The royal staff and snake's blood, having been kept in water all night, are carried to the temple after the sheep has been sacrificed and placed beside Poleramma. On the next two days the processions are resumed, and in the afternoon of the third day food is cooked, offered to the goddess and eaten by the villagers amid merry-making and a procession of gaily decorated carts and oxen round the temple. On the fourth and last day the principal event is the decapitation of a buffalo after the story-tellers have worked up the people to a great state of excitement, the head being placed before Poleramma to propitiate her.[75]

An almost identical rite is held for the same purpose in conjunction with the Great Mother Peddamma in the Telugu country, and with Ankamma, the Goddess of cholera, in the same district.[76] She too is represented by a stone image in a temple outside the village, and is the recipient of sheep and buffaloes amid wild dancing, drumming and horn-blowing. This too includes the impaling of live animals on stakes, the goddess being supposed to be propitiated by this terrible suffering and shedding of blood. Food is then poured out before Ankamma and the festival closes with the usual procession of carts round the temple.[77]

Mutteyalamma, whose main concern is typhoid fever, though

she is also a rain-goddess, has an almost identical cultus centred in the buffalo sacrifice, while Dilli Polasi is a village and household Mother who bestows prosperity on the farm and the herd. To renew their marriage a wife removes her *tali bottus* (marriage symbol), and her husband ties it again round her neck with a new string. Then they eat together and worship Dilli Polasi. As a public cult a group of families assemble, the head of one of them acting as priest. A sheep is sacrificed and then they go to the water and trace a pattern (*muggu*) on the ground with lime or rice-flour. Ropes and pots are taken from the water and carried in procession through the village. On reaching the house another sheep is sacrificed to drive away evil spirits before they enter to pay their respects to the image of the goddess and listen to the story-teller, who recites legends in the traditional manner. Her sister Bangaramma, 'the golden one', of the Madigas outcastes, is treated in much the same way as Poleramma and the other goddesses who have *jatara* offered to them with the buffalo sacrifice as the central observance, during the course of which the caste people are violently abused.

The special Madigas goddess, however, is Mathamma, who is greatly feared by all sections of the community. Her festival (*jatara*) follows the normal pattern, concluding with the cutting off of the head of a fowl and brushing away all the sacred marks on the image (*muggu*) in order to remove all traces of the evil proceeding from Mathamma. Her spirit is believed to possess an unmarried girl who henceforth becomes the Matangi in whom Mathamma is incarnate. Having been duly initiated by a Brahmin into her office and status, she rushes about ecstatically, spitting on all and sundry regardless of caste, touching them with her stick to purge them from uncleanness, uttering wild cries, prophecies and abuses, and using obscene language. Arrayed in a necklace of cowry shells, her face painted with turmeric powder, she walks behind the master of the ceremonies, continuing her invective and humiliations in the houses of the Brahmins, though only a few Brahmin families now acknowledge her allegiance.[78]

The origins of the supremacy of the Matangi is obscure, but

from the numerous Dravidian legends concerning her it would seem that the Brahmins only reluctantly adopted the aboriginal cultus since most of the stories describe how it was imposed upon them by dire necessity after they had refused to worship the embodiment of the Goddess Mathamma, their refusal having brought upon them all kinds of woes;[79] Mathamma being represented as a powerful demon as well as a bestower of life-giving and purifying qualities. Therefore, her touch and saliva are eagerly sought, but the Brahmin household is anxious to be rid of her as speedily as possible.

This dual nature of the Mother-goddesses is a characteristic feature of the cult everywhere. As Whitehead says, to the peasant of South India they are neither exclusively evil spirits nor unmixed benefactors. They are rather looked upon as beings of uncertain temper, very human in their liability to take offence.[80] When they cause trouble, as they are wont to do, they are greatly feared and have to be promptly propitiated and adequately worshipped. Even the deadly and dreaded serpent, so prolific and venomous throughout India, is venerated as well as propitiated, partly on account of the widespread belief in its periodic rejuvenescence by the renewal of its skin.[81] Thus, in Bengal, Manasa, the Snake-mother, has her four festivals, at three of which she is represented by her sacred Euphorbia-tree, having the power of repelling snakes planted in the court-yard of the house where the festival is held. This emblem of her, or a pan of water surrounded by clay images of snakes, is worshipped. Sheep, goats, buffaloes and pigs are offered to her, together with rice and milk, to prevent her wreaking vengeance by sending deadly serpents, particularly the cobra, to the houses of the people. On February 5th the festival known as Nagapanchami is held, and figures of snakes are then painted on the walls of the houses, but no image of the goddess usually is made apart from her symbol (the Euphorbia-tree, the pan of water, or an earthen serpent). As queen of the snakes she is the sister of Vasuki, king of the Nagas who upholds the world, and wife of a sage named Jaratkaru. One of the Naga kings, Sesha, a chthonic snake with a thousand heads, is represented as serving as a bed to Vishnu. Above him Shiva is seated on the half-moon, and below in the lower coil Vishnu reclines attended by Lakshmi, while Brahma springs from a lotus in the centre. Sesha, however, before he was incorporated in the Hindu Triad was a god of harvest and 'the plough-bearer', who presided over the in-gathering and the tillage of the soil, armed with a plough-share;[82] hence his surname, *Halabhrit*. As an agricultural deity he fulfilled the normal function of the serpent in its fertility aspect in the Goddess cult. It is this underlying motive that made the Snake-mother beneficent in spite of her venomous characteristics.

The Forest Mothers

The Forest Mothers, on the other hand, unlike the Village Mothers, not being connected with the agricultural stage in the development of civilization, are not propitiated with animal sacrifice. All that is required by way of recognition is for the passer-by to add a stick or a stone to the heap that marks the abode of the goddess. In the Rig-veda the jungle goddess Aranyani is invoked as the 'Mother of Beasts' and represented the forest as a whole,[83] abounding in food without tillage, and in weird and uncanny sounds heard in its numinous solitude. In Northern India, where she is known as Vanasparti in the form of Ban sapti Ma, 'Mistress of the wood', she is kept under control by flinging a stone or a branch on her cairn as a tribute to her dreaded presence.[84] Sometimes, however, a cock or goat or a young pig may be offered to her by village herdsmen who graze their herds in the forest, and with the spread of agricultural conditions Forest Mothers tend to acquire more and more the characteristics of the Village Mothers. Thus, among the Paniyans, a forest tribe, a goddess Kad Bhagavati (who also occurs as a sexless deity called Kuli) is a malignant and terrible being dwelling in a stone, a cairn or a tree,[85] resembling in its sinister features the fiercer types of Dravidian godlings.

In their earliest forms all these Mothers are local manifestations of either the Earth-goddess, beneficent, malevolent or chthonic, or of other aspects of fertility and natural phenomena in their benign or sinister activities. As they have become more specialized in their functions, from being agents of fecundity in general they have been associated with particular diseases and epidemics (e.g. smallpox and cholera) and practices (dancing, possession, etc.) until when they have been adopted by Brahmanic Hinduism they have lost their earlier local character in their original Dravidian cultus. As great goddesses they have developed a universal significance with unlimited spheres of action and influence. Nevertheless, in the Vedas they are subordinate to their male partners, until with the reinsurgence of the protohistoric agricultural civilization the Goddess cult again has come into greater prominence as a result of the rise of the Bhakti sectarian movement, notably in Saivism and Vaishnavism. Among the Dravidian tribes in the south they have survived little changed throughout the ages.

The Sacred Marriage

That the sacred marriage has been practised by many of these tribes both in the north and the south is shown by the periodic union of the Earth-goddess with her partner, as, for example, among the Kharwara of Chota Nagpur, who every third year celebrate the nuptials of Muchak Rani (the Earth-mother). A small stone painted with red pigment is brought out of a cave and dressed in wedding garments. It is then carried on a litter to a sacred tree, whence it is conveyed in procession to an adjacent hill, where the bridegroom is thought to reside. There it is thrown into a chasm in which an underground passage is believed to communicate with the cave from which the stone has been taken, and through which it is supposed to return for the repetition of the rites three years later.[86] The Oraons in the Ranchi and Palamau districts in the province of Bengal and the Orissa States celebrate the ritual marriage of the head of their pantheon, Dharmi, the source of life and light, with the Earth-goddess at the Khaddi festival held annually in the spring when the sacred *sal*-tree begins to blossom. The priest and his wife with some of the villagers repair to a grove occupied by a spirit Kalo Pakko, identified for the occasion with Dharti Mata, Mother-earth. After sacrificing a fowl and offering rice and flowers, he applies oil and vermilion to the roots of a *sal*-tree, and by tying a cord round the trunk unites the Earth-goddess to himself in the capacity of Dharmi. Daubing his own forehead, ears, arms and breast with the red pigment, he sacrifices another fowl and exclaims, 'O Kalo Pakko, may there be abundance of rain and fruitfulness in our houses and fields!' After further sacrifice of fowls to evil spirits a marriage feast is held with the customary carousing. In the evening the priest is carried back to his house where his wife meets him and washes his feet. The next morning he goes round the village, his feet again being washed by the women at the door of each house and an offering is made to him of rice and money. After he has danced with the women they throw water over him, and he gives them *sal*-flowers to put in their hair. His assistant throws water on every roof of the houses visited, some of which is taken inside to bring prosperity. Feasting, merry-making, dancing and the singing of obscene songs amid general licence brings the proceedings to an end.[87] In the United Provinces, Bansapti, the Forest-mother, is married to Gansam (Bansgopal), the phallic deity who is represented by a mud-pillar in the form of a *lingam*,[88] while in Khandesh during a ceremony lasting seven days the marriage of the Goddess Ranubai is performed, together with the investiture with the sacred thread of an image of her made of wheaten-flour.[89]

The Dravidian Malayalis in the Salem district marry their god Sevarayan to a goddess of the Canvery river every year in May. The emblems of the two deities are placed in two chariots bedecked with flowers, jewels and tapestries amid umbrellas and fans, and taken in procession to the temple on Canvery hill, the people throwing fruit, nuts and coco-nut water after the cars. Incantations are recited by the priest, and when the nuptials have been completed the procession re-forms and marches down the hill, halting at cairns erected for the purpose to enable the deities to invoke a blessing on the villages and their inhabitants to secure their prosperity.[90] In the Rajshabi district of Bengal the Sun is married to Chhatmata, the Sixth Day Mother, and a male image is wedded to Koila Mata, a Mother-goddess of Bishar, when a well is dug.[91] At the beginning of the ploughing season in Central India the Bhils at the Akhtij festival marry two wooden images representing the deities who control the rains, and throw them into a stream when the rains come.[92]

Although the conception of the Mother-goddess, derived mainly from that of the Earth-mother, is such an outstanding feature in the Dravidian cultus in the south, and a hardly less important element in that of the Northern and Central tribes, the sacred marriage seems to have been developed mainly under Brahmanic influence. Thus, in the Baroda State of Bengal the Goddess Tulasi, the impersonation of the sacred Tulsi plant, is married to Vishnu,[93] and in Kathiawar, in the peninsula of Gujarat on the west coast, it is married by Hindus to the *shaligram* ammonite in the Gir forest near Una, where Krishna is believed to have ravished Tulasi and was himself changed into the stone by her.[94] In the Bijaput district the marriage of the Goddess Parvati with Sangameshvar, the God of the sacred river, on the banks of which the Saivite temple is erected with its numerous *linga* and images of Shiva, and Jain figures, is celebrated annually on January 12th. A local Brahmin officiates as the bridegroom, and a priestess as the bride. The ceremony extends over four days and on the fifth day it concludes with a procession in which Sangameshvar is carried in a car through the village,[95] very much as in the Himalaya during the rainy season Parvati is solemnly married to Shiva at the Nandashtami festival to promote the well-being of the crops.[96] In the fourth compartment of the west porch of the Great Cave on the island of Elephanta (Gharapuri), about six miles from Bombay, the marriage of Shiva and Parvati is depicted showing Parvati standing at the right of Shiva adorned as a bride for her husband. At her left is a three-faced figure, apparently acting the part of the priest in the nuptial rite. The bridal pair are accompanied by Brahma, Vishnu and

Surya, the Sun-god, the mother of the bride and Saravasti, the goddess who blesses the union, as is shown in Cave XXIX of the group of Jain and Buddhist Cave-temples at Ellora in the Deccan, constructed and occupied from the fifth to the tenth centuries A.D.[97] Following this scene at Elephanta in the fifth compartment on the south side of the eastern portico, Shiva and Parvati are represented seated together on a raised floor, arrayed as in the other sculptures with a female carrying a child standing behind the goddess; doubtless a nurse with Skanda, the warrior son of Shiva.[98]

The Cult of the Cow

In all this iconography the emphasis is laid on the union of the primeval pair for the purpose of assuring the fertility of the soil and the increase of man and beast. In her benevolent aspect the close association of the Mother-goddess in India with the cow brings her into line with her counterparts in the Fertile Crescent and Western Asia. Like Neith and Hathor in Egypt, Nin-Khursag in Mesopotamia, and Anat in Syria, Lakshmi and Parvati became equated with the divine cow as the source of life and fecundity, though this was a relatively late development in Brahmanic Hinduism. As we have seen, it was unknown in the Rig-veda in the second millennium B.C., and in the Harappa civilization in the previous millennium cow-worship has not been detected in spite of the fact that it seems to have arisen in the indigenous Dravidian culture.

The first prohibition of cow-killing occurs in the compara-tively late Atharva-veda, a collection of hymns in which non-Aryan influences are apparent. In one of them 'Viraj, who verily was this universe in the beginning', is said to have come to gods and men who milk from her the calf, the milker and the milking-vessel. 'Manu son of Vivasvant was her calf; earth was her vessel; her Prithu son of Vena milked; from her he milked both cultivation and grain.'[99] This conception of the Earth under the figure of a cow was elaborated in a myth in the Puranas in which the Earth, assuming the form of a cow, was assailed by Prithu, son of Vena, a sacral king who endeavoured to recover its fruits when they had all perished. At length she yielded to him and undertook to fecundate the soil with her milk. He then flattened the surface, and having made the calf he milked the Earth for the benefit of mankind. As a result corn and vegetables have abounded ever since.[100]

Having attained this status the sanctity of the cow was such that every part of her body was regarded as divine and her hair inviolable. Even her excreta has become hallowed and cow dung is now regarded as the most stringent purifying agent in existence, sanctifying everything it touches and making sinners into saints.[101] Therefore, to kill a cow is the most heinous crime and sin imaginable, and those guilty of this sacrilege are doomed 'to rest in hell for as many years as there are hairs on the body of the cow so slain'.[102] For the Creator, Daksha, having drunk a quantity of nectar, became elated and from him an eructation proceeded that gave birth to a cow which he names Surabhi and who was his daughter. She brought forth a number of cows who became the mothers of the world; 'the means of livelihood of all creatures'.[103] Being the daughters of the heavenly Surabhi ('the cow of plenty') who was created by Prajapati from his breath,[104] they are divine in origin, attributes and function, and, therefore, the object of veneration and surrounded with an elaborate system of tabus. But although the cow became the centre of a peculiar worship with mantras and rites,[105] requiring the devotees of Surabhi to subsist on the five products of the cow (milk, curds, ghi, dung and urine), to bathe and to use dung as prescribed, no image has been used by Hindus in the cultus.

All are required annually to perform an act of worship in the cow-house before a jar of water, while the more devout may throw flowers daily at the feet of a cow after bathing and feeding her with fresh grass, saying: 'O Bhagavati eat!' They then walk round her three or seven times, making obeisance. In the Central Provinces a ceremony called Maun Charaun ('the Silent tending of Cattle') is observed in commemoration of Krishna feeding the cows in the pastures of Braj. Those taking part rise at daybreak, bathe, anoint themselves with oil and hang garlands of flowers round their necks, remaining absolutely silent throughout. They then go to the pastures, still in perfect silence, holding a peacock's feather over their shoulders to drive away demons. For several hours they remain in silence with the cattle and then return home.[106] The fact that Krishna is thought to have spent his early life among cowherds and become the lover of their daughters, especially Radha, has given an odour of sacredness to cows, Krishna being one of the greatest and most venerated of the *avatars* among Hindus.

Nevertheless, in spite of this extraordinary reverence now shown to cows, in the earlier Vedas the sacrifice of cattle to Indra, Varuna and other deities was enjoined, though it is said to have been abhorrent to public opinion, suggesting that they were already regarded as sacred animals by the non-Aryan population, as in Western Asia and the Fertile Crescent. It would seem that the cult arose in India in the indigenous Dravidian civilization when with the development of agriculture the cow as the source of milk needed for sustenance became essentially the emblem of fertility and general well-being hedged round with tabus, so that even in the Rig-veda, doubtless under pre-Vedic influences, the epithet *aghnyax*, 'not to be killed', was assigned to it.[107] This was carried a stage further in the Brahmanas where the eating of its flesh was prohibited, though Yajnavalkya admitted that he ate it provided it was tender![108] Indeed, as late as the time of the Sutras and Epics it remained an ancient rite of hospitality to offer to slay a cow for a guest, though in fact the gesture was steadfastly refused, 'the guiltless cow' being the Goddess Aditi, the Earth-mother. Formerly, however, the Aryans both ate and sacrificed oxen quite freely.

While the Vedic Indians were meat-eaters and engaged in agriculture, like their predecessors they were primarily a pastoral people with milk and its products as a very important elements in their staple diet. While the ox, the sheep and the goat were killed for food, and, like the horse, as sacrificial victims, the cow acquired an increasing sanctity by virtue of its being the source of the milk-supply. In Indo-Iranian times it was treated with care and respect, milked three times daily and kept in a stall during the night and when the sun was at its height. Bulls and oxen used for ploughing fertilized the land by their droppings and so played their part in the cultivation of the soil.

Thus, the bull became sacred to the non-Vedic god Shiva, who, as we have seen, had a fertility significance inherited from his prototype Pasupati, the Lord of Beasts, and the partner of the Mother-goddess. In his Rudraic aspect he was connected with the Storm-god, who throughout the Ancient East has been associated with the Weather-god and the Goddess cult. The worship of the bull was a feature of the Harappan civiliza-tion which in due course became a dominant element of non-Aryan origin in Brahmanism, and the female figurines leave little room for doubt that the veneration of the Goddess was a prominent feature in the domestic life of the Indus cities. With these emblems of the maternal principle the bull and the *lingam* were symbols of reproduction embodied in Shiva, at once the Reproducer and the Destroyer. In due course every bull and every cow came to be regarded as embodying the spirit of fertility. Therefore, to destroy cattle was to jeopardize fecundity at its source and to bring disaster upon the fruits of the earth everywhere. Hence the tabu gradually imposed on cow-killing in Vedic India which, in the last analysis, arose out of the Goddess cult in the pre-Aryan Indo-Iranian culture.

CHAPTER V

Crete and Greece

A SITUATION not unlike that which obtained in India recurred in Greece and the Aegean, where an Indo-European cultus was superimposed on that of the Minoan-Mycenaean tradition in which the Goddess was predominant. Thus, on the mainland and the adjacent islands she was the principal object of worship in the Bronze Age, especially in Crete, Cyprus and the Peloponnese, where her emblems and adjuncts abounded—those of the snake, dove, double axe, horns of consecration, phalli and obese female figurines, together with representations of sacred pillars, trees and mountains on which often she is depicted as accompanied by wild and fantastic beasts and horned sacrificial victims. These cult objects and scenes undoubtedly were for the most part of Asiatic origin and significance, having passed from the Near East through Anatolia to the Eastern Mediterranean region, while others made their way from Egypt to the islands and thence to the mainland. This, as we have seen, is very apparent in the Neolithic and Chalcolithic statuettes and bas-reliefs in the Troad, the Cyclades, Cyprus, Crete, Thessaly and the Peloponnese in the third millennium B.C.,[1] though the technique in some instances indicates independent developments and diffusions in the Eastern Mediterranean. Nevertheless, the Aegean was virtually an Anatolian province[2] which became an area of characterization of the Goddess cult before 3000 B.C. when Western Asiatic influences had penetrated to Crete.

THE GREAT MINOAN GODDESS

At Knossos the flat fiddle-shaped figurines were peculiar to the Middle Neolithic period (c. 3500 B.C.), but the stumpy steato-pygous type continued to the last phase of the Neolithic, and as Sir Arthur Evans says, in Crete it is impossible to dissociate these primitive statuettes from those that appear subsequently in the shrines and sanctuaries of the Minoan Goddess.[3] Therefore, the beginnings of the cult can be traced back in the island to the middle of the fourth millennium B.C. when connexions with Asia Minor had been established. It was not, however, until the Middle Minoan period (*c.* 2100–1700 B.C.), when these Asiatic relations increased, that the Goddess herself emerged as an individualized anthropomorphic figure in her threefold capacity of the Earth-mother, the chthonic divinity and the Mountain-mother, Mistress of the Trees, Lady of the Wild Beasts, and guardian of the dead, represented with her various symbols, associates and backgrounds. Eventually on the mainland her functions and attributes were divided among a number of goddesses, but in Crete she was essentially the Minoan goddess *par excellence*, Britomartis or Diktyanna, later identified with Artemis and her other Greek associates.

The Snake- and Earth-goddess

In the central shrine at Knossos she was arrayed with a high tiara, a necklace, a richly embroidered bodice with a laced corsage, and a skirt with a short double apron, made in faience. Her hair is shown falling behind her neck and on to her shoulders, her eyes are black, her breasts bare, and coiled round her are three snakes with greenish bodies spotted with purple-brown. In her right hand she holds out the head of one of them, the rest of its body curling round her arm, behind her shoulders with the tail ascending to her left arm and hand. Two more snakes are interlaced below the waist in the form of a girdle round the hips while a third runs up from the hips, over the bodice to the left ear and round the tiara.[4] At Gournia in East Crete the principal object in the shrine, which was a public sanctuary, is a more primitive unpainted figure of the Snake-goddess Eileithyia, with raised hands and a snake twined about the body, clad in a bell-shaped skirt in the conventional Minoan manner. In the centre stood a low earthen table with three legs and the base of a vase supporting a bowl, presumably for offerings. Around it were

three tubular vessels with a vertical row of three or four handles
on either side. Above a larger handle was a pair of horns of
consecration, and one of the vessels were entwined with two
snakes. Other representations of the Goddess included heads,
forearms and hands, a piece of a pithos decorated with a double
axe, and a round disk like the emblem of Hathor in Egypt.[5]

Tubular vases recur at the household sanctuaries at Kumasa
and Prinia, and in a small chamber known as the Snake Room
of a private house at Knossos, having attached to their sides
two pairs of cups. Ringed or grass snakes moulded in relief
were also placed on the sides and shown in the act of drinking
from the cups, which in all probability contained offerings of
milk or of some other liquid. With these tubular vessels were
also found a terracotta tripod or table, the upper surface of
which was divided into four separate compartments by grooves
and partitions to accommodate four snakes each of which was
represented drinking from the bowl in the centre of the table.
The conclusion drawn from these designs by Sir Arthur Evans
is that in the Snake Room the reptiles were venerated as 'the
visible impersonation of the spirits of the household'.[6]

In addition, however, to being the 'House-mother', in this
early form of the cult going back to the Early Minoan period
(*c.* 2500 B.C.), as he has pointed out, she is depicted in her
destructive chthonic aspect holding the venomous viper rather
than the harmless snake.[7] The beneficent Mother of the domestic sanctuaries would hardly have as her emblem so deadly a
foe of mankind as the adder. Therefore, when she appears in
this guise it is reasonable to suppose that she has acquired the
more sinister qualities attributed to the Goddess everywhere in
one of her phases. Moreover, at Gournia, which was neither
a house nor a palace shrine, although she was essentially the
Snake-goddess she was not apparently the centre of a domestic
cult as at Knossos, in spite of her similar representation and
equipment with a table of offerings surrounded by tubular
vessels, and the close association of the snake with the guardian
of the house. Here it would seem that she was rather the
chthonic Earth-mother in the dual aspect of the Goddess of

fertility and the Mistress of the nether regions. Thus, not only were cups absent from the vases but they were also hollow tubes through which doubtless offerings were poured on to the earth as libations to the chthonic Snake-goddess, very much as in the shrine at Asine a large jug decorated with parallel stripes was found upside down on the cult ledge the bottom of which had been deliberately broken off to enable it to be used for libations of some kind.[8]

The Chthonic Goddess of Fertility

Similarly, in the famous cult scene painted on the sarcophagus at Hagia Triada, two miles from Phaestos near the south coast of Crete, in a kind of chamber-tomb ascribed to the Late Minoan II and III, bottomless libation jars occur through which the blood of a bull sacrificed on an altar flows down into the earth. Above the altar are horns of consecration and a basket of fruit. In front of it stands an olive-tree with spreading branches, a pole painted pink with a double axe and a bird, and a priestess with a vessel of offerings and a libation jar. Then follows the sacrifice of the bull, its blood being collected in the bottomless pail. Behind the well is a figure playing the double pipes, and a priestess clad in the skin of a victim offers libations at an altar.[9]

Here the Goddess is represented in a funerary setting, it would seem, with her priestesses as the officiants in a sacrificial oblation on behalf of the deceased, the life-giving blood of the victim being conveyed to them by means of ritual jars which carry the offering to Mother-earth, regarded as the ultimate source of rebirth. Professor Pedersen, on the other hand, thinks the episode depicts the sacred marriage of Zeus with Hera and her bridal bath as a mythical expression of the spring rains renewing nature. The goddess, it is said, is carried away on a chariot with griffins before the end of the year and brought back in a chariot with horses in the spring to be united with the god in the form of a cuckoo, the two leaf-clad pillars symbolizing the union. The goddess then disappears and the pillar is denuded but the blood of the bull offered in sacrifice effects a renewal, the rebirth of nature being expressed by the offering of the bath and the calves.[10] Similarly, Miss Harrison maintains that 'the picture speaks for itself; it is the passing of winter and the coming of spring, the passing of the Old Year, the incoming of the New, it is the Death and Resurrection of Nature, her New Birth'. It is the springtime of man and bird and flower as recorded in the Hebrew Wisdom literature in the book of Canticles (ii. 10); the bridal song of the new birth of vegetation translated into ritual action in the seasonal drama.[11]

It is difficult, however, to avoid the conclusion that the drama represents the Goddess cult in its funerary setting, connected probably with the journey of the soul to its final abode, where in its royal status it may have received divine honours.[12] Evans thinks the sacrificial rites were performed temporarily to summon it back to the land of the living while the divinity was charmed down into its material resting-place aided by the music and ritual chants as well as the sacrifice.[13] As they occur on a tomb in which one of the Minoan priest-kings may have been buried, it is not unreasonable to think that the cult of a heroized member of the royal line was associated with that of the Goddess who combined chthonic and vegetation attributes as the author and giver of life, the symbolism suggesting a combination of mortuary ritual with that of the Minoan Earth-mother.

The Tree and Pillar Cult

As the patron of fertility she was very frequently represented in association with a sacred tree or pillar. Sometimes the branches of a tree loaded with leaves and fruit are shown spreading over a baetyl or a cairn with attendants holding libation jars. Thus, on the mainland in tholoi of the lower town at Mycenae, Professor Tsountas discovered two glass plaques with lion-headed daemons pouring libations from ewers; in one case on a heap of stones surmounted with a larger block, and in the other on a square pillar reminiscent of the anointing of the menhir at Bethel in the Jacob story in Hebrew tradition.[14]

Similarly, on a gem from the Vapheio tomb the same kind of daemons are represented watering a nursling palm-tree from two spouted vases, while on a third plaque from Mycenae the libation is poured into a kind of bowl resting on a column with three supporting legs.[15]

As baetylic stones and pillars are among the most prominent features of the Minoan-Mycenaean shrines, second only to horns of consecration and the double axe, and recur with great frequency on engraved signets and gems, very often associated with mythical animals and sacred trees, there can be no doubt that these aniconic ritual objects were regarded as the embodi-ment of an in-dwelling divinity like the mazzebôth and asherôth in Semitic sanctuaries. Hence the pouring of libations upon them in conjunction with the identical treatment of the sacred tree, so frequently found standing beside the menhir, or very intimately connected with it. The pillar, however, was not exclusively the aniconic image of a male god, as Evans supposed,[16] since it often has been the abode of a goddess like the asherah, and in the Minoan cult-scenes the presence of priestesses and female votaries performing ritual actions in honour of the Mother-goddess predominate. Moreover, some of the pillars at Knossos were structural rather than religious in their purpose, and it is not very likely that they were also venerated as sacred baetyls.[17] It was only those which were erected definitely as menhirs that can be regarded safely as cult objects. Therefore, without accepting the interpretation of the double axe merely as a mason's mark, which does not seem to be at all probable, everything containing this sacred sign need not have been a divine embodiment, any more than in Christian practice a sacramental meaning cannot be attached to all objects marked with a cross. But, in any case, the double axe was associated with the Mother-goddess as well as with the Sky-god.[18]

That anthropomorphic representations of the Goddess, or of goddesses impersonating the maternal principle, were an integral element in the earliest manifestations of the cult is clear from the widespread and continuous use of female figurines in this connexion from Palaeolithic times. Indeed, these Venuses are not infrequently described as 'idols'. Nevertheless, in Crete it appears to have been under the influence of the palace sanctuaries and their cultus that the earlier aniconic forms assumed an anthropomorphic guise in the Middle Minoan period (*c.* 2200–1600 B.C.). For example, in the Neolithic cave sanctuary of Amnisos near Herakleion, the old harbour town of Knossos four miles east of Candia, identified with the goddess of birth, Eileithyia,[19] two stalagmites in the centre surrounded with broken sherds and enclosed by a rough stone wall were venerated as her aniconic embodiment as a sacred pillar. But no figurines of any kind have been recorded in the site.[20] Similarly, in the double cave of Psychro on Mount Dikte in the lower chamber were stalactite columns with double-axe blades and a bronze object placed edgewise into the vertical crevices. This was in all probability the legendary birth-place of Zeus whither the Goddess Rhea carried her new-born babe;[21] she doubtless being in her original form the Minoan Mother-goddess,[22] represented in the Middle Minoan Age aniconically in the stalagmite pillar when the Dictaean cave began to be frequented.[23]

The Mountain-mother

How very deeply laid was this baetylic imagery is shown by its survival after anthropomorphic representation had become established in the Middle Minoan in the sanctuaries on mountain peaks, in sacred groves and in the palace cult. With the pillar, pines, palms, cypresses and fig-trees invariably occurred in the mountain shrines, sometimes in a stone enclosure and overshadowing the menhir. This is particularly conspicuous on the seal- and signet-engravings where the Earth-mother as at once the goddess of vegetation and the *Mater dolorosa* is depicted, often with her attendant lions or genii, and standing on a mountain, sometimes with her youthful male partner. Thus, on a gold ring from Knossos fig-trees are shown overhanging the entrance to a temenos with an obelisk in front of the sanctuary enclosed by a wall of masonry. Before the pillar is

a female figure with her hands raised in an attitude of incantation, while suspended, as it were, in the air is a male figure
holding out a staff or weapon, thought by Evans to be that of
the Young God summoned by his mother-paramour, the
Minoan Goddess.[24] She appears to be standing on a stone
terrace, possibly indicative of a mountain. In the middle of the
portal of the sanctuary a smaller pillar is set up having some
affinity with the Cypriote female baetyl.

On a Late Minoan signet from Mycenae the Goddess is
represented in a flounced skirt, apparently as the *Mater dolorosa*
bowed in grief engaged in lamentation over a kind of miniature
temenos within which stands a little baetylic pillar with a small
Minoan shield hanging beside it. To the right another figure,
apparently that of the Goddess repeated, is about to receive the
fruit of a sacred tree in a small sanctuary containing a pillar,
a young male attendant being shown bending the branches
towards her.[25] If the enclosure represents a tomb containing a
phallic stone, the scene is brought into line with the grave of
Attis in Phrygia and that of Zeus at Knossos.[26] Therefore, it
may be a Minoan version of the Suffering Goddess theme in
Western Asia in relation to the vegetation cycle; the coming of
spring being expressed in the budding leaves and ripening
fruits.

This is confirmed by the scene on a gold ring in the
Museum of Candia, showing the sacred tree in an enclosure
with scanty foliage. The stem is grasped by a woman with both
hands, and on the left is an almost identical female figure in a
flounced skirt with the upper part of her body naked, revealing
prominent breasts. She is standing with her back to the tree
and her arms extended to a third woman clad in the identical
manner as her companions. In the fields are chevrons.[27] Here
the barrenness of winter gives place to the epiphany of the
Goddess in its spring setting, as in the case of that reproduced
on a ring from a cist in a small tomb where an orgiastic dance
in a field of lilies by four female votaries in typical Minoan
garments is portrayed. Above the chief worshipper in the
centre is a small female figure, apparently rapidly descending,

and to the left a human eye which may symbolize the Goddess regarding the ecstatic dance being performed in her honour at the renewal of life in the spring of which the snake by the side of the central figure below the eye is an emblem.[28] The bull, again, as we have seen, has always been a potent emblem of reproductive power in nature, and in Crete it was the king-priest in conjunction with his consort as the Goddess who played the leading part in the slaying of the Minotaur to overcome death and renew life.[29]

On the ring from the Vapheio tomb near Sparta a female of the same type stands beneath the overhanging branches of a fruit-tree at the foot of which is a stone column. Rocks below suggest that a hill or mountain indicated the setting of the scene. A naked male figure is bending the branches either to pluck the fruit for the Goddess or to enable her to gather it herself.[30] On a Late Minoan ring, now in the Ashmolean Museum at Oxford, which is said to have come from this tomb, a kneeling woman is depicted bending over a large jar with her left arm bent at the elbow resting on the rim. Her head is inclined forward supported by her left hand in an attitude of mourning. Above her are the eye and ear symbols, and a little to the left in the air is a small rigid male figure holding an oval object that looks like a bow. Below is a richly dressed female figure with wavy hair, thought by Evans to be the Mother-goddess, while both he and Nilsson identify the small figure, high in the scene, as her young male partner armed as the youthful archer.[31] Professor Persson thinks that since the vessel signifies a pithos burial the theme is that of sorrow over death. The object next to the jar he interprets as an elliptical rounded stone with the leafless branches of a tree behind it, symbolizing, as he suggests, the dying vegetation in winter and man's sorrow over death; the gods by their epiphanies giving renewed hope of the resurrection of the dead in response to this display of grief and lamentation.[32]

As the 'Lady of the Dead' the Mountain-mother combined the office and functions of a chthonic divinity ruling the grim nether regions and guarding its denizens with those of the

Goddess of the upper regions, exalted in triumph on the grandeur of her mountain-peak, where in her lofty sanctuaries she was worshipped with upraised hands and received libations and votive offerings. In these shrines the sacred tree and pillar occupied a prominent position but not the snake, which was confined to the chthonic and household cult of the domestic Goddess. In a recess of the central court of the palace of Knossos fragments of a series of clay sealings made by a signet were discovered on the cement floor, which when restored showed the Goddess in a flounced skirt standing on a rock or mountain-peak guarded by two lions with her left arm out-stretched and holding in her hand a sceptre or lance. Behind her is a shrine with columns and sacral horns, and in front of her the figure of a youthful male votary or divinity, or, as Evans suggests, a priest-king.[33] In the eastern quarter of the palace a simpler seal impression was found in a chamber with the Goddess between two lions, and other standing goddesses with sacred animals reveal the Mother of the Mountains as the Mistress of the Beasts.

The Mistress of Animals

The lion-guarded Goddess, in fact, with her male satellite, shrine and cult objects is essentially the Minoan Mother repre-sented in her various forms, aspects and attributes on the sanctuary seals everywhere in Crete as well as on the Cypro-Mycenaean cylinders. Sometimes in addition to lions a dove is held, and groups of the cow and calf and wild goat and horned sheep appear on the faience reliefs of the Goddess shrine. On one clay seal from Knossos, reminiscent of that of the Mother of the Mountains, she wears a high peaked cap, a short skirt, and holds a spear and shield with a lioness or dog at her side.[34] No signs are shown, however, of a mountain or rocky peak, a pillar or a votary, in any of the eleven examples that have been found of this impression. But clearly they represent the same divine pair in an almost identical setting, belonging to Middle Minoan III.

In her capacity of Mistress of Animals she was intimately

associated with hunting and wild life in general. Although there are no indications of a Minoan-Mycenaean animal cult, the Goddess and her male attendant were constantly surrounded with real and monstrous creatures, among whom lions, doves, bulls, griffins and sphinxes predominated, sometimes in a hybrid form.[35] Daemons with the head of a horse and the body of a lion took the place of other fabulous beasts on seal impressions from the palace of Knossos. Besides the usual bulls, lions, rams, dogs and moufflons, there are flying fish and monsters, and a flounced goddess lays her hand on the necks of two lions, while on a gem from Kydonia a male figure grasps by their heads two lions sitting upright.[36] But the central figure usually is female and conforms in type to the Minoan Mother, and the animals and satyrs are her servants, sometimes represented, as at Hagia Triada, in the performance of her cult.

The Young Male God

The male god when he appeared at all was apparently a later addition venerated in a subordinate capacity, held less in honour as well as being later in time and youthful in age and appearance. His most conspicuous occurrence is on a lentoid beadseal of Spartan basalt, discovered near Canea, the site of the ancient Kydonia. There he is shown nude except for a girdle, standing between two sacral horns (a sure sign of divinity) with his arms folded. To the left is a daemon holding a libation jar, and to his right a winged goat with the tail and hindquarters of a lion.[37] This is a heraldic design devised to represent the Young God as the 'Master of Animals'—the male counterpart of the Goddess as their Mistress, portrayed in the same manner. On the Mycenaean gem from this site (Kydonia) he reappears, as we have seen, with his arms outstretched and supported by lions on either side, as well as on the signet ring in the Ashmolean Museum, where he is a small figure holding a spear, or on that from Knossos where he is represented descending from the air.

On an electrum ring from a tomb in the lower town at

Mycenae a nude youth holding a spear in his left hand extends his right hand to a goddess type of female, seated on a throne, whom Evans regards as the Minoan Mother in conversation with her consort.[38] With less probability it is interpreted by Furtwängler as the plighting of their troth.[39] The representation of a youth with uplifted arms wearing a mitre, standing erect before the Goddess, who is arrayed like the chryselephantine statuette of the Snake-goddess of Knossos in the Boston Museum clad in a flounced skirt with a series of small aprons contained by a narrow girdle of gold, a tight-fitting jacket exposing the breasts, and on her head a tiara with several peaks. She is holding out her hands towards the boy, and in them are two snakes coiled about her arms. This is interpreted by Evans as depicting an act of adoration of the Minoan Mother by the Boy-god, but the conjecture is by no means conclusive.[40] More significant is the scene on a signet-ring from a tomb at Thisbe in Boeotia, showing the Goddess vested on a throne with a child on her knee and holding out her left arm in response to two adoring male figures approaching her. In her right hand she holds a disk-shaped object with a central cup, while behind her a female attendant has a similar object, thought by Evans to be a bronze cymbal, which later was associated with the worship of Kybele.[41] Unfortunately, however, the hoard from Thisbe is such a 'mixed bag' of genuine and spurious contents that this scene is open to grave doubts, like the Ring of Nestor.

Nevertheless, although the available evidence is not impressive, that a young male divinity was associated with the Goddess in Crete and the Aegean certainly cannot be denied, even though he did not play a prominent or essential role in the Minoan-Mycenaean cult. Except as the Master of Animals he was seldom in evidence and when he did appear it was never on equal terms with the composite and complex Minoan Goddess. From her in one or other of her several forms and attributes aid was sought for the promotion of fertility, the well-being of the natural order and the protection of the house-hold. Furthermore, as a chthonic deity she was venerated in the nether world, while as the Mountain Mother her rule extended to the upper regions. When she passed from the island to the mainland she, like so many of her counterparts in the Near East, acquired warrior characteristics. Thus, on a painted limestone tablet from the Acropolis of Mycenae, ascribed to the Late Minoan I period, she may have been depicted covered by a large eight-shaped shield and venerated by two female votaries.[42] In its present mutilated conditon the figure is difficult to decipher, but it may represent an armed war-goddess, though in the Cretan scenes the divinities who carried weapons were connected with the chase rather than with warfare. The Minoans were relatively peaceful people, whereas the Mycenaeans in their fortified towns were constantly fighting, and, therefore, it is not at all improbable that the Goddess then assumed her familiar martial role as elsewhere. This certainly is suggested by the tablet from Mycenae, where she may have been the forerunner of Athena, very much as at Knossos she appeared as the 'Lady of the Sea', reposing on the waves which protected her island home.[43]

Whether in all these manifold functions and relationships she was one and the same composite goddess, like the Magna Mater in the Graeco-Oriental world, or that each manifestation represented an independent goddess with her own individuality and departmental concerns, is the recurrent problem of the cult. In favour of regarding the Minoan Mother as the one Great Goddess, Evans has contended that it is substantially the same form of religion as that so widespread at a later date throughout Anatolia and Syria. She can be identified with Rhea, the Cretan Mother of Zeus, and assimilated with the Syrian Goddess Ma and the Phrygian Kybele.

With the Young God as her paramour, son or consort, she is true to type, as she is in her chthonic associations, her dove, snake, guardian lions and double-axe symbols, her exposed breasts and her apparel. She was apparently the source of all vegetation, the Earth-mother, the Mistress of Animals and of the sea, and she hunted with bow and arrow like Artemis. It is not surprising, therefore, that Evans, Marinatos and many other scholars[44] have regarded her as a universal deity, the Goddess of nature, and that from her and her youthful male satellite in his customary role, the Cretan counterpart of Adonis, Kinyras, or Attis, the Hellenic pantheon developed with its gods and goddesses as distinct and independent figures, eventually brought together in the Olympian theology under the rule of Zeus, the father of gods and men.

Nilsson, on the other hand, argues in favour of a plurality of divinities from the beginning,[45] the Minoan Mother in her several guises being the syncretistic equivalent of Artemis, Rhea, Athena, Aphrodite and the rest of the Greek goddesses, each separate and distinct as an independent entity. While it is true that the Minoans had a number of lesser gods and spirits like other ancient peoples in much the same state of culture, it is difficult to conceive of the identical representation of the Great Goddess in so many forms recurring over such a wide area from Syria and beyond to Crete, unless there was a funda-mental underlying unity in the personification of the female principle. In any case, so far as Crete is concerned, the various aspects of the Goddess can hardly be differentiated as separate personalities. The syncretism and fusion were so complete that they can scarcely be explained other than as several forms of one and the same divine figure—the Minoan Great Goddess with her subordinate satellites.

THE GODDESSES OF THE GREEK PANTHEON
Rhea and Zeus

In Greece, however, this Minoan divinity unquestionably emerged in a plurality of goddesses with particular names and personalities as distinct developments of Rhea, Britomartis, Dictunna and Aphaia in pre-Hellenic Crete. Thus, Rhea, the Cretan counterpart of the Anatolian Kybele, and often indis-tinguishable from Ge or Gaia, Mother-earth, was a majestic if somewhat vague figure, with or without a partner. Crete was her original traditional home and the earliest seat of her worship, and it was there in the pre-Homeric period, probably after a Dionysian wave had passed over the island, that the birth and infancy of Zeus were associated with its caves and attributed to Rhea. Then the Sky-god of the Homeric tradition was represented as the son of the Cretan goddess who hid him in a cave in the mountain called Aigaion, and where later he was said to have been suckled by a goat. From this cavern, according to a curious tale, every year a fire flashed when 'the blood from the birth of Zeus streamed forth', suggesting in all probability, as Nilsson says, that 'this child is the year-god, the spirit of fertility, the new life of spring'.[46]

This Cretan Zeus was a much more primitive figure than the Indo-European Sky-god. He embodied the processes of fecundity on earth rather than renewed them by sending the vitalizing rain from the heavens. It is not surprising, therefore, that he should be represented as the son of Rhea in this version of his birth and infancy, and that around this tradition a vegetation legend and cultus should have developed. Thus, the aetiological story of the Cretan Kourites mentioned by Euripides in the *Bacchae* (lines 119–25), and repeated by later writers and inscribed on coins and monuments in the Hellenistic period, clashing their shields and swords in their ecstatic dance to drown the cries of the Zeus-child concealed from the vengeance of his father Kronos, as Strabo recognized,[47] was simply the orgiastic worship of the Asiatic Mother-goddess as a fertility rite related to the rearing of Zeus. This is now clear from the inscription containing the hymn to the Dictaean Zeus discovered in the ruins of the temple at Palaikastro on the east coast of Crete.[48] Although it was composed in the Hellenistic Age, it seems to constitute a revival of a fertility cult practised before the temple was deserted after the break-up of Minoan power in the second millennium B.C.

That a Sky- and Weather-god should be identified with the flocks and herds is not surprising. Such a coalescence frequently had occurred in the Near East from the Fertile Crescent and Anatolia to the Indo-Iranian region, and when the Olympian myth and ritual of the Indo-Europeans reached Greece and were fused with the Goddess worship of the Aegean basin,

Zeus continued to exercise his customary functions without any substantial change, in combination with those of the indigenous chthonian vegetation cultus.

Moreover, under Dionysian influence, before he attained his exalted position in the Hesiodic and Homeric tradition he was engaged in the overthrow of the Titans, an earlier group of gods from whom he was himself descended through his father Kronos and his mother Rhea. Here there may be a reminis-cence of a historical situation when the Olympian Sky-religion defeated to some extent the chthonian Goddess cult of the soil, but only to incorporate many of its essential traits in the same way as the human race was alleged to have imbibed a Titanic element in its ancestry in combination with the divine nature derived from Zagreus-Dionysus. This dual character of Zeus is recorded in his celestial aspects and attributes, brought into relation with his vitalizing functions in connexion with the fertility of the earth and of vegetation, when the invaders had to live on the produce of the soil of the land of their adoption after their settlement on the plains of Thessaly.

The various unions of Zeus with Earth- and Corn-goddesses —Hera, Dione, Demeter, Semele and Persephone (Kore)— suggest that in the background of these traditions lay the wide-spread conception of the marriage of Heaven and Earth in which he played the role of the Sky-father in alliance with his many consorts. When the local legends were correlated in the Epic literature one of the brides was exalted to the status of the official wife of Zeus while the rest were regarded as his mis-tresses, this being more in accordance with the custom that prevailed in the Greek States where monogamy was established but concubinage was tolerated as an accepted irregularity.[49] In this way Zeus was accredited with a considerable number of illegitimate offspring, partly divine when born of goddesses, and partly human when their mothers were mortal women. But behind this adaptation of the mythology to the existing social practice lay the sacred marriage of Heaven and Earth, interpreted in terms of the fertilization of the ground by the life-giving rain.[50]

Hera

With the fusion of the Olympian and the chthonian cults, whereas in the Minoan-Mycenaean cult the male god was subordinate to the Mother-goddess, Zeus as the Sky-father became predominant. Therefore, henceforth his consorts were relatively minor figures so that often it is difficult to determine to what extent they were his wives. His legitimate consort unquestionably was Hera, but in fact her cult had little to do with Zeus, and her union with him was merely the result of her having been the chief goddess, and so the fitting partner for the chief god, in spite of his previous nuptials with other Earth- and Corn-goddesses like Demeter, Semele and Themis.

Originally Hera seems to have been mainly concerned with birth, marriage and maternity, though occasionally she was regarded as a perpetual virgin and as a widow.[51] She was essentially the goddess of women and of fecundity (particularly though not exclusively of childbirth),[52] and consequently of every side and aspect of female life and its functions and attributes. This doubtless accounts for her close association with the earth and its uterine capacities, even though apparently she was not actually an Earth-goddess and only indirectly associated with vegetation.[53] Her connexions with the moon also were very secondary and derived from its supposed influence on the life of women.

Nevertheless, her union with Zeus in myth and rite at many places was represented in terms of a sacred marriage ($\iota\varepsilon\varrho\grave{o}\varsigma$ $\gamma\acute{a}\mu o\varsigma$) which, as we have seen, normally everywhere had for its object the renewal of the life in nature in the seasonal cycle. That it had no such significance in Greece is contradicted by the union of Demeter with Iasion and by the mystery ritual. Indeed, as Professor Rose agrees, such weddings had for their object the production of fertility, especially that of the soil. Moreover, he recognizes that 'it is not without reason that a reminiscence of this is found in the famous passage of the *Iliad* in which all manner of flowers and also thick soft grass spring up to make a marriage-bed for Zeus and Hera on Mount Ida'.[54]

The rite can hardly be separated from its usual purpose

elsewhere, especially as there is no reason to suppose that the ancient Greeks until well after the sixth century B.C. discriminated between fecundity in mankind and in that of the rest of the natural order. Therefore, since Hera was the goddess of birth and maternity her life-bestowing powers cannot be excluded from the fertile soil and its products. Thus, she stands in the Cretan Rhea tradition with its Minoan background, though her own origin is obscure. From time immemorial she was the Great Goddess of Argos—'Argive Hera' of the *Iliad*[55] —but Samos also was her traditional birthplace and a very important seat of her cult, going back, it was alleged, to the time before she contracted her alliance with Zeus.[56] In Crete at her shrine near Knossos, Diodorus maintains that her sacred marriage was still celebrated annually in the first century B.C.,[57] and in Greece her very ancient cult (including the ἱερὸς γάμος) was widely practised, especially in the sites of the oldest civilization (e.g. Argos, Mycenae, Sparta), except in Thessaly and the northern coast.[58] In Argos and Samos she attained the dignity of a city-goddess, and among all the divinities connected with birth and marriage she was supreme as the wife of Zeus, and doubtless, by virtue of her own ancestry, in the Goddess cult 'guarding the keys of wedlock'.[59]

Thus, the goddesses of childbirth (Eileithyiai) were called her daughters,[60] and in Argos she was venerated as both maid and mother, since by bathing in the spring Kanathos at Nauplia she renewed her virginity every year.[61] That her matrimonial affairs were not always regarded as running smoothly[62] may be an indication that her cult and that of Zeus had separate origins and were in opposition to each other. Originally, like her Cretan and West Asiatic prototypes, she may have had either no male partner or only a very subordinate satellite.

Athena

Similarly, as Nilsson has shown, Athena almost certainly was a survival of the Minoan-Mycenaean household goddess bearing a shield, who protected the citadel and the person of the king. Thus, in the *Odyssey* she is represented as having had her dwelling in the palace of the Prince Erechtheus,[63] and in her own city, Athens, she lived on the citadel, her temple being the site of a Mycenaean palace.[64] Having become the patroness and protector of the city that bore her name, she assumed a martial character, though originally in her pacific Cretan surroundings she was primarily a household and civic divinity, with fertility attributes revealed in her snake and tree symbolism. Her association with craftsmanship (τέχνη) was derived from her domestic Minoan prototype[65] as the goddess of the household, and it was not until she was brought into the service of the Mycenaean princes on the mainland that her more warlike characteristics became dominant. Then gradually she was transformed into the bellicose Athena of the Homeric poems, far removed from the peaceful domestic pre-Hellenic goddess of fertility and skill in the arts in which she excelled. Always, however, she was a dynamic figure, the goddess of action and wisdom, helper of craftsmen, the protectress of the home and the citadel, and eventually of heroes.

Her name as well as her character is probably of pre-Greek origin, with its non-Hellenic suffix -*na* as in the place-name *Μυκῆναί*, whose goddess *Mykene* (a heroine) in the *Odyssey*[66] may have been ousted by Athena.[67] In any case, she was a tutelary goddess of the Cretan and Mycenaean princes, subsequently raised to the dignity of the goddess of the republican State, the important Attic city being named after her. As its patroness, taking the place of the king, she became involved in its wars and acquired a military character, until eventually she was a mighty and furious war-goddess fighting all and sundry.[68] But she never abandoned her earlier female attributes and functions, and continued her interest in the arts and crafts, of which she remained the highly skilled master, until ultimately she was regarded as the personification of wisdom.[69] Her title Pallas, probably a form of the Greek παλλακεία, 'concubinage' in its ritual sense, was later applied to maiden-priestesses, and the image of Pallas Athena that Zeus sent down from heaven was called the Palladion.[70] These designations may refer to a Greek maiden-goddess of Indo-European origin who was absorbed by the non-Hellenic Athena and incorporated in her cultus. Be this as it may, she (Athena) was subsequently depicted as a beautiful and stately virgin, whether or not, like her prototypes, she was a Mother-goddess.

Aphrodite

More glamorous and voluptuous than the dignified, wise and comely Athena, the Mistress of the home, family and city, was Aphrodite, another goddess of the mother-type, who made her way into Greece from Cyprus. Originally she was the Western Asiatic Goddess, akin especially to Ishtar and Astarte.[71] Therefore, in name and personality and function she was un-Hellenic, and in contrast to Athena she was not really Hellenized when the Homeric poems were written, for there she is thoroughly anti-Achaean, and treated with little respect. Nevertheless, she is represented as the daughter of Zeus and Dione, and as the faithless wife of Hephaestus.[72] Ares, who later is described as her husband in the *Odyssey*, is her para-mour,[73] and Aeneas became her son by the Trojan Anchises.[74]

Primarily she was the goddess of fertility and love with the usual emphasis on the sexual characteristics of generation, being the personification of the maternal principle in proto-historic Asiatic fashion. In her Oriental guise her beloved was the youthful vegetation god Adonis ('the Lord'), described in the Greek myths as the handsome young hunter killed by a boar, represented as Ares in disguise. According to another version of the story, she hid him as an infant in a chest which she entrusted to Persephone, the spouse of Hades. So enrap-tured was the queen of the underworld with the babe that she refused to return him to Aphrodite, even though the goddess went herself to the nether regions to reclaim him. It was not, in fact, until Zeus decreed that Adonis should spend part of the year on earth with Aphrodite and the rest with Persephone in the lower world that the dispute was settled. Thus, Adonis assumed the role of the Babylonian Tammuz, and Aphrodite that of the Hellenic Demeter, resembling the Eleusinian god-dess in her searching for and bitter grief and lamentation at the loss of her beloved, whether this was brought about by a wild boar in the chase, or by abduction on the part of the queen of Hades.

It was this death and resurrection theme that was celebrated annually at Byblus on the coast of Syria with a period of mourning followed by rejoicing at the restoration of the youth-ful vegetation-god in the spring in the figure of Adonis.[75] Similar rites which included ritual prostitution may have been held at Paphos in Cyprus, where at Kuklia there is an ancient sanctuary of Aphrodite.[76] In the *Adoniazusae* of Theocritus, however, there is no reference to the restoration of the god in the account of the nuptial ceremonies which were held annually in Alexandria to commemorate the sacred marriage of Adonis and Aphrodite.[77] Images of the god and goddess on two couches were displayed and the next day the figure of the dead god was carried to the sea-shore amid lamentation and thrown into the sea, apparently in the rather vain hope that he would come back again. Similarly, in Attica at the height of summer, effigies of the dead Adonis were carried in procession to the strains of weeping and wailing,[78] while in Athens the 'gardens of Adonis' (i.e. baskets containing earth in which cereals had been sown) were exposed to the sun during the eight days of the festival in the spring or autumn. When they had withered they were flung sadly in the sea or in springs to typify the decease of the god.[79] Adonis, therefore, was essentially a dead god, but he was always worshipped in conjunction with Aphrodite as the goddess of vegetation.

Her lovers, however, were numerous and when she reached Greece she found herself faced with serious well-established rivals, such as Hera, Athena and Artemis, with whom she had to contend, though in fact she had very few cult con-nexions with the major Hellenic deities, apart from Hermes, from whom she conceived and brought forth Hermaphro-ditus.[80] Her festivals also were of little importance except in Cyprus, and at Delos in the Cyclades, the legendary birthplace of Artemis and Apollo, where she absorbed the cult of Ariadne, the daughter of Minos.[81] It was in Cyprus, however, that according to her myth she first came ashore when she arose in her exquisite beauty from the foam and was carried in a sea-shell to Kythera, an island off the coast of Sparta, whence she was driven by the tide to her Cypriote resting-place. There as she stepped on the ground the earth blossomed under feet and the gods received her joyfully and arrayed her in divine regalia.[82] Although she emerged within the sea and came forth from it, she was not a sea-goddess as Poseidon was a sea-god. It was from the foam, the generative organ of Uranus, that Kronos had mutilated and thrown into the sea, that she was born, and, therefore, she was regarded in Cyprus as 'the Celestial', her origin being connected with the cosmic myth of Heaven and Earth. In this status she turned to flight the winds and the clouds of heaven, making 'the levels of the ocean smile, and the sky, its anger past, gleams with spreading light'.[83] So she was called Goddess of the Sea, like several of her predecessors (e.g. Anat), and she became the patroness of sailors.

Similarly, she also had warlike qualities in Cyprus and particularly in Sparta, and at Delphi, where a statue of her was called 'Aphrodite of the Tomb',[84] she assumed chthonic characteristics. At Corinth she retained her Cypriote title of Urania ('Celestial'), and had in her service a retinue of sacred prostitutes, thereby preserving her original nature as the goddess of love, sexuality and fecundity. In fact, all her other aspects were true to type inasmuch as they were features common to the Great Mother, matron or virgin, everywhere; being essentially the author and giver of life and its restorer through the natural processes of birth and rebirth. She was the Lady of the spring blossoms in the *Pervigilium Veneris* (13 ff.), and wherever she went the flame of love was kindled and new life was generated.[85] 'Through seas and mountains and tearing rivers and the leafy haunts of birds and verdant plains' she struck 'fond love into the hearts of all, and made them in hot desire to renew the stock of their races, each after his own

kind',[86] regardless of all restrictions in an abandon of ravish-
ment and voluptuousness. Her girdle, indeed, could render
those who wore it irresistible,[87] imparting as it did all her
unconquerable passion of love and desire, irrespective of the
consequences for good and ill. Such were her gifts to mankind
and the world, bringing peace and joy, light and life, confusion
and strife, darkness and death.

Artemis

Another pre-Hellenic virgin goddess who appears to have
been of Minoan origin[88] long before she became the sister of
Apollo and while she was still an Earth-mother and Mistress
of the Beasts in the forests and hills in which she roamed,
hunted and danced before she became a city-divinity. As a
daughter of Zeus she was 'Lady of the wild animals' ($\pi \acute{o} \tau \nu \iota \alpha$
$\theta \eta \varrho \tilde{\omega} \nu$), and as sister of Apollo she was a huntress[89] who,
nevertheless, protected the young of all creatures, was tender
to cubs of lions, pregnant hares and all suckling and roving
beasts,[90] because she had been their mother in her original
guise. This role is given prominent expression in her Ephesian
temple-statue with its many breasts, and as a goddess of fertility
she assisted females of all species to bring forth their young and
helped women in the pains of childbirth. She was, therefore,
often called Eileithyia and Kourotrophos, though her precise
functions in these respects are obscure.

In Crete and Lakonis, Eileithyia was worshipped as an
independent goddess of childbirth with a cultus of her own
which became widespread in Greece and the neighbouring
islands,[91] while in Homer, as we have seen, she was called
the daughter of Hera.[92] Her association with Artemis was the
result of their common functions in connexion with midwifery,
though Artemis, who was the most popular goddess in Greece
among the peasantry[93] and in whom the life of nature became
centred, had a wider significance, preserving the main characteristics of the Great Minoan Goddess well into classical times.

In her earlier manifestations she was chiefly an Earth-goddess
associated principally with wild life and human birth whose

beginnings must be sought in her Minoan-Mycenaean background rather than, as Farnell supposed, in her Greek forms.[94]
The ecstatic dances so prominent in her worship connect her
with Phrygia and Kybele, as do the lions with which so often
she has been flanked.[95] At her festival, the *Ephesia*, in the
spring her creative and all-sustaining powers were stressed in
her many-breasted image believed to have fallen from heaven,
with its outstretched arms and lions and rams (or bulls), and
in the orgiastic and sacrificial rites which included a sort of
bullfight (*taurokathapsia*) reminiscent of the Minoan bull-
games.[96] She was the πολύμαστος—the multimammia—like
her Anatolian counterpart, served by virgin priestesses and a
high-priest (Megabyzas) who was a eunuch and was vested
in the same manner as the eunuchoid priests on Hittite bas-
reliefs. It is not improbable, in fact, that as in the case of the
Asiatic Goddess Ma in Komana, her cultus included wild
orgies in which her votaries castrated themselves in dedication
to her service.[97]

Similarly, another female companion Hellenized as Britomartis, with whom Artemis was identified, was of Cretan
origin.[98] Having escaped from King Minos, who had pursued
her for nine months, she leapt over a cliff into the sea, where
she was caught in fishermen's nets, and so it was alleged she
was called Diktynna, 'the net', from δίκτυον. But in all
probability under this name she was venerated in Western
Crete because originally she was the goddess of Mount Dikte,
the most conspicuous mountain on the island. Subsequently
Diktynna was interpreted etymologically in terms of a net in
the late aetiological myth told by Callimachus to account for
her designation, and to explain why henceforth she was worshipped as Aphaea in Aegina, where in a grove of Artemis
she was said to have sought refuge after she had again escaped
from Minos.[99] But in fact Diktynna, like Britomartis, at first
was a Cretan Mother-goddess—an aspect of the Minoan
Mother—called after the most striking mountain on which she
was worshipped before they were both brought into relation
with Artemis and the Greek Goddess cult.

Hekate

The chthonian goddess Hekate has been confused with Artemis since she too was a goddess of women with lunar features intimately connected with fertility, victory in war, skill in games, horsemanship and fishing, as well as with the under-world, cattle-breeding and the nurture of children. Here, again, it seems that an ancient Earth-goddess of obscure origin acquired a number of aspects and attributes when she became established in Greece, which often made her indistinguishable from Artemis. The Greeks, however, were themselves much perplexed about her and her dual connexions with the earth, the nether regions and the moon; with Artemis and Selene, Demeter and Persephone, and with Hermes.[100]

No mention of her occurs in Homer, and in the Hesiodic *Theogony* she suddenly emerges as the daughter of the Titan Perses and Asterie, daughter of Koios and Phoebe.[101] In Mousaios she is represented as the daughter of Zeus and Asterie.[102] Elsewhere her mother is said to have been Leto, Night,[103] while in a Thessalian myth her parents are Admetus and a woman of Pheraea.[104] According to the Hesiodic frag-ment incorporated in the *Theogony* she was a fully formed great divinity having neither brother nor sister, described as μουνομενής (i.e. from a single parent) mighty in heaven, on earth and in the sea, endowed with frightening magical powers exercised in sorcery.

Although her cultus was firmly established in Boetia, parti-cularly in Aegina, and was widespread in the northern and southern islands of the Aegean coast, in Asia Minor, Italy and Sicily, she was almost unknown in Arcadia.[105] Her name seems to be a Greek epithet signifying 'one from afar', if it is derived from ἑκατγβόλος, 'far-darting' or 'shooting', although this title was applied to the archer-god Apollo with whom Hekate was never associated. But if she were actually of Hellenic origin her cult must have been obscured and even-tually was revived in the north of Greece, which may have been her cradleland. There she was an ancient goddess of fertility who, as so frequently has happened, became connected

with the underworld and the dead. Hence her chthonic associations and functions, often of a sinister nature. It was doubtless because she ruled over ghosts and demons that she was
regarded as the goddess of the cross-roads who drove away the
evil influences from these dangerous spots. Therefore, at night
under a full moon, ritually prescribed food offerings, known
as 'Hekate's suppers', were placed at the parting of the ways to
placate her if and when she appeared with her hounds of hell.[106]

Demeter and Kore

Very different was the Goddess Demeter, the daughter of Rhea
and Kronos and the mother of Kore (Persephone), who
became the abducted wife of Hades. In the Homeric *Hymn to
Demeter*, assigned to the seventh century B.C.,[107] the story is
recorded for the purpose of explaining the origin of the
Mysteries celebrated in honour of Demeter at Eleusis when in
the autumn the fields were recovering from the drought of
summer, and preceded in the spring by lesser preparatory rites
at Agrai on the Ilissus. Behind the narrative lay a long and
complex history, going back to ancient seasonal rustic rites at
the critical junctures in the annual sequence of sowing, ploughing and reaping. While from her name Demeter seems to have
been of Indo-European origin, if as is very probable the last
two syllables ($\mu\dot{\eta}\tau\eta\varrho$) mean 'mother'. $\varDelta\eta$ is more difficult to
determine. Its meaning is very uncertain. It could be rendered
as 'earth' by transposing it into $\gamma\eta$, but for this there is no
adequate evidence.[108] Mannhardt, on the other hand, has
interpreted it as a form of $\zeta\epsilon\iota\dot{\alpha}$, 'spelt', akin to the Cretan $\varDelta\eta\dot{\alpha}\iota$,
'barley', and so has made Demeter the 'Spelt-mother'.[109] This
too is conjectural as Demeter is not at all intimately associated
with either barley or with Crete.

However, as Nilsson has urged, there are grounds for thinking that she was the Greek Corn-mother, and it is by no means
improbable that the Eleusinian Mysteries arose, as he suggests,
out of a very ancient agricultural festival celebrating the bringing up of the corn from the silos in which after threshing in
June it had been stored away until it was ready to be sown in

October.[110] During the four summer months in which it was below ground the fields were barren and desolate until the autumn rains began. Then the ploughing season opened in Attica, the corn was sown and immediately the fields became green again as the crops sprouted in the mild winter months (except in January). The flowers, having appeared in early spring (February–March), by May the grain was ready to be reaped and threshed at the beginning of the dry season (June).

Though it is a matter of debate whether Demeter was the goddess of the earth and of fertility in general, or exclusively the Spelt- or Corn-mother, with her daughter Kore, the Corn-maiden embodying the new harvest, unquestionably she was concerned with the vegetation cycle. At Eleusis her cult was essentially an agricultural ritual which doubtless centred very largely in the cultivation of the grain on the Rarian plain. Moreover, if she was, as is almost certain, originally a Greek divinity, nevertheless behind her and her mysteries lay the Minoan Goddess cultus in which were incorporated the various aspects of the seasonal sacred drama celebrated to promote the growth and harvesting of the new crops and the rebirth of nature. Therefore, while they may have begun as a corn ritual, suggested perhaps by the stowing away of the grain in the subterranean silos after it had been threshed in June, interpreted eventually in terms of the descent of Kore to the realms of Plouton, the god of the wealth of corn in the grain and of other fruits of the soil, they acquired a wider and deeper significance.

In the fulfilment of the role of the Great Goddess, Demeter had functions that ranged beyond the cornfields of the Rarian plain. She was the giver of all vegetation and of the fruits of the earth to whom the myrtle, the briony and the narcissus were sacred.[111] And when the seasonal cycle was brought into relation with the sequence of human life here and hereafter, Kore was identified with Persephone, the queen of Hades and wife of Pluto whose name easily could be confused with that of Plouton, to whom probably Kore was married at first before she was associated with Demeter. When this transference was accomplished the way was opened for the legend to describe the abduction of the daughter of Demeter as she was gathering flowers in the meadows with the daughters of Okeanos in the rich plain of Phatos. Appearing suddenly in his golden chariot, the amorous Pluto bore away the protesting Persephone to his nether realms. Thereupon the sorrowing mother wan- dered far and wide in search of her, carrying a torch to light up the deep recesses where she might be concealed. Such was her grief that she withheld her fructifying gifts from the earth so that universal famine was threatened.

As the story in the Homeric hymn continues, disguising herself as an old woman, Demeter went throughout the land until at length she came to Eleusis. There she sat down near the wayside well called the Fountain of Maidenhood, and was encountered by the daughters of the wise lord of Eleusis, Keleos, to whom she told a fictitious story about her escape from pirates. Having won their confidence, she was taken to the palace and became nurse to Domophoon, the infant son of the queen, Metaneira. To make the child immortal, which was Demeter's intention, unknown to his parents she anointed him with ambrosia, the food of the gods, and breathed upon him by day, and at night hid him in the fire to consume his mortality. As a result of this treatment he grew like an immortal being until, disturbed one night at her fiery operations by Metaneira, who screamed in terror when she saw her son in the fire, Demeter revealed her identity.

Although in her wrath at her plans for Domophoon having been upset she refused to complete the process of immortaliza- tion, or to continue her stay in the royal household, before she left the palace she commanded the people of Eleusis to build a sanctuary in her honour on the hill above the Fountain of Maidenhood where she first met the daughters of Keleos, and there the rites she would teach her votaries should be performed for the purpose of bestowing immortality on all who hence- forth would be initiated into her mysteries. After another terrible year of drought and famine, which even deprived the

gods on Olympus of their sacrificial sustenance, Zeus intervened on behalf of Kore. Sending a messenger to the underworld in the person of Hermes, it was arranged that she should
be released provided that she had not eaten of the food of the
dead. Pluto, however, had forestalled this by giving her
surreptitiously some pomegranate seeds. This bound her to
him for the third part of the year, and had the effect of producing the decline in vegetation while she was in his realm. For the
remaining eight months she lived with her mother in the
upper world, and during this period Demeter allowed the earth
to bear its fruits again. Triptolemus, one of the young princes
of Eleusis, was commissioned to go all over the world in his
chariot to teach men how to cultivate the soil under the
direction of the Goddess, and how to perform her rites.[112]

In the form in which the cult legend is told in the Homeric
hymn, there is a good deal of confusion and intermingling of
myths. That the ritual and its story are pre-Hellenic in origin is
suggested by the Mycenaean foundations of the sanctuary at
Eleusis dating from the middle of the fifteenth century B.C. in
the second half of the Mycenaean Age,[113] and the primitive
character of the agrarian rites with their affinities to the ancient
Thesmophoria, celebrated by women at the autumn sowing.
Indeed, Demeter was herself called *thesmophoros*, and she and
Kore were the two *thesmophoroi*.[114]

At first they seem to have been held in the open air as a
fertility festival to promote the growth of the crops before they
were given a more personal application as an esoteric mystery
cult to secure a blissful immortality for those who underwent
the elaborate process of initiation, after the final union of
Eleusis with Athens had taken place between 650 and 600 B.C.
Then they acquired an urban character and a more profound
sacramental significance giving to those who underwent the
experience a new philosophy of life that transcended the things
of time and space.[115] Being open to everyone who could speak
and understand Greek, regardless of sex or social status, they
became a pan-Hellenic institution, though they were under the
direction of the Archon of the ancient Eleusinian clans,

assisted by the priestly families, the Kerykes or the Eumolpidae, who were in charge of the rites.

What form the *dromena* took when the cult was first estab/ lished in its later guise is very largely a matter of conjecture as the available information comes mainly from relatively late and not very reliable sources, apart from the archaeological material recovered from the sanctuary. Being an esoteric mystery its secrets were carefully guarded with dire penalties meted out to any who divulged the things revealed during the protracted process of initiation.[116] From the few vague references to what took place that have survived it seems that after engaging in the lesser mysteries at Agrai in the spring, the *mystae* underwent a course of instruction in the knowledge to be imparted to them in the chief celebration in the month of Boedromion (Septem/ ber), together with purifications and asceticisms of various kinds. On the 19th day of the month they were led forth in procession along the sacred way from Athens to Eleusis, accompanied by the statue of Iacchos and the relics of Demeter guarded by her priestesses. At the shrines, temples and baths *en route* pauses were made to perform the prescribed rites at each of them. On arrival at Eleusis, after Iacchos had been cere/ monially received, they bathed in the sea and roamed about the shore with lighted torches in imitation of Demeter's search for Kore recorded in the myth.[117]

On the 22nd day of Boedromion, which coincided with the autumnal sowing, after a nocturnal vigil the neophytes repaired to the *telesterion*, the remains of which have now been excavated within the sacred precincts. In the large square hall, 54 metres in length with stone steps on all four sides, and with two doors in each of three of the four walls, the roof supported by forty/two columns arranged in rows of six at right angles to the main axis, the final rites took place with great solemnity. Veiled in darkness and in complete silence, sitting on these rows of steps, which perhaps were covered with sheep/skins, the *mystae* beheld the sacred sights in the *anaktoron*, the inner shrine of the Goddess in the centre of the hall in which her relics were deposited and the mystic rites were performed by the hierophant, vested in the official robes of the high-priest of Eleusis. It seems that they may have included certain mystic and symbolic utterances (*legomena*), and the revealing to the neophytes of cult objects (*deiknymena*), as well as the enactment of *dromena* in the form of dramatic perform-ances depicting the abduction of Kore, episodes in the wanderings of Demeter, her experiences at Eleusis, and her reunion with her daughter. Thus, in the museum at Eleusis there is a scene showing on a tablet an initiate in process of being led by the *mystagogoi* (i.e. sponsors) to Demeter, and Kore seated in their sanctuary, while on reliefs in front of the wall in the room near the entrance the rape of Persephone is represented. In another relief Demeter is seated and Kore standing near her holding torches, with votaries approaching. The circular box on which the Mother-goddess is sitting may be a sacred chest containing the holy symbols revealed to the *mystae*.

The mission of Triptolemus to teach the people how to cultivate grain is also prominent in the iconography, where he is shown holding a sceptre and seated on a magnificently carved throne drawn by dragons. In his right hand he holds the ears of corn and looks intently at Demeter in an attitude which suggests listening to her instructions. On a later very large plaque dedicated by the priest Lakrateides in the first century B.C., put together from fragments found during the excavation of the *ploutorion*, he is represented holding out his left hand to take the ears of corn from Demeter, who is seated before him. Between them is Kore holding torches, and close to her Pluto with his sceptre as king of the underworld. To the right is a god on a throne, and a goddess with a sceptre, who, as Kourouniotis suggests, may be the ancient divinities wor-shipped at Eleusis before the cult of Demeter was established there and whose names were unknown.[118] At the back is the upright figure of a young man carrying a torch, probably the Young God Eubouleus or Iacchos, to whom it is dedicated.

On a red-figured vase from Rhodes, now in the museum at Istanbul, the Earth-goddess is shown rising from the ground and lifting a cornucopia on the top of which sits a male child whom she presents to a goddess standing to the right holding a sceptre. To the left of Demeter is a figure, possibly that of Kore, and above her head is Triptolemus in his winged car.[119] Nilsson identifies the child as Plouton,[120] the fruit of the fields and representative of vegetation, while Triptolemus was a revealer of the secrets of Demeter, the promoter of agriculture and bestower of bounty, who invariably stands by the side of the divine pair, the Corn-mother and Earth-goddess, and her daughter.

It is possible that some of these iconographic scenes give some indication of the nature of the *dromena* at Eleusis. In the late literary sources reference is made to the drinking of barley, gruel, taking certain sacred things from the chest, tasting them and placing them in a basket, and from the basket into the chest as 'the password of the Eleusinian mysteries'.[121] This suggests that a sacramental meal occurred during the course of the rites and may have been re-enacted in the passion drama in the *telesterion*. But what the drinking of the *kykeon* signified is not known. Dr Farnell thinks that the votary felt a certain fellowship with Demeter who had herself partaken of it, though, as he says, it does not appear that it was consecrated on an altar, or that 'the communicant was ever penetrated with any mystic idea that it contained the divine substance of the goddess'.[122]

According to the post-Christian writer Hippolytus, an ear of corn was reaped in a blaze of light before their wondering eyes, and the birth of a divine child, Brimos or Iacchos, was solemnly announced.[123] This has led to the assumption that the *dromena* concluded with a sacred marriage between Zeus and Demeter symbolized by the union of the hierophant and the chief-priestess in an underground chamber when the torches were extinguished.[124] But the excavations have not revealed any such chamber in the sanctuary, and Hippolytus seems to have confused the Attis rites with those of Demeter.[125] If a corn-token, in fact, was one of the sacred objects shown to the initiates such a marriage would be in place in the vegetation setting of the mystery as part of the seasonal drama. The germinating ear would be at once the symbol of the harvest of the grain and that of the rebirth to immortal life of the neo-phytes. This background is demonstrated in the iconography and seems to be presupposed by the documentary data. More-over, as Farnell has pointed out, the formula in Proclus when the worshippers gazing up to the sky exclaimed 'Rain (O Sky), conceive (O Earth), be fruitful'[126] savours of a very primitive liturgy resembling the Dodenaean invocation of Zeus and Mother-earth. Late though it is (fifth century A.D.), it may well be 'the genuine ore of a religious stratum sparkling all the more for being found in a waste deposit of Neoplatonic metaphysic'.[127]

Therefore, while the sacred marriage as an integral element in the Eleusinian mysteries cannot be demonstrated, and the conjectures on which the assumption rests are based on very uncertain, confused and later literary sources, nevertheless it is highly probable that the theme of the seasonal drama lay behind the Eleusinian *dromena* and *teletae*, vested as a hereditary posses-sion in the ancient priestly families. When they had become transformed into a death and resurrection ritual centred in the pledge of a blissful immortality, for more than two thousand years it would seem they gave to their initiates hope and confidence alike in this life and beyond the grave.

CHAPTER VI

The Magna Mater

THE IDAEAN MOTHER OF PHRYGIA

THE affinity of the 'Lady of Ida', the *Mater Idaea*, as her official title suggests, to the Ephesian Artemis, Hekate and the Cretan Rhea has long been recognized. Thus, Strabo regarded the Goddess of Asia Minor as identical or very closely connected with her counterparts in Northern Greece, Thrace and Crete.[1] In her original Phrygian home, in fact, she was virtually indistinguishable from the Great Mother in the Ancient Near East, being primarily the goddess of fertility, mistress of wild life in nature responsible for the health and well-being of man and the animals, the protector of her people in war, and the recipient of orgiastic ecstatic worship in her chief sanctuary at Pessinus. With her youthful lover Attis, the god of vegetation, she was the guardian of the dead, perhaps under Thracian influence, associating her with the Earth-mother, while she was at the same time the *Dea domina Dindymene*, the goddess of the mountain in her Asiatic home, and later she acquired astral and celestial characteristics. Attended by her Thraco-Phrygian daemonic Korybantes, she was a Dionysian figure, just as Phrygian and Bacchic cults were fused in Rhea and her worship. Similarly, the lions yoked to her car had their counterparts in the guardian lions with which the Goddess was accompanied in Crete and the Aegean.

Attis and Kybele

Attis, again, played much the same role in relation to Kybele, the *Mater Idaea*, in Phrygia and Lydia as did Adonis to Astarte in Syria. Both are said to have castrated themselves, and Agdistis, the hermaphrodite monster, was afterwards deprived of male organs by the gods. From these genitals an almond-tree was said to have sprung up from the fruit of which

Attis was conceived by his virgin mother Nana.[2] When later Agdistis fell in love with him, to prevent his marrying Ia, the king's daughter, she struck him with madness and caused him to emasculate himself under a pine-tree, where he bled to death.[3] In a Lydian version of the story, like Adonis, he was killed by a boar,[4] but both agree that he met an untimely end through misadventure.[5] Ia, after wrapping the body in wool and mourning over him, killed herself, and Kybele took the pine to her cave, where she in company with Agdistis (with whom she was identified in the version of Arnobius) wildly lamented Attis. The corpse remained undecayed and was consecrated at Pessinus, where rites were instituted and performed annually in his honour.

The Cultus in Asia Minor

In Anatolia the worship of the Mother of the Gods and her consort was the predominant feature from the fourth century B.C. Notwithstanding local variations in names, epithets and forms, the two central figures retained their identities and maintained their position in spite of their syncretisms with the goddesses and gods of Asia Minor and the Aegean. The wild and savage nature of the Thraco-Phrygian cultus with its ecstatic revels and mutilations, barbaric music and frantic dances, reminiscent of the Dionysian orgies and indicative of consider-able antiquity, reveals its original character and significance.

The rites being designed for the purpose of establishing a highly emotional communion with the deities on the part of their frenzied votaries, the *gallos* was called κυβήβος because he was regarded as the male embodiment of the Goddess Kybele and the high-priest at Pessinus was himself Attis.[6] In this capacity he was a kind of sacral king who owed his status and influence to his union with the god whom he incarnated for the time being during the course of the ecstatic ceremonies. The votaries underwent a process of regeneration which appear to have included a sacramental meal, eating from a timbrel (drum) and drinking from a cymbal; both of which instru-ments were used in the orchestra of Attis.[7] A more drastic

method of securing rebirth was the well-known taurobolium
graphically described by Prudentius,[8] when the initiate into
the Mysteries of Attis in the spring was required to stand
in a pit beneath a grating over which a bull was stabbed
to death with a consecrated spear. Saturated with its blood
in every part of his body, he emerged born again and cleansed
from every stain of impurity, sealed with the seal of the
Goddess.

The Taurobolium

Our knowledge of this grim rite comes from post-Christian
sources when it was practised in the Roman world in and
after the second century A.D. in conjunction with the Attis
Mysteries. Then it had acquired a more lofty spiritual re-
interpretation of rebirth, in spite of its crude setting, and was
regarded as efficacious for twenty years, until eventually one at
least who underwent the experience was said to be *in aeternum
renatus*.[9] By A.D. 134 it was established in the cult of Venus at
Puteoli, and from the Phrygian sanctuary of Kybele on the
Vatican hill near the present basilica of St Peter it spread to
Ostia, Narbonensis, Aquitania, Spain and North Africa.[10]
Its origins are obscure, but, like the rest of the Attis-Kybele
cultus, it was completely foreign to the Roman religious
tradition. The priests were Asiatics and at first no Roman
citizen was allowed to take part in any of these alien rites.

Unquestionably the cradleland of the cult of the Magna
Mater must be sought in Phrygia just as that of Ma Bellona,
with which later it became largely fused, was Cappadocia,[11]
and that of Atargatis was Syria.[12] The ecstatic dances, outlandish music, the Phrygian pipes and cap, the emasculated
priests, the lion-drawn chariot, the sacrifice of the bull or ram,
and the sacramental meal from the drum and the cymbal, with
Attis called the 'cornstalk' in the liturgy; all these features point
to a Western Asiatic source of the Attis-Kybele cultus as do
the eunuch priests at Ephesus and such cult objects as the
astragaloi (which may have been attached to their scourges), the
pine-cones, pomegranates, the cymbals, tambourines and

sheep skins. All these, so closely connected with the Magna
Mater cultus, indicate its provenance.

Although there is no positive evidence that the taurobolium
and criobolium were practised in Phrygia in this connexion,
that they came from Asia Minor, and were related to the
worship of the Magna Mater, is very probable. Cumont,
having abandoned his earlier suggestion that originally it was
held in honour of the Eastern Artemis Tauropolos, and the
deities closely allied to her[13] (e.g. Anaitis and Ma Bellona)
later deduced the name from the lassoing of wild bulls.[14]
Without adopting this conjecture since the word signifies the
sacrificial slaughtering of a bull, it may have arisen where wild
bulls were hunted, and having acquired a fertility significance
they may have been slain ritually and the blood drunk or
applied sacramentally to give a renewal of life. In this event
the practice would be associated very readily with the Goddess
cult as an integral part of the process of regeneration and
purification, especially in the case of her chief priest, the *gallus*,
who had sacrificed his virility in her service. Thus, in the
Roman Empire it was performed for the welfare of the
Emperor and the community until it was given a wider and
more personal application in the third and fourth centuries A.D.
It may well have been, therefore, that when it first arose it was
confined to the chief priest of the Magna Mater.

THE MAGNA MATER IN THE GRAECO ROMAN WORLD
The Hellenization of the Goddess

While, as we have seen, from the fifth century B.C. the Phrygian
Magna Mater was identified with the Cretan Aegean Rhea,
and after her importation from Asia Minor the two cults
merged more and more, yet it was in her Hellenized form that
the Goddess functioned in Greece itself where none of these
Thraco Phrygian religions had much vogue until in the
Hellenistic Age, largely under Semitic influences in Asia
Minor, they had undergone a very considerable modification,
like the Orphic Dionysiac. Thus Attis was represented as a
hunter who was killed by a boar like Adonis,[15] or who

mutilated himself under a pine-tree,[16] while Kybele was equated with the less orgiastic Rhea, Hekate and Artemis and her Semitic counterpart Ishtar or Astarte.[17] In a terracotta relief from the neighbourhood of Smyrna she is represented in a shrine (*sedicula*) caressing one of her lions and wearing a chiton and mantle. Below her are two Marsyas playing flutes, while an attendant (possibly Attis) pours out a libation from a jug. At the sides are figures in a frenzied attitude, and at the base a frieze of lions and bulls.[18]

As the ecstatic emotional worship became increasingly popular among the unsophisticated masses it was regarded with disapproval and disdain in Hellenic circles, both on account of its character and content, and of its alien origins and significance. It was condemned, for example, by the Pythagorean Phintys as inconsistent with female modesty.[19] Nevertheless, it was too closely allied to the Dionysia of Thracian origin to fail to secure a considerable popular following in Greece without fundamentally changing the essential character of the cult. Once the Dionysiac religion had become established in post-Homeric times as a foreign intrusion, in spite of the hostility it aroused in traditional Achaean circles, the way had been opened for the worship of the Phrygian Magna Mater to take root because it supplied what was lacking in the prosaic heroic cult of the Indo-European ruling classes with which it became assimilated.

For an agricultural and pastoral people fertility in its various aspects was a vital necessity, and it was this which the Great Mother provided, summing up in her complex personality the office and functions of the goddess connected with the maternal principle in nature, giving life to the crops, the flocks and herds, and to mankind. Her male partner was of secondary importance in this process and so he occupied a subordinate position in relation to her, Attis, like Tammuz, being the young god or servant, or high-priest of Kybele, the Ishtar of Asia Minor and the Aegean. Her prototype Rhea, it is true, was the mother of Zeus and the other children of Kronos, and was overshadowed by her illustrious offspring. Nevertheless, the fact remains, as Nilsson has maintained, that the youthful paramour of the Minoan Nature-goddess was a year-god, embodying the new life of spring,[20] fulfilling the role of the consort of the Magna Mater. Their joint function was the promotion of the fertility of nature, especially in connexion with the revival of vegetation interpreted in terms of the reunion of the son-lover and his mother-spouse after their separation, typified by the decline of virility in winter and its renewal in the spring.

The Spring Festival

Thus, as the androgynous Kybele was alleged to have sprung from the ground, and from her several male genital organs an almond-tree arose, the fruits of which gave birth to Attis by Nana, the daughter of the river Sangarios, so in the Spring Festival the genitals of her emasculated priests were consecrated to her to renew fecundity by the potency in them. For the same purpose a fir- or pine-tree was wrapped round with bands of wool, decorated with violets, and on it an image of Attis was hung as the embodiment of the vitality which dwelt in the tree, which was then buried amid lamentation. After three days it was dug up and preserved until at the end of the year it was burned. According to Diodorus these rites were performed at the command of Apollo, who taught the Phrygians the ritual,[21] thereby giving this very ancient cultus some status in the Olympian tradition in Greece, notwithstanding its non-Hellenic character.[22]

Behind it lay the long and complex history and development of the Goddess cult in its manifold forms. Thus, before it was introduced into Phrygia, leave alone Greece, it was already firmly established in its main features and purposes. From its cradleland in the Ancient Near East it appears to have been diffused to the Aegean, chiefly by way of Anatolia and Asia Minor, where similar influences produced an almost identical cult in Northern Syria. Thus, the Goddess Kubaba, corresponding to the Greek Kybele, was primarily the queen of Carchemish represented in relief seated on a lion, and mentioned in Cappadocian tablets as Kubabat.[23] Elsewhere in texts she is only a minor Hurrian goddess but as the Magna Mater she assumed the status and function of the Sumerian Mother-goddess Nintud under the name of Hannahanna (the 'Grandmother'), though without the Phrygian orgiastic rites practised at Pessinus.

The Galli

On the other hand, the *galli* of the Syrian goddess Astarte of Hierapolis at the Spring Festival lacerated their arms and scourged one another to the accompaniment of the beating of drums, playing on pipes and the utterance of deafening cries. Many of the young men were caught up in the frenzy, stripped off their clothes and emasculated themselves, running through the city with the severed organs and throwing them into any house. In exchange they received female attire and ornaments.[24] Throughout Phrygia, Syria, Lydia, Cappadocia, Pontus and Galatia, where the Magna Mater reigned supreme, with or without her youthful partner, reckless ecstatic passion of this nature was of common occurrence at the Annual Festival, involving acts of sexual mutilation to secure complete identity with the Goddess. But although Attis was a Thraco-Phrygian figure and Adonis a Western Semitic form of Tammuz, the orgiastic element in their cultus was not a Mesopotamian feature in the Spring Festival. Lamentation there was with 'women weeping for Tammuz', but the celebration of the death of the year-god of fertility never excited the frenzy in the Euphrates valley it produced in Western Asia, any more than devotion to the Goddess led to the sexual madness it created in Phrygia and Anatolia. The same is true of Crete and Greece, where in the Minoan-Mycenaean religion and its aftermath the Goddess cult was relatively restrained, dignified and sober until it came under Thraco-Phrygian influences.

Castration was regarded as a foreign extravagance in the Graeco-Roman world, to be either prohibited altogether or to be kept strictly within the limits of the aliens who practised the unedifying rites. A eunuch-priesthood was forbidden by Hellenic, Babylonian and Judaic law, and, as in primitive society, those who served the altar, be it of the Goddess or of any other deity, must be virile and free from blemish like the victims they offered to the source of all life. Therefore, *galli* were excluded *ex hypothesi* from temple-worship, as in the Code of Lesbos. How or when self-emasculation arose in Phrygia is an unsolved problem, but it seems to represent an extreme expression of an ardent desire for communion with the Magna Mater which became a mental aberration. Thus, the frenzied eunuch-priest was called Κύβηβος, and, as the male counterpart of the Goddess, by sacrificing his virility he assimilated himself to her so completely that he shared in her life-giving power.[25] Henceforth he adopted female attire, having consecrated him-self to her service even at the cost of his manhood.

The practice may have long preceded its mythological inter-pretation in relation to the Kybele-Attis cult legend, especially as there are indications of Anatolian eunuch-priests in addition to those associated with the Ephesian Artemis, Atargatis and Hekate, not to mention the reference to the castration of the gods (e.g. Uranus and Kronos). These have little in common in this respect with the Attis story and its ritual, the closest affinities being with the Adonis and Astarte cultus. Neverthe-less, as have been demonstrated, self-mutilation in some form or another was a recurrent element in the Goddess cult, and in that of the Magna Mater it reached its height in the Phrygian frenzies.

The Coming of Kybele to Rome

Even when her worship gained access to Rome in the third century B.C., just before the end of the Hannibalic war (204 B.C.), the orgies had by no means spent their force. Whether or not the true nature of the Phrygian Great Mother and her rites was properly appreciated, in response to the recommendation of the prophetess of the Sibylline books, it was decided to bring to the capital the small black meteorite in which the Goddess was embodied. The situation was becoming desperate. The war had lasted for twelve years and its end was still nowhere in sight. Furthermore, there had been recently several ominous showers of pebble rain, portending, as it was thought, some approaching calamity. These events led to the oracles being consulted, with the result, according to Livy, that it was declared that 'when a foreign foe had invaded Italy it could be driven out and vanquished if the Idaean Mother were brought from Pessinus'.[26] It was decided, therefore, to follow this oracular counsel and to dispatch at once an envoy to the sacred Phrygian city to convey the precious symbol of the Mother of the Gods to Rome.[27]

After some demur on the part of Attalus, the king of Pergamos, who then had the custody of the stone, the request for its removal was granted. Placed in a special ship, it was borne to Ostia, where there were strange happenings on its arrival. The boat was grounded on a sand-bank in the mouth of the Tiber, from which, after all efforts to release it had failed, a Roman matron of noble birth, Claudia Quinta, drew it off quite easily after having prayed to the Goddess, and thereby clearing her character of charges of unchastity that had been made against her.[28] It then proceeded up the river to Rome, where on April 4th, 204, the sacred stone was received with due reverence by matrons who carried it to the temple of Victory on the Palatine hill. There it remained until in 191 B.C. the temple of the Magna Mater was erected in her honour on the hill.[29]

As soon as she had been installed in her temporary sanctuary her influence was felt, for that summer produced a bumper harvest,[30] and the following year Hannibal left Italy for Africa, having made his last stand in the mountains of Bruttium. The prediction of the Sibyls had come true, for Kybele, it seemed, had rid the land of the invaders. It is not surprising, therefore, that the people of Rome brought their gifts to her shrine in return for her beneficence, and instituted a festival to be held on April 4th in her honour in recognition of the services she had rendered to them. At it a *lectisternium* (sacred banquet) and *ludi* (games) were held,[31] which ten years later took the form of scenic performances—*Ludi Megalenses*.[32] After the erection of the temple on the Palatine, dedicated to the Magna Mater Idaea on April 10th, 191, the *Megalesia* were included in the State calendar, and so were given official recognition.[33]

In due course they were elaborated and occupied the entire week from April 4th to April 10th, being celebrated by the whole nation. On the first day the *praetor urbanus*, representing the State, made a solemn offering to the Goddess in her temple,[34] and *mutitationes* (entertainments) were given by *Sodalitates*.[35] Plays were performed on the third day,[36] and on the last day races were run which eventually became the most popular event.[37] Merry-making and licence, reminiscent of the Saturnalia in December, remained a feature of the observance,[38] even after the wilder aspects had been brought under control and sobered.

The Ecstatic Procession

At first the strange spectacle of the Phrygian Magna Mater, being conducted in her chariot drawn by lions through the streets of Rome by her *galli* leaping and dancing and gashing themselves amid strains of outlandish music, must have been no small embarrassment to the Senate. If the Goddess had brought relief from the Hannibalic hosts she had introduced a very dangerous element of ecstatic fanaticism completely foreign to the Roman tradition and temperament, but none the less capable of becoming a serious menace and alarmingly infectious. The scene has been described by Lucretius and confirmed in great measure by Ovid.

'Borne from her sacred precinct in her car she drove a yoke of lions; her head they wreathed with a battlemented crown, because embattled on glorious heights she sustains towns; and dowered with this emblem even now the image of the divine mother is carried in awesome state through great countries. On her the diverse nations in the ancient rite of worship call as the Mother of Ida, and they give her Phrygian bands to bear her company, because from those lands first they say corn began to be produced throughout the whole world. The mutilated priests they assign to her, because they wish to show that those who have offended the godhead of the Mother, and have been found ungrateful to their parents, must be thought to be unworthy to bring offspring alive into coasts of light. Taut timbrels thunder in their hands and hollow cymbals all around, and horns menace with harsh-sounding bray, and the hollow pipe goads their minds in the Phrygian mode, and they carry weapons before them, the symbols of their dangerous frenzy, that they may be able to fill with fear through the goddess's power the thankless minds and un-filial hearts of the multitude. And so as soon as she rides on through great cities, and silently blesses mortals with un-spoken salutation, with bronze and silver they strew all the path of her journey, enriching her with bounteous alms, and snow rose-blossoms over her, overshadowing the Mother and the troops of her escort. Then comes an armed band, whom the Greeks call the Curetes, whenever they sport among the Phrygian troops and leap in rhythmic movement, gladdened at the sight of blood and shaking as they nod their awesome crests upon their heads, recall the Curetes of Diete.'[39]

Making due allowance for Lucretius having borrowed much of the embellishment of his narrative from the songs of the 'learned poets of the Greeks in the days of old', the procession, nevertheless, must have put the civil authorities in a quandary between the respect due to the Goddess who had demonstrated her power in delivering Rome from the Carthaginians and giving fruitful seasons, on the one hand, and the maintenance of dignified, decent and orderly behaviour on the part of its citizens, subject to these wild and violent orgies in their main thoroughfares, performed by a motley crowd of foreigners in their unfamiliar garments, and with their outlandish tam-bourines. Under the circumstances the rites could not be either suppressed or ignored. Therefore, with their genius for statesmanlike compromise, and forewarned by the unedifying Bacchanalia in which Roman citizens already had become involved they facilitated the building of the temple for Kybele on the Palatine as a separate edifice so that the cultus could be confined as much as possible within its own sacred enclosure. For the rest, the presence of the *praetor urbanus* at the rites, while giving the *Megalesia* official recognition, enabled him to exercise a watching brief over the proceedings. Furthermore, it was strictly forbidden for any Roman citizen to become a *gallus*, to hold any office in the service of the Goddess, or to take part in the processions.[40]

These limitations and regulations had the effect of isolating the cult and its observances, confining it to Phrygians and their emasculated priesthood, who for the most part had been brought over from Asia Minor for the purpose. Soon, regarded merely as a spectacle, the procession appears to have lost a good deal of its novelty for Romans, and, shorn of its Oriental extravagances, the *Megalesia* became in due course little more than a holiday celebrated in honour of the Magna Mater. Indeed, by the end of the Republic it had so far declined in public esteem that when a high-priest from Pessinus appeared in the Forum arrayed in his vestments and ornaments to demand a public expiation of an alleged profanation of the statue of the Goddess, he was mobbed by the populace.[41]

The Hilaria

It was not until the establishment of the Empire that the cult was revived and given a new status. Then the temple on the Palatine, which had been burned down in A.D. 3, was restored by Augustus, though it was not until the reign of the Emperor Claudius (A.D. 41–54) that the Phrygian worship was incorporated in the State religion of Rome, and the Spring Festival of Kybele and Attis was inaugurated in a series of observances in March.[42] These began with a procession of *cannophori*, or reed-bearers, on the fifteenth day of the month in commemoration of the finding of the youthful Attis by Kybele in the reeds of the river Sangarios in Phrygia, intended perhaps originally to secure the fertility of the fields.[43] A six-year-old bull carried in the procession was sacrificed by the *archigallus*, and after a fast from bread for a week a sacred pine-tree was felled in the wood of Kybele outside Rome, wrapped in linen to represent the dead Attis, garlanded with violets because violets were said to have sprung from the blood of the vegetation deity Attis, with his effigy tied to the stem, and then taken to the Palatine temple.[44]

When these ancient agrarian rites of Phrygian origin had been duly performed, the next day a strict fast was observed in preparation for the solemn celebration of the *Dies Sanguis* on March 24th. This was the day devoted to lamentation for the death of the god, with piercing cries, the blowing of pipes, and the making of an incision in his arm by the *archigallus*, symbolizing the self-mutilation of the neophytes in the earlier Phrygian rite.[45] The rest of the *galli* scourged and cut their flesh to unite their blood in a common offering to the sorrowing Magna Mater and her dead lover, doubtless as a survival of an ancient renewal and funerary rite.

In the evening the lamentation was renewed and continued during a night of fasting and vigil (*pannychis*) until, presumably at dawn on the 25th, the longed-for announcement was made by the priest, 'Be of good cheer, neophytes, seeing that the god is saved; for we also, after our toils, shall find salvation.' Sorrow was then turned into joy because the initiates were united with the Goddess in the relationship of a new Attis, and the restoration of the dead god in all probability was an earnest of the resurrection of those who shared in his triumph over death.[46] The *Dies Sanguis* became the *Hilaria*, the Festival of Joy (which has given its designation to the whole Spring Festival), celebrated in Rome as a carnival with feasting, merriment, wanton masquerades and universal licence, saturnalian in its absence of all restraint and respect for authority, which nearly cost one emperor his life.[47]

The excesses of jubilation, not uncommon at the end of an observance of this nature at the vernal equinox, which so often reached its climax in a sacred marriage and the attendant ceremonies, were followed by the *lavatio* after a day of

much-needed rest on the 26th (*requietia*). Thus, on the morning of the 27th the image of the Goddess in a wagon was
drawn by oxen in procession to the river Almo outside
the Porta Capena, preceded by barefooted nobles, and to the
accompaniment of the music of pipes and tambourines. On
arriving on the banks of the river near the walls of the city the
archigallus, vested in purple, washed the image and the wagon,
and the other sacred instruments in accordance with an ancient
rite.[48] With these ablutions the festival concluded, the wagon
and the oxen, still adorned with spring flowers, returning with
the mysterious meteoritic image in its silver setting to its shrine
on the Palatine hill, there to remain in virtual isolation until
the crude Phrygian Easter drama was again re-enacted when
the festival recurred the next year.

THE HELLENIZED ISIS CULT

Rites of this nature, however, were not confined to the Kybele-
Attis cult. Closely associated with them were the lamentations
and rejoicings of the Isis votaries in the autumn when they
celebrated the scattering of the remains of Osiris by Seth (or
Typho as he was called in the Graeco-Roman world), and
their recovery by Isis and restoration to life, thereby giving
assurance of a blissful immortality in union with Osiris-
Serapis and 'the Goddess of many names'.[49] By the fourth
century B.C. her worship had been established in Greece by
the Egyptians in the Piraeus, often combined in the Aegean
with that of Serapis, Anubis and Harpocrates, and sometimes
along with that of Selene and Io, Demeter and Aphrodite,
while her son Horus was equated with Eros. As she became
more and more syncretistic she was almost a universal goddess
and, true to type, her husband-brother Osiris then assumed a
subordinate position. In her several roles she was the beneficent
Mother, who conceived, brought forth, and nourished all life
in this world, renewed vegetation at its source, and restored
the dead beyond the grave. She was the personification of the
maternal principle, and the highest type of the faithful wife and
loving mother.

This became most apparent in and after the Ptolemaic period when Alexander, having completed the conquest of Western and Southern Asia Minor, defeated the Persians at the battle of Issus in 33 B.C., placed Egypt, Palestine and Phoenicia under the control of Ptolemy I, Soter (306–285 B.C.). The cult of Serapis and the Hellenized Isis was then instituted by mingling the Egyptian and Greek elements into a composite whole. Although its origins are obscure,[50] the worship of the Memphite Apis bull, brought into conjunction with that of Isis in the Serapaeum he founded in Alexandria, spread rapidly over the Graeco-Roman world. Greeks and Macedonians in the military and commercial services may have been largely responsible for its propagation, and an Egyptian priest of Heliopolis, Manetho, was actively engaged in its formation and dissemination. But by the time that the flood of Eastern divinities poured into the West, especially towards the end of the Roman Republic, Isis had eclipsed Serapis to a very considerable extent. Even in Alexandria she soon became the more important of the two deities, and it was her festivals in a Hellenic setting, rather than those of Serapis, which were more frequently celebrated.

According to Plutarch, Ptolemy Soter employed Manetho and Timotheus, a member of the Eleusinian family of the Eumolpides, to formulate this syncretistic Hellenized Isis mystery cult in association with Serapis who was identified with Osiris. The priesthood remained Egyptian and when some of the ceremonies were performed by Greeks they shaved their heads and wore white robes like Egyptians. Although Greek became the common language for the ritual, the liturgy was Egyptian, and reference is made by Apuleius, as late as the second century A.D., to a liturgical book in use in the Mysteries at Corinth, written in hiero-glyphics.[51] The cult-legend was brought into relation with the Osirian doctrine of immortality, and its counterparts in Western Asia and Anatolia, while Isis became the compre-hensive 'Goddess of many names', like the Phrygian Magna Mater. In the iconography she was represented frequently in

Greek designs, and as Hathor she became identified with Aphrodite.

The aim of the Ptolemaic syncretism was to create a divinity in whom both Egyptians and Greeks could unite in a common worship at Alexandria and wherever the cult was established in the Graeco-Roman world. When this was accomplished Isis came to be more and more all things to all men, completely overshadowing her male partner, Serapis; her worship combining the features of a public ritual and an esoteric mystery. The success of the effort was due very largely to the fact that the composite figure met the fundamental needs which the Goddess cult in its various aspects supplied. Moreover, in the Graeco-Roman guise Isis Mysteries had undergone a spiritual refinement and spiritualization which differentiated them from the original drama at Abydos while retaining the essential death and resurrection theme and all that this offered as a warrant of rebirth and future existence for the individual initiated, and the wider implications for the well-being of mankind. Temples were erected for the conduct of the rites in Athens, at Halicarnassus near Corinth, and at Antioch, and after having gained a foothold in Cyprus as well as in Syria and Asia Minor, Isis in due course obtained official recognition in the Roman Empire equal to that enjoyed by Kybele.

From the Eastern Mediterranean the syncretistic cult made its way to Rome through Sicily in the third century B.C., and having become established at Syracuse and Catania it reached Pompeii and Pozzuoli, the port of the Campania, in the next century. In spite of several attempts by the Senate to suppress it in the capital as a corrupting influence and perversive of piety and moral behaviour, the popular demand was such that it could not be withstood. Therefore, when the destruction of statues and altars of Isis on the Capitol on five consecutive occasions between 59 and 48 B.C. proved to be wholly ineffectual, temporary recognition was given to the cult in 43 B.C.[52] Subsequently it was equated with the allies of Antony and Cleopatra and again suppressed by Augustus,[53] but the decree was reversed by Gaius on his accession in

A.D. 37. It may have been in his reign that the Isiac was first celebrated in a temple in the Campus Martius in Rome,[54] but it was not until about A.D. 215 that Aurelius Caracalla (A.D. 188–217) gave the Goddess a place in the Roman pantheon with a magnificent temple on the Capitoline hill.[55]

The Initiation Rites

The unprecedented victory of the cultus over official opposition and its persistence during the first three centuries of the Christian era are a testimony to the deep and genuine religious emotion aroused in the initiates by the ritual. This is shown very clearly in the graphic account of the conversion of Lucius given by Apuleius in the middle of the second century A.D. in his *Metamorphoses* (i.e. *The Golden Ass*). In this curious romance based apparently on a Greek folk/tale in the first instance, the adventures of its hero (Lucius) are narrated with a strange combination of witchcraft and magic asceticisms, revelations of secret mysteries and profound religious experi/ences, brilliantly written with humour and imagination. Opening with the young man Lucius having been changed into an ass accidentally by a charm he was handling, the mysterious sights he sees and the things he hears are recorded while he is in this state before he regains his human form. Some are grotesque, fantastic and unedifying; others are truly religious and almost certainly represent the actual experiences of Apuleius when he was himself initiated into the Isiac. Thus Lucius is represented as being required 'to abstain from profane and evil foods that he might more rightly approach the secret mysteries of this, the purest of religions'.[56]

As he proceeds he encounters Isis, who declares that she, 'nature's mother, queen of the dead, primal offspring of the ages, mightiest of deities', the single form of all divinities, is much moved by his supplications, and encourages him to go forward with his initiation. 'When thou shall have run the course of thy life and passed to the world beneath,' she said, 'there too in the very vault below the earth thou shalt see one shining amid the darkness of Acheron and reigning in the secret domains of Styx, and thyself dwelling in the fields of Elysium shalt faithfully adore me as thy protector.' No wonder then that the spectators cried, 'Happy and thrice blessed is he who by the innocence and constancy of his former life has won so nobly an inheritance from heaven, that he should be reborn and forthwith devoted to the service of the sacred rites.'[57]

Initiation appears to have consisted of three stages. The first was that of Isis, the second of Osiris-Serapis, and the third of admission to the priesthood. The climax was reached when Lucius (i.e. Apuleius) was at length taken to the inner chamber of the temple at night. There with the aid of sacred drama and occult methods he was brought face to face with the gods to receive mystic revelations and to witness rites which unfortunately could not be divulged, being an integral part of the esoteric mystery. He says, however, that he 'penetrated to the boundaries of the earth; that he approached the borderland of death and setting his foot on the threshold of Proserpine [Persephone], when he had been borne through all the four elements he returned again; at midnight he beheld the Sun gleaming with bright light; and came into the presence of the gods below and the gods above and adored them face to face'. In the morning he was presented to the people clad in the gorgeous vestments of a Sun-god, with twelve stoles, a coloured garment of linen, and a precious scarf on his back, all decorated with animal designs. In his right hand he carried a burning torch, and on his head he wore a crown of palm leaves. Thus adorned he was shown forth for the admiration of the adoring crowd. A year later he was advanced to a higher status, that of the invincible Osiris, and then to that of the priesthood and membership of the sacred college of *pastophori*, dedicated to the service of the Goddess for the rest of his life.[58]

Making due allowance for the fanciful character of this novel, unquestionably it was based on inner knowledge of the Isiac initiation rites and their significance. Enough has been revealed to show their strenuous demands on those who underwent 'a voluntary death' to obtain the sure and certain 'hope of salvation'. Unlike those of the Phrygian Magna Mater, the emphasis was on subduing the flesh as a means of obtaining clearer spiritual perceptions, not infrequently to the despair of husbands whose wives were votaries of Isis. Thus, they regarded with dismay and apprehension the approach of the *puri dies* of the Egyptian Goddess when their spouses slept apart on their chaste couches in preparation for her rites.[59]

At first these abstinences from sexual intercourse, and from flesh and even bread, and the repeated ablutions before taking part in the ceremonies, doubtless were designed to rid the worshipper of ritual impurity and to ward off malign influences. At the beginning of the Christian era, however, they had acquired a more ethical and spiritual significance. Thus, Lucius was said to have abstained from 'profane and evil foods' in order 'rightly to approach the secret mysteries of the purest of religions'.[60] Similarly, Plutarch maintained that the purpose of the asceticisms was moral and practical,[61] cleanliness of body being conjoined with purity of heart. Therefore, in the first three centuries of the new era those who were invited to 'sup at the couch of the Lord Serapis' and his chaste spouse in the temple of Isis may be accredited with finding behind the prescribed ablutions and abstentions, and the subsequent esoteric ritual observances, a deeper meaning which enabled them to gain renewal and strength from the Goddess in this life, and in the world to come everlasting bliss through the immortal glory of Osiris.

The Goddess of Many Names

The mystery cult of a goddess differed from that of a god in that the one was the mystery of birth and generation, of life issuing from life; the other was the mystery of death and rebirth, of life rising renewed from the grave. Therefore, originally Osiris was the lord of the dead and the god of vegetation, whereas Isis was the 'throne-woman', the mother of Horus the reigning king. So in due course she became the protector and patroness of the living, summing up the attributes of the Mother of the Gods in her various manifestations—as Kybele, Demeter, Athena, Venus—but purified of the orgiastic elements of the Phrygian cult of the Magna Mater and its survivals in the Aegean. Like the sublime Virgin Mother who eventually was to dethrone her, she was the 'goddess of many names', the queen of heaven, mother of the stars, first-born of all ages, parent of nature, patroness of sailors, star of the sea, and *Mater dolorosa*, giving comfort and consolation to mourners and those in distress, and finally, in the *Metamorphoses*, 'the saviour of the human race', the redemptrix. Thus, it was said of her that 'the Phrygians called her Mother of the Gods (Magna Mater), the Athenians Minerva (*sc.* Athena), the Cyprians Venus, the Cretans Dictynna, the Sicilians Proserpine, the Eleusinians Ceres (*sc.* Demeter), others Iuno, Bellona, Hecate, or the Goddess of Rhamnus (Nemesis), but the Egyptians called her by her right name, the queen Isis'.[62]

In fact, however, as we have seen,[63] Isis in Egypt was not the Mother-goddess, and it was only in her Hellenized guise that she became equated with the Magna Mater, and personified as the female principle in nature, 'the Goddess of ten thousand names'.[64] But although her votaries claimed that she was a universal divinity rather than merely a national goddess, the source of all life and beneficence, of law and order, imperfectly worshipped by the barbarians under another name, the Isiac mysteries never really exercised the profound influence over the Graeco-Roman world in its declining years comparable to that of the Magna Mater of Asia Minor. Her appeal, it is true, was universal, and her temples in all the larger centres of the far-flung Empire were thronged with devotees, the women in particular finding in the young and gracious queen-mother a mystic object of devotion who met their universal needs as did none other goddess. With Mithraism, its male counterpart, her cultus was the most effective rival to Christianity from the second century onwards, and during the temporary revival of classical paganism in Rome in A.D. 394, it was her festival that was celebrated with great magnificence.[65] Even after the closing of the Serapaeum in Alexandria three years later, her temple on the island of Philae in the first Cataract survived until 560, when the worship was prohibited and finally brought to an end by the Emperor Justinian.

Nevertheless, popular and attractive as the Goddess of many names and attributes was, she was essentially a syncretistic divinity, Egyptian in origin and mode of worship, but un-Egyptian in character. By amalgamation with Greek and Asiatic names, titles and mythologies she secured and retained her position in the Roman world because she absorbed the qualities and functions of all other goddesses. Moreover, she gained dominion not only over nature but also over the hearts and lives of those who dedicated themselves to her service. In these ways and capacities she fulfilled the role of the Great Mother, but she was rarely identified in worship with any Hellenic deity, and the gods of Egypt, Greece and Rome had too little in common to be capable of any true blending. At the most it was but a crude and imperfect fusion that was achieved. Even at Alexandria, with its cosmopolitan population drawn largely from Greek and Egyptian sources, the eclectic figure of Serapis, while bringing into conjunction the two main streams of religious ideas and worship current in the capital, was predominantly Hellenic and reduced Osiris to a subordinate position.

For the populace, however, he had little influence on their daily life, being essentially the official supreme creator and controller of the universe. It was to his consort, Isis, that men, and especially women, turned for the satisfaction of their personal and domestic needs. But even so, she never possessed the same influence as Kybele because, unlike Serapis, she retained her Egyptian affinities. Her temples, though numerous and widespread, were small except at Philae and Alexandria, and the worship in them often was localized in its character, intentions and distinctive epithets, conducted by priests and priestesses of Egyptian extraction or appearance, sometimes not wholly above suspicion of engaging in licentious practices in the pursuit of their office. The suppression of her cultus, rightly or wrongly, was in fact attributed to the scandalous behaviour in her temples necessitating their destruction and the cessation of her private worship. Even her statue was removed from the Capitol, and when subsequently the restrictions were lifted, her sanctuaries were only allowed outside the pomoerium.[66] These may have been merely rules imposed on foreign institu/ tions regarded with suspicion, like those applied to Christianity for similar reasons. But whether or not they were justified, it was not until the time of Vespasian (A.D. 60–79) that the Isiac became firmly established and took its place in the Magna Mater tradition in the Roman world.

THE CAPPADOCIAN MA/BELLONA

Among the new cults that had close affinities with those of Kybele and Isis was that of the Cappadocian Ma (i.e. Mother), identified with Bellona, the Roman war/goddess associated with Mars. Like those of the Magna Mater her priests were Asiatics, and Roman citizens were forbidden to take part in her fierce ecstatic rites in which the *bellonarii* (as the priests or *galli* were called) armed with swords and axes worked them/ selves into a frenzy by outlandish music and dancing. This orgiastic cult in all probability was introduced by soldiers who had come into contact with it during the campaigns of Sulla and Pompey in Asia Minor. In the last half/century of the Republic it was practised in Rome more or less secretly, or at any rate privately. Indeed, it did not receive recognition until the third century A.D., although the first temple to Bellona was vowed by Appius Claudius in 296 B.C. during the war against the Samnites, and erected somewhat later in the Campus Martius near the altar of Mars.[67] At the pillar columna bellica in front of it declarations of war were made symbolically by launching a spear over it.

The Goddess, however, had no festival or flamen, her priests (*bellonarii*), as we have seen, being Asiatic ecstatics (*fanatici*) who, clad in black vestments, gashed themselves with their swords to the sound of drums and trumpets and sprinkled the statue of the Goddess with the blood as it gushed forth. In a state of delirium they foretold the future, but the main purpose of the ferocious rites was to arouse a warlike spirit in themselves and so to become invincible. Later the cult was brought into conjunction with that of the Magna Mater, and the same people often might combine the priesthood of Bellona with that of Kybele.[68] But although in a subordinate capacity it was very closely associated with the worship of the Magna Mater, and adopted the *Dies Sanguis* and the Taurobolium as its own rites, even after the restrictions upon its activities had been withdrawn at the beginning of the Christian era, it had only a very brief period of popularity, and never exercised a distinctive influence in the welter of foreign Oriental cults that arose in the declining centuries of the Roman Empire.

Atargatis, the Dea Syria

It was those introduced from Syria by slaves and traders that made a much deeper and more permanent impression. Thus, on the Janiculum there were successive temples to Syrian deities, and from Northern Syria came Atargatis who in Rome was known as the *Dea Syria*, popularly called Diasuria, or Iasura, the goddess of Hierapolis-Bambyce near the Euphrates. Her origins are obscure, but from the description of the cult and of the temple at Hierapolis to the south of Carchemish, given by Lucian of Samosata in the manner of Herodotus in the second century A.D., we are left in no doubt about its licentious nature; equipped as it was with its phallic symbols, eunuch-priests and ritual prostitutes, dedicated to the service of the Goddess.[69] Nevertheless, although its debauched character is strongly emphasized, it conforms to the general pattern of the Mother-goddess cultus in Western Asia, be it in Phrygia, Anatolia, Mesopotamia, or Syria. Indeed the worship of Atargatis as a fertility-goddess, the counterpart of Aphrodite, with her consort Hadad, the Mesopotamian equivalent of the Hurrian and Hittite Weather-god, is merely the localized version of that of the Magna Mater throughout the region.

In all its essential features the priests, rites and sanctuaries are true to type, and differ little from the account given of the worship of the *Dea Syria* in the Roman world by Apuleius.[70] Moreover, these descriptions have been confirmed by the numismatic evidence from the time of Alexander to the third century A.D., and that of Macrobius, who wrote about A.D. 400. Thus, the local coins portray the Goddess seated on a lion or on a throne supported by a lion, while the male deity survives in his bull symbol as a counterpart of the lion-goddess on the obverse side. But sometimes the bull is shown in the grip of the lion, suggesting the ultimate triumph of the Goddess cult. Again, inscriptions in Delos, where Syrian slaves abounded and the cult was firmly established, on a number of votive inscriptions dating from just before the Christian era the name of Atargatis and Hadad are combined, the Goddess being identified with Aphrodite, and her priests called 'Hiera-politans'.[71] Fishes and doves were sacred to her, and she was said to have been changed into a fish and her daughter, Semiramis, into a dove.[72]

In the Lucian narrative this temple is said to have been the largest and richest in Syria, equipped with oracular statues, huge stone phalli, a bronze altar, and in an inner shrine to which only certain priests had access there were three golden images. The first of these was that of Atargatis, having the attributes of Hera, Athena, Aphrodite, Rhea, Artemis, Selene, Nemesis and the Fates, carrying in one hand a sceptre and in the other a distaff. On her head, surrounded with rays, she wore a tower as a crown, and round her waist the girdle of Aphrodite, as on the coins, and she stood on lions.[73] The second image is described as Zeus, but actually it was Hadad sitting on bulls, as Macrobius indicates in his account of the cult.

'The Syrians [he says] give the name *Adad* to the god which they revere as first and greatest of all. They honour him as all powerful, but they associate with him the goddess names *Adargatis*, and assign to these two divinities supreme power over everything, recognizing in them the sun and the earth. Without expressing by numerous names the different aspects of their power, their predominance is implied by the different attributes assigned to the two divinities. For the statue of *Adad* is encircled by descending rays which indicate that the force of heaven resides in the rays which the sun sends down to earth: the rays of the statue of *Adargatis* rise upwards, a sign that the power of the ascending rays brings to life everything which the earth produces. Below this statue are the figures of lions, emblematic of the earth: for the same reason that the Phrygians so represent the Mother of the gods, that is to say, the earth, borne by lions.'[74]

Between these two images stood a third deity different from the others, the sex of which Lucian failed to determine. It was without name, and he could obtain no information about its origin or form. It was called σημήιον, 'sign', but this was an error on his part, as almost certainly the divinity represented was Ate, the Aramaic 'Atar', the second element in Atargatis. The identity of this deity has been a matter of considerable conjecture, and falsely it has been confused with Astarte. The most that can be said with any degree of certainty is that this ancient Semitic divinity, whatever may have been its precise name and nature and location, was associated with the Mother-goddess under her various designations—being the local form of Ishtar-Athtar—and it is possible that Attis, the consort of Kybele, is another variation of the name.

As to the origin of the temple it was attributed to Deucalion, Dionysus, Semiramis and Ate, Lucian inclining to Dionysus.[75] Its priesthood was divided into classes according to the functions performed. The eunuchs were the most conspicuous, and in the description of the rites given by Lucian and Apuleius the crowd of painted young men, who paraded the streets in female attire, with an ass bearing the image of the Goddess, were led by an old eunuch of dubious reputation. Under his guidance they worked themselves into a frenzy, aided by their Syrian flutes, and flagellated themselves before seeking lavish rewards from the wondering spectators. The gifts included jars of milk and wine, flour and cheeses, as well as bronze coins. Lucian regarded the orgies as having been borrowed from the cult of Attis, who was the traditional original founder of the shrine at Hierapolis. Thus, it was an image called Ate that was taken to the sea-shore twice each year when a procession went to bring thence jars of sea-water taken to the temple where the water was poured into a hole in the precincts.[76]

Moreover, Lucian repeats the tradition that Atargatis was Rhea, by which designation was meant Kybele, not the Cretan goddess, just as the shrine was the work of Attis. Now this Attis, he says, was a Lydian, and it was he who first taught the sacred mysteries of Rhea (i.e. Kybele). 'The ritual of the Phrygians and the Lydians and the Samothracians was entirely learnt from Attes. For when Rhea deprived him of his powers, he put off his manly garb and assumed the appearance of a woman and her dress, and roaming over the whole earth he performed his mysterious rites, narrating his sufferings and chanting the praises of Rhea.' In due course, he reached Syria, and there erected a temple at Hierapolis in which the rites of the Magna Mater were held in the prescribed manner. As in her Phrygian cradleland she was drawn in her chariot by lions holding a drum in her hand and carrying a tower on her head. Her priests castrated themselves in her honour, like her own *galli*, and behaved in the same frantic way in their wild exercises.[77]

There can be little doubt that the 'omnipotent and all-producing Syrian goddess' was in fact the Magna Mater, however she might be described and worshipped, indistinguishable from Kybele and her counterparts.[78] As the local form of the universal figure she controlled birth, vegetation and fertility in all its various aspects, and taught mankind law and the worship of the gods. With the rest of these goddesses she shared the same emblems (e.g. doves, lions, fish and sexual symbols), and was associated with the life-giving waters. Her Syrian cult-centre would appear to have been Hierapolis, and there she was venerated as Atargatis. Thence her cult was diffused in the wake of the worship of Astarte, and so penetrated westwards until at length it reached the Greek islands, the Mediterranean littoral and the Graeco-Roman world in the Hellenistic period.

Historically Atargatis and Astarte were distinct, and it is now clear that the *Dea Syria* and the North Syrian Goddess cults had been subjected to Anatolian influences.[79] Thus, on a coin from the earliest levels at Hierapolis the figure of a priest-king is depicted designated Abd-Hadad, the 'servant of Hadad', vested in a Hittite robe and hat, while at Boghaz-Keui a similar representation is clad in a toga-like garment holding a curved lituus and wearing a Hittite pointed cap.[80] The Hierapolitan cult-images (e.g. the bull, lion, double axe) are Anatolian connecting the *Dea Syria*, usually seated and robed, with the Idean Mother, the Phrygian Kybele or Rhea, with the Greek Hera the consort of Zeus. Therefore, in what was once the Hittite capital on the Euphrates she inherited many of her Anatolian features which distinguished her from the more specifically Astarte and identified her with the Magna Mater *par excellence*.

The Magna Mater Cultus in May Day Celebrations

This syncretistic ecstatic cultus of the Mother of the Gods, originally indigenous in Phrygia, when subsequently it found expression in the Roman Empire after the introduction of Kybele in 204 B.C., spread along the northern coast of Africa into Spain, and throughout Southern Gaul, along the Rhône valley to Autun, into Germany and Mysia.[81] While, as we have seen, the highly emotional character of the orgiastic rites was considerably modified when they were given official recognition in imperial times, in their Romanized form the story of Attis and Kybele was enacted as a sacred drama in the month of March. This no doubt was current in Asia Minor in the second millennium B.C. long before it acquired a place in the Attis Spring Festival in Rome.[82] But in the form in which it was presented from the 15th to the 27th of the month, the pattern was set which down to modern times survived in Central and Northern Europe in folk tradition, transferred from the vernal equinox to May 1st.

This transition was effected apparently by the confusion in reckoning of the dates in the pre-Julian and our present calendars. Thus, our May 1st every alternate year is the same day as March 25th in the pre-Julian calendar,[83] and just as March 25th, commonly called Lady Day, is set apart in the Christian Year for the commemoration of the Annunciation of the Incarnation to the Madonna so the month of May has now been dedicated to her. With the rise of Christianity in the Roman world in the fourth century and the suppression of the pagan cults, the popular festivals were retained in their less obnoxious aspects, and so far as possible given a new inter- pretation. As a result of this procedure the traditional customs continued little changed in their outward form and character, whatever modifications they may have undergone in their doctrinal theological interpretation and popular presentation.

In the case of the Magna Mater celebrations, the rites having been shorn of what remained of their ecstatic frenzies by incorporation in the cult of the Empire, Lady Day, which invariably falls in Lent and occasionally coincides with Good Friday, was not an appropriate day for making carnival. Moreover, the more solemn aspects of the Hilaria—viz. the *Dies Sanguis*—were observed in their Christian interpretation in Holy Week culminating in the Easter death and resurrection sacred drama. While this concluded with manifestations of rejoicing, they assumed their later forms when in and after the eleventh century they were celebrated on May 1st, with its calendrical connexions with March 25th. It was then that Kybele reappeared in the guise of the May Queen with Attis as the Green Man, and the May-pole decorated with greenery as his symbol. Moreover, the ceremonies conformed to the observances in the Roman celebration of the Hilaria. Thus, as the sacred pine-tree representing the emasculated god Attis was taken in procession by the dendrophori from Kybele's wood to the temple of the Magna Mater on the Palatine hill on March 22nd,[84] so it has been a common and widespread custom in peasant Europe for youths to go out to the woods after midnight, cut down a tree, lop off the branches, leaving a few at the top, and after wrapping it round with purple bands to decorate it with violets like the figure of Attis.

It was then taken back to the village at sunrise on May Day to the accompaniment of the blowing of flutes and horns, together with either young trees or branches which were fastened over the doors and windows of the houses, while the May-pole was erected on the village green or in some central place, often near the church. Sometimes a doll has been fixed to the tree, like the Attis image, mentioned by Firmicus Maternus,[85] bound on the middle of the sacred tree. Alternatively it has been carried in a basket or cradle from house to house by young girls, or dangled in the midst of two hoops at right angles to each other and decorated with flowers as the May Lady.[86]

The May-pole often has stood more than sixty feet high, and, like Kybele in her car drawn by a yoke of lions or oxen, it has been conveyed in a wagon by from twenty to forty oxen, each adorned with garlands on the horns, followed by men and women and children 'with great devotion'.[87] On its arrival at the selected spot in the village it was erected, very much as the pine-tree was exposed for veneration and set up near the temple of the Magna Mater on the Palatine,[88] and around it dances were held. Sometimes those taking part in them were confined to lovers, though frequently all the younger members of the community joined in the merry-making. In England long streamers are now attached to the top of the pole, each held by a child, and as they dance round it the ribbons are twined round it, to be untwined when the dancers reverse. These may be survivals of the bands of wool on the Attis tree.

Not infrequently the May Queen herself has been taken in triumph to the village green in a decorated cart drawn by youths or maids of honour, and headed by the May-pole. After she has been crowned and enthroned, the dances and revels have been held before her rather than around the May-pole. Moreover, during her year of office she has presided at all the gatherings and revels of the young people in the village.[89] The May King, who has often been associated with her, has been represented by a man, usually a chimney-sweep, clad in a wooden framework covered with leaves in the guise of the

Jack-in-the-Green. Sometimes he has been taken to the village on a sledge, or on horseback with a pyramid over him, surrounded by a cavalcade of young men. The leader might be a clown with coloured fringes and frills on his blouse, and hanging from his beaver-hat, who amused the crowd by his gestures and hilarity.[90]

Sometimes the symbolism was that of a sacred marriage of the May Queen and the May King, united to each other as bride and bridegroom, thereby unconsciously fulfilling the role of their prototypes, Kybele and Attis. As Kybele was responsible for the flowering of the fields, so the May Queen sat in an arbour wreathed with flowers, or in the porch of the church, resembling Kybele seated at the entrance of her mountain abode and receiving floral offerings from her votaries.[91] Her spouse, the Green Man, has been treated in a similar manner because in him Attis, the beloved of the Goddess, has lived on in undying folk tradition and its immortal seasonal customs.

It is true that May Day observances that have survived in the peasant cultures in Europe have lost their serious character and become merely an occasion for merry-making and the collection of *pourboires* from the houses visited by the processions, led by the May King and Queen and the May-pole. The principal roles now often are played by children, as, for example, in Warwickshire where the Queen is a small girl wheeled with a 'mail-cart', or perambulator, by an older girl. The May-pole, with its conical framework and hoops covered with flowers, is borne by four boys, and a young girl carries a money-box as the children go from house to house singing their traditional songs and collecting money for their tea and treat in the afternoon.[92]

Nevertheless, although the ancient rites have degenerated into little more than picturesque popular pastimes, clownish burlesques and children's diversions, they have retained their original figures and traits little changed through more than two thousand years during which they have persisted, however much their purposes and functions may have become de-sacralized. So ingrained in these customs and observances were the myth and ritual of the Phrygian Magna Mater and her consort that centred in the Spring Festival, known in Rome as the Hilaria, that the enactment of the theme has been handed down throughout the ages. If in the meantime the annual rebirth of nature in the spring in the popular mind has become less dependent upon the performance of this ancient cultus, the May Queen and the Green Man have survived true to type in their respective roles, even though the fruitfulness of the earth may no longer be thought to rest upon the fulfilment of their time-honoured offices. Behind them and their symbol, the bedecked May-pole, are the shadowy forms of Kybele, Attis and the resurrection drama in Western Asia, the Eastern Mediterranean and the Aegean, and in the cultus of the Magna Mater so widely distributed and firmly laid in the Roman Empire.

CHAPTER VII

The Mater Ecclesia and the Madonna

THE MATER ECCLESIA IN PHRYGIA

As the missionary enterprise of the Early Church was particularly active from Apostolic times in Asia Minor, where the cult of the Magna Mater was so very deeply laid and very prominent, it is not surprising that it was in this region that the pagan conception of the Mother of the Gods influenced its Christian counterparts. This is most apparent among the more obscure Gnostic sects, such as the Naassenes, the Nicolaitans, the Collyridians and the Montanists, in which the female principle was identified with the Holy Ghost bringing forth the male principle (Sophia or Prunicus) as the Gnostic *Aeon matres*.[1] Indeed, as Bousset maintained, there are grounds for regarding Gnosticism as in the main a cult of the Asian Magna Mater.[2]

Gnostic Mother Divinities in Phrygia

These sects flourished very prominently in the Fertile Crescent and Asia Minor in the opening centuries of the Christian era, and became a syncretistic excrescence of the worship of Kybele, Isis and Demeter. This found expression in a complex cosmological mythology in which the mother-element was predominant. As Irenaeus remarked, 'their Aeons they insist upon terming "gods" and "fathers" and "lords" and "heavens", along with their Mother whom they call both "Earth" and "Jerusalem", besides applying a host of other names to her'.[3] In this miscegenation of pagan and Judaeo-Christian elements the creative aspects of the Goddess were combined with the Isaianic-Pauline conception of fecundity of the Heavenly Jerusalem; the universal Mother nourishing the children she has brought forth.[4] Even Christ did not refrain from referring to the Holy City in personal maternal terms.[5] Similarly, the Church was represented as the Bride of Christ[6] very much as Israel was described as the Spouse of Yahweh.[7] So deeply laid was this ecclesiastical symbolism in the Early Church that it was inseparable from the allegory of the two Jerusalems in St Paul's Epistle to the Galatians (iv. 21–31), the 'Church-spouse' being 'the mother of us all', the Second Eve, and the means whereby the mystical union between its members and its divine Head is maintained.

Now it was this imagery that in sub-Apostolic times was developed by the Gnostics when they incorporated it in their syncretisms, equating the role of the Graeco-Oriental Mother-goddesses with that of the Holy Ghost and the celestial and polymorphous Mother. In the case of some of the more exuberant sects the Phrygian prototypes were taken over little changed. Thus, the Naassenes, according to Hippolytus, derived their name from the figure of the serpent (Naas) adored in Eden,[8] the connexion being with the cult of Sabazios, and, as we have seen, the symbolism was very prominent in that of the Minoan Mother.[9] But, notwithstanding their designation, serpent worship was only a minor feature in the group of anonymous Gnostic sects called Ophite. From such information about their speculations as is available, derived mainly from Origen's *Contra Celsum* (vi. 24–38), and from the *Adversus Haereses* of Irenaeus (i. 30), together with references by Epiphanius[10] and the pseudo-Tertullian,[11] it appears that their gnosis consisted in the Primal Man, or Universal Father, self-existent in the primeval abyss, holy and inscrutable, projecting from himself the Son of Man, with the female principle ($\mu\dot\eta\tau\eta\rho$) brooding over chaos. It was this Primal Woman who became the mother of the being who to effect the work of redemption descended to rescue the fallen divinity, Sophia, a very obscure figure in the earlier forms of the cult. In the later developments Prunicus-Sophia was represented as emerging as a potency from the left side of the female principle, or divine spirit, which eventually produced seven powers among whom was the Demiurge, identified with Ialdabaoth, the hostile god of the Old Testament. It was he who created Adam and gave him Eve whom Sophia seduced through the agency of the serpent to induce her to rebel against the Demiurge. In the great conflict between Ialdabaoth and Sophia the serpent (together with Cain, Esau, the Sodomites, Korah and Judas; i.e. the victims of the wrath of the God of the Old Testament) was extolled and venerated, and in those sects in which the Redeemer occurs (e.g. the Naassenes), some attempt was made to relate the Heavenly Mother to the Christ as an Aeon. The association of Sophia with his redemptive work was a concesˈsion to the identification of the Judaic conception of Wisdom with the Hellenistic Logos doctrine, and the Christian interˈpretation of the Incarnation in terms of the Theotokos.

The Ophite sects appear to represent an early form of primitive Gnosticism, as Hippolytus maintained,[12] in which Anatolian, Syrian, Mesopotamian and Iranian influences were predominant, though late Gnostic and Christian accretions also were added in course of time.[13] In origin, however, they seem to have been preˈChristian, and to have preserved among the various features of pagan belief and practice those borrowed from the Goddess cult. Thus, the Nicolaitans, mentioned in the Johanˈnine Apocalypse,[14] or, as is more probable, a later Gnostic sect of the name, are said to have worshipped the Magna Mater,[15] and to have engaged in immoral practices which included ritual prostitution.[16] Their purpose, however, appears to have been to prevent the sexual propagation of the human race in order to bring to an end the perpetuation of evil. A good deal of confusion has arisen by the identification of a later Gnostic group with the Johannine Balaamites, the alleged followers of Jezebel, and of Nicolaus, the proselyte of Antioch of an earlier period.[17]

The Montanist Ecstatic Cultus

Of the movement initiated by Montanus in the middle of the second century in Mysia adjoining Phrygia, who had been a pagan ecstatic before his conversion to Christianity, we are better informed. In course of time he was joined by two prophetesses, Maximilla and Prisca, or Priscilla, who also claimed to have the same charismatic powers, and together to have fulfilled the promise, as it was affirmed, of a new out-pouring of the Holy Spirit.[18] But although the ecstatic pheno-mena were represented as the coming of the Paraclete as at Pentecost, in fact the prophesyings were indistinguishable from those of the frenzied votaries of the Goddess, except that they worked themselves into a state of intense emotion—a deliber-ately induced madness—to excite to repentance and penitence.[19] Montanus, indeed, claimed to be the mouthpiece of the Paraclete, and at any rate after his death the prophetesses were regarded as having taken his place in this capacity.

At first, however, the movement does not appear to have been unorthodox in its Christian teaching, however ecstatic and Phrygian may have been its methods. Nevertheless, it provoked a good deal of criticism, suspicion and opposition on the part of the Thraco-Phrygian episcopate. One bishop from Anchiale in Thrace attempted, in fact, to exorcize Prisca. All efforts at restraint, however, proved to be of little avail, and the vast majority of Phrygian Christians became Montanists in spite of confutations by Apollinarius, bishop of Hierapolis, and others, denunciations of synods and excommunications, culminating in the expulsion of the movement as a whole from the Catholic Church not later than the year 177.[20] But the Phrygians, accustomed to the orgiastic worship of Kybele, found Montanist Christianity congenial with its ecstatic prophesyings, asceticisms, sadistic love of suffering, and cult of martyrdom. From all the remote villages they flocked to the headquarters of Montanus at Pepuza, located by Ramsay west of Eumenia near Pentapolis,[21] in the expectation of an imme-diate Parousia taking place there. Virginity was strongly urged and chastity strictly enforced as a preparation for ecstasy, and as became those who belonged to the spotless Bride of Christ. Women assumed the offices of bishops and priests as well as of prophetesses,[22] though Tertullian would not allow them to 'speak in the church, nor to teach, to baptize, nor to offer, nor to assume any function which belongs to a man',[23] thereby rejecting Phrygian practice. He was equally strenuous in his opposition to pagan accretions in Asian Montanism.

In the west it was Gaul, notably in the Rhône valley at Vienne and Lyons, that the influence of the movement was most apparent, and attempts were made to resolve the schism.[24] The absence of a Phrygian background doubtless in some measure accounts for the reluctance of the Christians in this region to accept Montanism as readily as their brethren in Asia and Phrygia, and prompted them to act as ambassadors for 'the peace of the churches' by taking letters to Rome expressing their view of the movement. Indeed, they were described by Eusebius as 'pious and orthodox',[25] even though they approved of the ecstatic prophesyings and the right of women to engage in these exercises. In its setting and techniques the cultus was essentially Phrygian, deeply rooted in the orgiastic antecedents centred in the worship of Kybele. Thus, Priscilla claimed that Christ visited her and slept by her side at Pepuza, though she discreetly added that he did so in the form of a woman, 'clad in a bright garment, and put wisdom into me, and revealed to me that this place is holy, and that here Jerusalem above comes down'.

The Mystical Conception of the Mater Ecclesia

As Christ was regarded as the Spouse of those who were filled with the Spirit, in Gaul and North Africa the Church was called Mater Ecclesia.[26] This nuptial symbolism, in fact, may have been diffused in Lyons and Vienne by its contacts with Phrygia and Asia Minor based on the conception of Christ as the divine bridegroom standing in a marital relationship with his Bride the Church, as Irenaeus stressed.[27] After his lapse into Montanism, Tertullian emphasized the virginity of the Church without spot or wrinkle as a virgin free from the stain of fornication.[28] Nevertheless, the nuptial symbolism remained his predominant theme, and he developed the Pauline tradition in relation to the underlying Goddess cultus in Asia Minor, interpreted in terms of Christ as the source of all true life. As physical life came through Adam, so it was maintained that the Church is the Second Eve, 'the true Mother of the living',[29] through whom spiritual life was mediated from Christ, the Second Adam, first by the waters of baptism and then not infrequently in the much-coveted baptism of blood in the arena.

Clement of Alexandria (150–220) adopted an allegorical interpretation of the converts who by virtue of their baptismal rebirth had become children of the Virgin Mother the Church.

'She alone had no milk because she alone did not become woman, but she is both virgin and mother, being undefiled as a virgin and loving as a mother; and calling her children to her, she nurses them with holy milk, because the Logos was milk, giving nourishment to this child fair and born in His own house, the Body of Christ, the youthful band, whom the Lord Himself brought forth in labour of the flesh and whom the Lord Himself swathed in His precious blood. The Logos is all to the child—father, and mother and tutor and nurse, "Eat ye my flesh", He says, and "Drink my blood". Such suitable nourishment does the Lord minister to us, and He offers His flesh and pours out His blood; and nothing is wanting for the children's growth.'[30]

As Virgin and Mother the Church is thus represented as undefiled by false doctrine and ever loving and watchful of those who come within her affectionate embrace, sanctifying them as children of God, training them on earth and so preparing them to attain to citizenship in heaven.[31] In fact, as St Paul maintained, every baptized person was called to reproduce in himself the life of Christ, born, nourished and sustained by the Church, under the symbolism of his Mystical Body and Spouse.

'The Lord Christ, the fruit of the Virgin, did not pronounce the breasts of women blessed, nor selected them to give nourishment; but when the kind and loving Father had

rained down the Word, Himself became spiritual nourishment to the good, O mystic marvel! The universal Father is
one, and one is the universal Word; and the Holy Spirit is
one, and the same everywhere, and one is the Virgin
Mother.'[32]

For Origen (*c.* 185–253), the pupil of Clement at Alexandria, all who are mystically united with the Logos in a spiritual
marriage constitute the visible Church on earth, the true
Bride of Christ, though it is composed of all *credentes*, many of
whom are far from having attained perfection.[33] But the desire
of the soul must be to be joined to the Logos and to enter into
the mysteries of his knowledge and wisdom as into the chamber
of a heavenly Bridegroom, there to experience spiritual intercourse (*κοινωνία*) and the parturition (*τόκος*) of good works.[34]
The womb of the soul is opened by God that it 'begets His
Logos and becomes His mother'.[35] Similarly, Macarius, the
first anchorite in Egypt (*c.* 389), uses the same nuptial termi-
nology in describing how a soul

'putting away the shame of her face, and no longer mastered
by the disgrace of her thoughts nor caused to commit adultery
by the evil one, has communion with the heavenly Spouse, as
being herself simple (*μονότροπός*); for, wounded with His
love, she languishes and faints (if I may dare to speak thus)
for the beauteous spiritual and mystical commerce in the
incorrupt union of communion in holiness. Blessed indeed
and happy is such a soul, which, conquered by spiritual
love, has been worthily affianced to God the Word.'[36]

Therefore, 'the five wise and prudent virgins could all go
together (*συνέλθειν*) into the heavenly Thalamos'.[37]

Methodius, another third-century mystic who apparently had
lived in Asia Minor,[38] adopted much the same interpretation
of the espousal to Christ of faithful souls as 'virgin helpmates'.
From him they conceive 'the pure and fertile seed of His
doctrine' brought forth 'as by mothers in travail', and

'regenerated unto the greatness and beauty of virtue'. When 'by the process of their growth in their turn have become the Church, they too co-operate in the birth and nurture of other children, bringing to fruition in the womb of the soul as in the womb of a mother, the unblemished will of the Logos.'[39] Thus, St Paul is quoted as an example of the new-born initiate, nourished after his baptism by the milk of the Gospel, who on attaining manhood was made 'a helpmate and bride of the Logos. Receiving and conceiving the seeds of life', and so becoming 'the Church and a mother'. In this state of spiritual perfection he 'laboured in birth of those who through him were believers in the Lord, until in them also Christ was formed and born'.[40]

Similarly, the Johannine apocalyptic vision of the Woman in travail that appeared in heaven clothed with the sun and bearing a crown of twelve stars, and having the moon for her footstool, was interpreted as 'our Mother, being a power of herself and distinct from her children'. In other words, the Church, called by the prophets 'sometimes Jerusalem, sometimes a bride, sometimes Mount Sion, sometimes the temple and tabernacle of God', is always labouring to bring forth her children, and then gathers them to her from everywhere, running to her 'seeking their resurrection in baptism'.[41] Adorned as a bride and a queen in her garment of light proceeding from the Logos, with a diadem of stars, she stands on the moon, symbolizing 'the faith of those who are cleansed from corruption in the bath of baptism'. Being in labour, she is the Mother

'regenerating sensual men. For just as woman conceives the unformed seed of a man and in the course of time brings forth a perfect man, in the same way, one may say, does the Church ever and ever conceive those who flee to the Logos, forming them in the likeness and form of Christ, and in the course of time make them into citizens of those blessed eternities. Whence must she of necessity stand over the bath of baptism, and bringing forth those who are washed in it.'[42]

The likeness and form of the Logos being stamped upon them and engendered in them, the baptized receive the characteristic features and manliness of Christ, so that in each one He is born spiritually. For this reason the Church as their Mother is pregnant and in labour until Christ is formed and born in each of the saints, making them very Christ's (anointed ones); the spiritual children of Sion, illuminated and trans⁄formed in the Logos.[43] But like the 'Devouress' waiting to consume the soul, should the scales not balance in the Egyptian Judgment scene, the Dragon is represented in the vision as waiting to devour the man⁄child of the Woman as soon as it is born, because the Devil is ever on the alert to destroy the Christ⁄possessed soul after his baptism. Hence the need of the protection of 'our Mother the Church, uninjured and undefiled by the wrath of the Beast, that, like the wise virgins, all faithful souls may keep their virginity secure through all the arduous struggle'.[44] Thus, at length they may join the ranks of the martyrs, imitating their Mother, the Mater Ecclesia, by courage⁄ously brooking 'the burdens and vicissitudes and afflictions of life'.[45]

In all this nuptial imagery the Phrygian cradleland in which it arose is clearly in the background. Behind it lies that of the Goddess cult in Asia Minor interpreted in terms of the mystical thought and language of the motherhood of the Virgin Church conceiving children spiritually through the natural process of parturition with its attendant labour and travail. The female principle, originally personified in the Magna Mater, became the Mater Ecclesia, at once the Bride and Body of Christ, the Mother of the faithful proceeding towards perfection, in whom the Bride is merged. Shorn of its cruder symbolism and Asian emotionalism, the nuptial element remained an integral feature in Catholic mysticism in the West as in the Byzantine tradition. After the time of St Augustine, who made the marriage of Christ and the Church the central theme of his Christology,[46] it was brought into relation with the Roman claim of universal sovereignty, and notably by St Bernard of Clairvaux (1090–1153), its mystical aspect was concentrated mainly on the Canticles. This collection of Hebrew erotic lyrics, whether or not they had any connexion with the cult of Ishtar as Meek has suggested,[47] were treated in a highly spiritual and emotional manner and coupled with chivalrous romantic love which became increasingly popular in the Middle Ages.

For St Augustine 'all the Church is Christ's Bride, of which the beginning and first-fruits is the flesh of Christ, because there was the Bride joined to the Bridegroom in the flesh'.[48] 'The nuptial union is that of the Word and the Flesh; the bridechamber of this union, the Virgin's womb. For the flesh itself was itself united to the Word: whence also it saith "Henceforth they are not twain, but one flesh". The Church was assumed unto him out of the human race: so that the flesh itself, being united to the Word, might be the Head of the Church: and the rest who believe members of the Head.'[49] In the Virgin's womb the Bride had already been united to Christ and made Head of the Church so that at His nativity the Church already was His Body.[50]

THE MADONNA

Although Mary was held in very high esteem by St Augustine and her perpetual virginity and impeccability were maintained in spite of his doctrine of original sin,[51] as the instrument of the Incarnation she occupied a secondary position in the capacity in which the Lord Christ deigned to dwell and become consubstantial with her. Indeed, during the opening centuries of the new era the influence of the Magna Mater tradition on Christian thought and practice was confined for the most part to the imagery of the Mater Ecclesia. It was only in the Gnostic Ophite sects that the Virgin herself was actually worshipped as a goddess, and as late as the fourth century, as we have seen, Epiphanius condemned in no uncertain terms the Collyridians who offered cakes to her as the Queen of Heaven. Thus, he declared that 'the body of Mary is holy but she is not God; she is Virgin and worthy of great honour but she is not given to us in adoration, rather she adores Him Who is born of her flesh'. Consequently, 'let Mary be honoured but let the Father, Son and Holy Spirit be adored. Let no one adore Mary.'[52] Similarly, Ambrose whose influence on St Augustine was very considerable, maintained that 'Mary was the temple of God not the Lord of the temple. Therefore, only he is to be adored who worked within the Temple.'[53]

The Virgin Church and the Cult of Mary

Undoubtedly popular veneration of the Virgin, which ran to extravagant lengths in the Phrygian sects, was widespread in the Conciliar period, especially in the Byzantine Empire, after Constantine's adoption of Christianity. For those who accepted the doctrine of the Incarnation with its stupendous claims, involving nothing less than the Creator of the universe assuming a human body in the womb of a mortal woman, the vehicle of this amazing event of necessity must be regarded as a unique personality to be held in the very highest esteem. Therefore, in an age in which the Goddess cult was so deeply laid the Mother of the Redeemer hardly could escape being assigned a position which in many respects corresponded to that of the Magna Mater in the pagan world, particularly in those areas in which she had been predominant. Nevertheless, to assume that the cult of Mary was merely the Christianized version of its pagan prototype is a simplification of a complex situation which is not supported by the evidence.[54]

Christianity moved in a very different world of thought, belief and practice from that which lay behind the 'Goddess of many names', and Marian doctrine and piety emerged and developed within their own theological and historical context. To some extent no doubt in some of their modes of expression they represent the universal psychological reactions to the Great Mother archetype—the archetypal Feminine—the symbolism of which in recent years has been the preoccupation of those engaged in psycho-analytical interpretation and fantasy[55]—an aspect of the phenomenon which lies outside the range of our present inquiry. But regarded from the anthropological, historical, comparative and theological standpoints, in so far as the

Early Church was influenced by the cult of the Magna Mater primarily, as has been demonstrated, it was in its conception of the Mater Ecclesia rather than in that of the Madonna. Thus, for example, in Armenia even the title Theotokos in the first instance was applied to the Virgin Mother and immaculate Bride the Church, and not until much later to the physical mother of Christ, after her cultus had become established in the twelfth and thirteenth centuries. The assumption of the Virgin, again, was transformed from the exaltation of the Church by the risen and ascended Christ to that of Mary as the Queen of Heaven.[56] This process of transmitting attributes of the Church to the Madonna was responsible for a good deal of the confusion of the one with the other, and gave Mary certain aspects which she inherited from the Bride Church rather than directly from the Mother-goddess. But the concept of the Church as a hypostatic heavenly being, coeval with Christ and on a level with Wisdom and the Word of God (the Logos), was too unrealistically mystical to remain the final interpretation of the pagan Magnae Matres mystery *dromena* and *mythoi* in Christendom. It was only a question of time, therefore, before the Madonna as a living personality of unique status in the divine revelation was apostrophized as not only the mother but also as the bride of Christ with all that this involved in the subsequent developments of Marian thought and piety.

Ante-Nicene Mariology

In the beginning, however, it was not so. In the canonical scriptures of the New Testament surprisingly little is recorded which throws light upon the problem. Apart from the Lucan infancy narratives there are only two or three incidents in the Gospels in which Mary is mentioned, and after the Day of Pentecost she does not again appear in the literature, with the possible exception of the strange vision of the Woman with Child in the twelfth chapter of the Johannine Apocalpse. In both the Matthaean and Lucan narratives she is represented as having conceived by an act of faith and obedience without the aid and intervention of human paternity, and so brought forth Him who was to be the Saviour of mankind.[57]

If St Paul was aware of the doctrine of the Virgin Birth he makes no reference to it in his extant letters, even when he developed his theme of the Two Adams[58] and of the birth pangs of the new era based on the Genesis Fall story.[59] In his somewhat involved typological arguments he could have introduced Mary as the Second Eve with great advantage. Instead he made the Church the new Eve in the role of the bride and mother married to the new Adam, with whom she was 'one flesh',[60] set against the background of creation personified as Mother-earth undergoing the travail of Eve in the process of the rebirth of a new humanity.[61] Similarly, in the Pauline allegory of Sarah as the mother of the faithful[62] she was identified not with Mary but with the heavenly Jerusalem like the Bride-church.

This imagery of course is capable of interpretation in terms of Marian theology and cultus, as later writers have shown, but it was not so represented by St Paul. If he had been familiar with it he could hardly have failed to have seen its relevance for his allegorical themes and to have developed his doctrine of the two Eves accordingly, and indeed more convincingly, since the Eden story occupied such a conspicuous place in his typology. But in fact it was not until the post-Apostolic period, from the second century and onward, that the Marian cult began to be formulated and gradually to take definite shape in Christian tradition.

At first references to Mary continued to be very few. In the earliest literature (e.g. the Didache, Clement of Rome, Hermas, Polycarp, Tatian) there is no mention at all of her, and only very occasionally by Ignatius, Aristides, Justin Martyr and Irenaeus. It was in reaction to Gnostic Docetism, in which the real humanity of Christ was denied, that she was brought into relation with Eve by Justin and Irenaeus, her obedience being represented as loosing the knot of Eve's disobedience, and setting free by her faith what her prototype had bound fast.[63] Having received faith and joy at the annunciation to her unique vocation by the angel Gabriel, there was born of her 'He by whom God destroys both the serpent and the angels and men that resemble it, and frees from death those who repent of their bad deeds and believe.'[64] Thus, she was assigned the place and function in the process of redemption inherent but not expressed in the Pauline allegories. Origen and Tertullian adopt the same attitude towards her maternal office and its significance,[65] and if her perpetual virginity was a matter of dispute, the reality of her maternity was maintained even to precise anatomical details.[66]

In the struggle first against Gnosticism and Docetism, and then in opposition to Arianism, Mariology came into increasing prominence since the role played by the Blessed Virgin in the work of the Incarnation and of redemption was one of the principal contentions in the prolonged controversies of the period. As Irenaeus affirmed, without a mother of God, God would not have recapitulated in Christ His creation that had fallen.[67] Upon this issue the struggle against Arius was pursued because if Mary was not the mother of the Logos he could not have been consubstantial—*homoousios* in the formula of Athanasius—with the human race.[68] Therefore, she became the key figure in the doctrine of the Incarnation and in orthodox Christology at a crucial moment in the formative period of the Early Church when on the one hand the divinity and on the other the humanity of Christ were being denied. To meet this attack and safeguard the Catholic faith, that Mary was the real mother of Jesus had to be affirmed and established beyond doubt. Against the Docetists and the Arians it was equally important, if the orthodox position was to be maintained that her status should be made absolutely secure. It was out of this Christological controversy that the title Theotokos, Mother of God, was conferred upon her at the Council of Ephesus in 431.

Behind the Ephesian Mariology lay the testimony of the earlier Apologists, beginning with Justin Martyr, Irenaeus and Tertullian, in which the 'Eve-Ave' doctrine was developed, based on the Eden typology in relation to the Second Adam. Out of it emerged the emphasis on the perpetual virginity of

Mary, her sinlessness, and her instrumentality in the redemptive process. That the cultic reaction to this developing Marian theology arose earlier in the East than in the West is not without significance in our present inquiry, since, as has been abundantly demonstrated, it was in this region, especially in Asia Minor, that the Magna Mater was so firmly established. Hence the grave warning against treating Mary as a goddess issued by Epiphanius in the fourth century to prevent the incursion of the pagan cultus into what easily could have become its Christian counterpart. 'Let Mary be honoured, but let the Father, the Son and the Holy Spirit be adored.'[69] In the West where these heresies and accretions were much less insistent the defence of the perpetual virginity sufficed. The Latin Fathers in particular were primarily concerned to uphold the orthodox position respecting the nature of Christ in its dual aspects of perfect God and true man, and to this Mariology was incidental.

Theotokos

Nevertheless, the defeat of Arianism at the Council of Nicaea in 325 and the establishment of the 'consubstantiality' of God the Son with the Father confirmed the title Theotokos assigned to the Virgin by Athanasius because, as he had proclaimed, 'from the flesh of Mary the Son of God by essence and nature did proceed'.[70] Actually it had been in use, probably from the time of Origen, before it was adopted by Athanasius to express the divine humanity of Christ against the Arian denial of his full Godhead. It was, in fact, difficult to confute the current heresies respecting his real manhood while maintaining his divinity except in terms of God as his father and Mary as his mother. Therefore, Nestorius, the Patriarch of Constantinople, raised a crucial issue when in 428 he opposed the use of the title on the grounds that in Holy Scripture Jesus is called Christ or Lord but not God. Mary, he said, should be described as *Christotokos* 'because giving birth to the Son of God she gave birth to a man who, by his union with the Son of God, can be called Son of God'.[71] But although the inference may have been mistaken, he gave the impression of contending that Christ actually was two persons, one human and the other divine; a kind of dual personality divided between the earthly and the heavenly orders of manifestation. Catholics, on the other hand, maintained that he was a single person uniting humanity and divinity completely in himself. It was in the first instance to safeguard this doctrine that the title Theotokos was steadfastly upheld.

In continuing the controversy, in a series of sermons Nestorius repeated his assertion that 'that which is born of woman is not solely God or solely man, but humanity united to divinity'. He was prepared to accept as a formula that 'the two natures which perfectly united with each other and without confusion are adored in the one person of the Only Begotten'.[72] But this could too readily be given a monophysite interpretation of Christ having one nature and that divine, to be acceptable at that juncture. Against it Cyril, the Patriarch of Alexandria, employed all the resources of Nicene orthodoxy in support of the hypostatic union of the human and divine natures in the One Christ when he addressed the Fathers of the Council of Ephesus assembled in the basilica of the Theotokos in 431. There, if anywhere, in the city so notorious for its devotion to Artemis, or Diana as the Romans called her, where her image was said to have fallen from heaven,[73] under the shadow of the great temple dedicated to the Magna Mater since 330 B.C. and containing, according to tradition, a temporary residence of Mary, the title 'God-bearer' hardly could fail to be upheld. St Cyril, however, took no risks, and opened the Council on June 22nd without waiting for the arrival of the Syrian bishops led by John of Antioch, who were most likely to take a sympathetic view of Nestorius.

Having assumed the presidency, Cyril, after the recitation of the Nicene Creed, caused his second letter to Nestorius to be read. This he declared to be in accordance with the faith set forth at Nicaea, and then proceeded with the excommunication of the Patriarch of Constantinople, which was confirmed amid immense public exclamation. As a result Nestorius was 'excluded from all episcopal dignity and from every assembly of bishops', before either the Syrian bishops or the papal envoy from Rome had arrived. John and his party replied by anathe-matizing Cyril and his partisans, accusing them of the heresy of Apollinarius in virtually denying the manhood of Christ by excluding from him a rational soul. Thus, once again the controversy turned on the Christological issue, which through-out the dispute over the title Theotokos remained the funda-mental question. Mary was declared by Cyril to have been truly the Mother of God because she was the 'indestructible temple, the dwelling of the Illimitable Mother and Virgin, through whom he is called in the holy gospels "blessed who cometh in the name of the Lord"'.[74] Nestorius, on the other hand, maintained that she was the mother of the man Christ Jesus who by his union with God could be called the Son of God.

However right from the Alexandrian standpoint Cyril may have been in upholding at all costs its conception of the pre-existent divine Logos taking human nature to himself as the divine Word through Mary as the Theotokos, this interpre-tation of the Incarnation in fact had the effect of making the Saviour of mankind somewhat remote. Therefore, the need of some more intimate and truly human intermediary became increasingly felt, and in this role the sorrowing and glorified Mother of God made a strong appeal to popular imagination and requirements. And in the early developments of the Marian cultus devotion to Our Lady was popular rather than scholarly; Alexandrian and Byzantine rather than Augustinian and Roman. Although the Nestorian heresy only concerned Mary incidentally, being centred upon her Son, nevertheless fresh emphasis was given to her as mediatrix. But, as when the Gnostics denied the manhood of Christ she became the Pleroma of all Pleromas, and even sometimes a Mother-goddess, so when the Council of Ephesus vindicated the title Theotokos it gave theological expression to the growing devotion to the Virgin as the Mother of God, especially in the East.

As a result her divine maternity and perpetual virginity were further stressed, having become the touchstone of Catholic orthodoxy in the Nestorian controversy, and been defended by Hilary of Poitiers (*c.* 315–67), the 'Athanasius of the West', and St Ambrose (*c.* 339–97), among other Latin Fathers in the fourth and fifth centuries. Though she was not actually designated mediatrix (μεσῖτις) until the term was applied to her by John of Damascus in the eighth century, to all intents and purposes she had long fulfilled this role in Asia Minor and the Eastern Mediterranean. But the cult of Mary was not as rapid in its growth after the Council of Ephesus as might have been expected, even where the ground had been so well prepared by the pagan votaries of the Magna Mater. This no doubt was because it arose and developed in the first instance within the context of the doctrine of the Incarnation in which she occupied a unique position; not from the pre-Christian veneration of the feminine principle in divinity which, as we have seen, found expression rather in a deified Mater Ecclesia.

Marian Iconography

Nevertheless, the Council of Ephesus gave a powerful impetus to the Marian cultus which was represented almost at once in iconography. Thus, alleged authentic portraits of the Virgin began to appear of which the *Hodegetria* (Ὁδηγητρία) attributed to St Luke is a well-known example, said to have been sent from Jerusalem in 438 by the Empress Eudocia to her sister-in-law Pulcheria, who placed it in the church of the Hodegin in Constantinople.[75] This was venerated in the East for centuries as an imperial palladium and carried to battle in a car, very much as the image of Kybele had been borne in like manner in the streets of Rome. Actually, however, it is a conventional Byzantine representaton of the Madonna of the sixth century, showing her standing erect holding the Holy Child seated on her left arm. With his right hand he is in the act of blessing, and in his left hand he carries a roll. In another portrait of the same type in a church built by Pulcheria at Blachernae, near Constantinople, she appears as an orante with extended arms interceding for the faithful.[76]

Of the likeness of Mary we know nothing, as Augustine affirmed.[77] In her earliest representations in art she was shown as a member of a group in scenes such as the Annunciation, the Visitation, the Nativity, the Presentation, and especially the Adoration of the Magi. In the vast mosaic on the western face of the triumphal arch in S. Maria Maggiore in Rome (c. A.D. 433) she is, however, seated in a chair with two winged angels in attendance, the dove hovering in the air above, and Gabriel flying towards her to deliver his message.

Churches Dedicated to the Madonna

Indeed, it is true, that at the end of the fourth century and at the beginning of the fifth century, when churches began to be dedicated to her honour, in iconography frequently she was enthroned in the manner and likeness of Isis and Horus, wearing the mural crown of Kybele, and having the gorgon at her breasts like Athena, with the Holy Child sometimes enclosed in a sacred mandala on her breast.[78] Nor was such representation confined to Byzantine Mariology. In the apse of the cathedral at Parenzo in Istria on the Adriatic a Virgin enthroned at the centre of the conch of the apse was set up, probably by workmen from Ravenna, about 540. On either side is an angel with saints in the background who include Bishop Euphrasius, the founder, and Claudius his Arch-deacon. Below on the vertical wall of the apse are scenes of the Annunciation and the Visitation, but these may be rather later. In 1944 frescoes of this period in a Hellenistic style depicting the life of the Virgin, the Annunciation, Visitation and proof of her virginity were found in the little church at Castelseprio near Milan.

In the catacombs a fresco of the third century in the cemetery of Priscilla shows the Annunciation, and in a painting of the next century in the *Caementerium majus* the Holy Child is repre-sented at his mother's breast with outstretched arm. Above their heads are two stars, and to the left a male figure, probably one of the prophets, pointing to the star. The Annunciation forms the subject of two paintings, one belonging to the end of the second century and the other to the third century. The Virgin is seated, the angel stands before her in human form. Only once is the Nativity depicted, and this is on a fresco of later date in the catacomb of St Sebastian. Usually Mary is seated on a throne holding the Holy Child forward, sometimes to receive the adoration of the Magi. On a fresco in the cemetery of St Castulus, outside the Porta Maggiore in Rome, the Virgin is with the infant Jesus between two of the Magi, while near the crypt of St Emerentiana in the *Caementerium majus* in the Via Nomentana, on a fresco of the fourth century in which Byzantine features are beginning to occur, she is represented as an orante interceding for those in the tomb. It can hardly be later than the beginning of the fifth century, but the recurrence of Mary in the very early art and iconography shows the gradual development of her importance and significance in Christian theology and devotion.

By the sixth century Madonnas had become a standard product of art in Christendom, with the Holy Child or standing as an orante with upraised hands and arms interceding. As early as the first quarter of the fifth century gilded glasses from the catacombs bore the name 'Maria' and showed the Virgin standing between St Peter and St Paul in the attitude of prayer, and bas-reliefs of her as an orante occur in the church of Santa Maria in Porto in Ravenna, and in mosaic pictures over the altar of the archiepiscopal palace there, as well as in the chapel of St Venantius in the Lateran in Rome (*c.* 642). Justinian turned to the Theotokos for protection for what was left of the Empire, very much as in the fourth century B.C. it was to the Phrygian Magna Mater that recourse was made to save the eternal city in its hour of need. Justinian's general, Narses, sought her advice on the field of battle much as the Sibylline books were consulted for divine guidance during the Hannibalic war; and as the sacred meteor of Kybele was brought in triumph to Rome so Heraclius bore in the fray a banner of Mary with her image on it. In a catacomb on the Appian Way near Albano her hands are outstretched in prayer, and in the corridor in the Wall of Aurelian near the Appian Gate (Porta di San Sebastiano) a Byzantine Virgin and Child of the sixth century may have been depicted for the benefit of the troops of Belisarius during the siege of the city by Vitiges in 538, when the fortifications were repaired. Even as far from the Byzantine world as Britain the Marian cult seems to have flourished in the monastic centres in these isles. Thus, it appears that the monks of Glastonbury invoked the Virgin in their liturgy, and when Ambrosius revived imperial sentiment they acquired a Madonna in the Byzantine style. The ancient historic church, around which legend has been so rife, is spoken of as an 'oratory of Peter and Paul', but eventually it was rededicated apparently, to 'Our Lady St. Mary of Glastonbury'. This probably was the first centre of the Marian cult in Britain.

In Rome the basilica of Santa Maria sopra Minerva, near the Pantheon, was superimposed on a former dedication to Minerva as the name indicates, and close by was a sanctuary of Isis. But Santa Maria Maggiore on the Esquiline Hill is the largest of the eight first and great churches in Rome dedicated to our Lady. It was built originally in the fourth century by Pope Liberius, when it was called the basilica Liberian. In the seventh century, if not earlier, it was known as Santa Maria ad praesepe because beneath the high altar the relics of the crib are alleged to rest. It is said to have been erected on the site of a temple of Kybele, while a few hundred yards away was a temple to Juno Lucina, protectress of pregnant mothers.[79] On the Capitoline Hill with all its sacred associations with the Goddess cult stands Santa Maria in Ara Coeli, called originally Santa Maria in Campitolio, in which in the chapel of the Presepio is the famous praesepe. In this crib the *Santo Bambino di Ara Coeli*, rudely carved in olive wood and said to have come from Palestine, is exposed from the Eve of the Nativity to the Feast of the Epiphany, adorned with jewels of great value. In a grotto behind are the Virgin with the Bambino on her knee, and St Joseph with the ox and the ass behind. The shepherds, the Magi and the women bringing their offerings of fruit in the background complete the scene with remarkable effect. Above, God the Father is represented with angels and cherubs, and formerly St Augustine and the Sibyl pointed to the Holy Child. This depicted the medieval legend of Greek origin that the Incarnation was foretold in the Sibylline books, and an altar was erected on the site of the church by the Emperor Octavius, who, when consulting the Tiburtine sibyl, heard a voice saying 'this is the altar of the First-born of God'. In the Benedictine chronicles it is said to have been built by Gregory the Great in 591, and such is its antiquity that its foundation traditionally was assigned to Constantine, suggesting that it was one of the earliest churches erected in Rome, and, therefore, placed on the Capitol and dedicated to the Mother of God. Similarly, in Athens when the Erechtheum on the Acropolis, sacred to Pallas, was converted into a church it was placed under the patronage of the Madonna, as was the Anthenaion, the Roman temple in Syracuse.

The superimposing of churches dedicated to the Virgin on the Goddess sanctuaries marks the development of the Marian cultus, and doubtless involved the transference of at least some of the beliefs and practices connected with the pagan occupants of the shrines in popular piety. This was almost inevitable, however desirable and necessary the procedure may have been in the circumstances in which it occurred. It certainly made for the localization of the Madonna rather along the lines of the earlier 'Goddess of many names', though of course it was never supposed for a moment that Mary was other than one person, the Theotokos. Nevertheless, her office and functions tended to be departmentalized so that she became not only the patroness of churches with special characteristics in their earlier associations, but also the protectress of particular cities, towns, sanctuaries and localities, with titles, such as our Lady of Zaragoza, Mount Carmel, Glastonbury, Walsingham and, since the authorization of the apparitions to Bernadette in 1858, Notre Dame de Lourdes, as well as of occupations like that of sailors in her capacity of Star of the Sea.

MARIAN FESTIVALS

The Assumption

Another aspect of her cultus found expression in the place assigned to her in the calendar. Again, it was in the East that the principal festivals were first observed—the Assumption, the Annunciation, the Purification and the Nativity. Of these the Dormition, or 'Falling Asleep of Mary the Mother of God' (ἠκοίμησις, or *Dormitio*), is said by Nicephorus Callistus to have been instituted by the Emperor Maurice (582–602)[80] on August 15th, though it may have been observed in the previous century round about that time in Syria and Palestine, according to the life of St Theodosius (d. 529). In Egypt and Arabia it was celebrated in January, and in the sixth century in the Gallican Liturgy it was observed by the monks in Gaul on January 18th until the Roman rite was introduced. In fact, although it became the principal Marian feast its universal observance was only very gradually established outside the Byzantine East.

That it arose as a commemoration of the dedication of a church is more probable than that it was the outcome of the Council of Ephesus, or that it was introduced in Rome by St Damascus. If this were so, then behind it doubtless lay a long tradition lacking definition or general acceptance. Thus, according to a Gnostic and Collyridian legend the body of Mary was wafted on a cloud to Jerusalem at the time of her death, and in the presence of the apostles her soul was taken from her body to Paradise by Gabriel. But when they proceeded to lay her mortal remains in a tomb in the valley of Jehoshaphat, Christ himself appeared and reunited them with her soul, which had been brought back from Paradise by Michael and an angelic host. This story in the apocryphal *De Obitu S. Dominae*, and in the book *De Transitu Virginis Mariae Liber*,[81] falsely ascribed to St Melito of Sardis, was confuted by Epiphanius, who said, 'search the Scriptures, you will not find either the death of Mary or whether she died, or that she did not die, or that she was buried or was not buried'. That her death and burial were surrounded with the honour her virgin purity merited, and that her holy body was blessed and glorified, he affirmed, but 'no one knows her end'.[82] Such, indeed, was the ignorance during the first six centuries respect⁄ ing the date and place of her 'falling asleep' that the way was open for speculation and the growth of a legend which was condemned as heretical in the *Decretum de Libris Canonicus Ecclesiasticus et Apocryphis*, attributed to Pope Gelasius in 494.

It was not until after the Council of Ephesus that credence was given officially to these fabulous traditions when in the sixth century the Nestorian controversy had brought the venera⁄ tion of the Theotokos into such prominence that her corporeal assumption became a widespread 'pious belief'. Attempts were then made to support it by attributing the heretical treatises to St John Melito of Sardis, Athanasius, St Jerome and St Augustine, all of which in fact are spurious. The Chronicle of Eusebius was made to assert that 'in the year 48 Mary the Virgin was taken up into heaven as some wrote that they had it revealed to them' in order to receive his authority for the doctrine that was then in process of formulation. Gregory of Tours recorded the apocryphal story of the *Liber de Transitu* in his De Gloria Martyrum (i. c. 4), and as related by him it was incorporated in the Gallican Liturgy. The title 'assumptio' first appeared in the canons of Bishop Sonnatius of Rheims (*c.* 630), and under this designation it occurred in the Gelasian Sacra⁄ mentary. Duchesne maintains that like the other three festivals of the Virgin it was a Byzantine importation, and that the countries of the Gallican rite knew nothing of them until they were adopted in the Roman Liturgy.[83] But the absence of any mention of the legend in the Gelasianum may suggest that a Mass commemorating the death of the Virgin was said on August 15th, since the feast seems to have been observed in Rome at Santa Maria Maggiore in the sixth century. By the time of Sergius I (700) it was a major festival, subsequently observed with an octave except in the Ambrosian rite in Milan. It was not, however, until as recently as 1950 that the increas⁄ ingly widely held belief that 'when the course of her earthly life was run' the Mother of God was 'assumed in body and in soul to heavenly glory', was declared *ex cathedra* by papal decree to be a *de fide* article of faith.

The Annunciation

Since the Marian cultus rests on the unique status and office claimed for the Virgin in the Incarnation of the Son of God, attention could hardly fail to have been concentrated upon the supreme moment when she was confronted with the archangel Gabriel and called upon to make her momentous decision upon which the salvation of mankind depended. That this event should have been a major commemoration in the calendar was inevitable, though there is no historical account of the institution of the Feast of the Annunciation.

As the generation of the Christ-child always has been held to have been a normal physiological process extending over nine months, once the date of the Nativity was fixed in the West on December 25th that of the Annunciation naturally fell on March 25th. This, however, raised a problem in the East, since the Council of Laodicea in the fourth century forbade the keeping of holy days in Lent, except on Saturdays and Sundays.[84] The situation was relieved by an exception being made in favour of its observance at the Council of Trullo in 692. In the West when it was first kept in Spain it was held at different dates in different places until the Council of Toledo in 656 fixed December 18th as the day of the festival because, as it was explained, it could not be held in Lent or Eastertide. But in the Mozarabic rite the same Mass is appointed for both December 18th and March 25th.[85] It was not until much later that this procedure was adopted in Rome, and no mention of the feast occurs among the festivals ordered by the Council of Metz in 813 (can. xxxvi).

It would seem, then, that the commemoration of the Annunciation arose about the time of the Council of Ephesus in 431, as it was not known apparently when the Synod assembled at Laodicea in 372, and the first mention of it in the West is in the Sacramentary of Gelasius in a seventh-century manuscript, and in a manuscript of the Sacramentary of St Gregory in the next century. Therefore, in Rome the feast very likely was a product of the seventh century,[86] though it was observed earlier in Spain and in the East as a Dominican rather than a Marian festival, the emphasis being on the virginal conception of the Incarnate Christ. It was not until the Marian cultus developed that it was held primarily in honour of the Mother of God. Originally, in fact, in the West it was only in countries of the Gallican rite that any such feast was celebrated, and then it was confined to that held for the purpose in the middle of January.[87] As a special commemoration the Annunciation has never been rigidly fixed to March 25th, as might have been expected. Thus, in the Ambrosian rite it was assigned to the last Sunday in Advent while the Armenians kept it on the Eve of the Epiphany (January 5th) until they transferred it to April 7th.

The Purification

Like the Annunciation, the Purification of the Blessed Virgin Mary, or Candlemas as it has been commonly called, originally was a Dominical festival and has so remained in Eastern Christendom. Its Byzantine origin is shown in the title, 'Hypapante', designating the 'meeting' of Christ with Simeon and Anna at the presentation in the Temple. In the West it was the Purification of Mary according to Jewish custom[88] that was emphasized, and since the commemoration coincided with a pre-Christian Feast of Lights when candles and torches were carried in procession, held at the beginning of February as a protection against plague, famine, pestilence and earthquake, it came to be known as Candlemas, the symbolism being interpreted in terms of the Nunc Dimittis in the Biblical narrative. In the fourth century (*c.* 385) a solemn procession was held on February 14th (*Quadragesima de Epiphania*) at Jerusalem in the church of the Anastasis, to which reference is made by a pilgrim of Bordeaux, Etheria or Silvia.[89] But no mention occurs of the Purification of the Virgin in connexion with it. Cedrenus, an historian of the eleventh century, assigns the institution of the festival to the Emperor Justin of

Constantinople in the year 526,[90] and it was then, or in the reign of his successor Justinian in 541,[91] that it became estab-lished on February 2nd, after the Feast of the Nativity had been transferred to December 25th under Latin influence in Byzantium. When it was introduced into Rome is obscure. Baronius attributes it to Pope Gelasius (492–6) as the Christian counterpart of the Pulercalia,[92] but this was mere conjecture.

Although it was described by the ancient writers as a *lustratio* or *purificatio*, it did not bear any very obvious connexions with the Candlemas procession. The Lupercalia was a fertility rite in which two parties of youths clad in a girdle of goatskins ran round the boundaries of the Palatine Hill, striking women with thongs of goat-hide to make them fruitful. Therefore, it was the prototype of the Rogationtide procession rather than that of Candlemas. Nevertheless, it is true that behind the symbolism of the Feast of Lights lay the ancient perambulations associated with the return of the Goddess from the underworld and the rebirth of nature in the spring and of that of the neophytes in the Mysteries. Thus, in the Eleusinian rites they carried lighted torches in commemoration of the search of Demeter for Kore as a part of the purification ritual in prepara-tion for the sacred drama in the *telesterion*.[93] Similarly, it was amid a blaze of torches that 'the fair young god Iacchos' was borne along the sacred way from Athens to Eleusis. Or, again, in the Lesser Mysteries at Agrai, which began on the eleventh of the month Anthesterion (March 2nd), when Kore was supposed to return from the underworld in the young corn and bring with her lengthening days, a procession assembled during the afternoon of the second day of the festival, and at six o'clock in the evening started with torches in celebration of the return of life and light after the death and darkness of the year's decline.[94]

While the Eleusinian Mysteries could have exercised only an indirect influence on Christian practice, nevertheless the Early Fathers were by no means unaware of their rivalry, especially after the Emperor Julian, whom they described as the Apostate, had himself become an initiate at Eleusis in reaction to his Christian upbringing and education. Indeed, as has been considered, a good deal of our information concerning these rites comes from Christian sources, such as the writings of Hippolytus. The reverse process, therefore, cannot be ruled out arising from the spiritual condition of the world in which Christianity arose, and which favoured the spread and persistence of the Graeco-Oriental Mystery religions. This certainly is not least apparent in the Marian cultus after the Virgin as the Theotokos replaced the Mater Ecclesia as the Magna Mater of Christian tradition, and herself was installed as the central figure in the festivals of the Goddess cult with their long-established ceremonial. Thus, in the case of the Feast of Lights, February 1st was the day on which fires had been lighted and torches left burning all night as life-giving agents; customs which were so deeply rooted that they survived in the Christian era long after their original significance had been abandoned, at any rate 'officially'. In Scotland, for example, the sacred fire of St Bride, or Bridget, was carefully guarded, and a bed made of corn and hay on the Eve of Candlemas surrounded by candles as a fertility rite.[95] Here St Bride played the role of Kore, and the fire symbolized the victorious emergence of the sun from the darkness of the departing winter.

As candles were emblems of the divine vitalizing power of the sun, not inappropriately they were blessed and carried in procession at the end of the Christmas festival to commemorate the presentation of the 'sun of righteousness' in the temple of his heavenly Father. Furthermore, as the sacred light became a symbol of the Holy Child who was declared to be the 'light to lighten the Gentiles and the glory of his people Israel', so as Mary came into greater prominence as the 'light-bearer', the Mystery significance of the festival was complete. The procession depicted the entry into the world of the true light; the blessing and distribution of the candles to be carried round the church anticlockwise (i.e. in the penitential manner) symbolized his illumination of the whole earth; and the Mass of the Purification of the Blessed Virgin Mary which followed brought the Incarnation, which 'translated mankind from the power of darkness into the clear light of his beloved Son', into relation with the pure Virgin who was the 'light-bearer'. The penitential character of the procession was in accord with the purificatory preparation in the mystery ceremonial, while the candle ritual was derived from the ancient torch and light symbolism which was brought into conjunction with that of the Virgin Mother, presenting herself in the Temple with her divine Son, not as a goddess like Ishtar or Isis but making the simple peasant offering of a pair of turtle-doves or two young pigeons. Once again the Church superimposed its own faith and practice on the established cultus in the culture in which Christianity emerged, adapting it to and interpreting it in terms of its cardinal doctrines, and so formulating its own myth and ritual as a living reality.

The Feast of the Nativity

Thus, the festival of the Incarnation, which taken as a whole was spread over forty days from the Nativity to Candlemas, illustrates this process. While the determination of the date of Christmas Day is very obscure,[96] that it was observed at the winter solstice when the rebirth of the sun as the author and giver of life and light was celebrated is beyond question. More-over, whatever may have been the cause, the selection of December 25th as the Feast of the Nativity in the West in the fourth century brought it into direct relation with the *Dies Natalis solis Invicti* of Mithraism—the annual commemoration of the victory of light over darkness. This was not an inappro-priate occasion for the Church to celebrate the 'rising of the sun of righteousness with healing in his wings', even though it involved the fact that in the background lay the earlier associa-tions of the pagan winter festival. It was then that in Egypt the Sun-god was born anew like Horus, son of Osiris, in the arms of Isis, who 'when his arm was strong' fought against Seth and prevailed at the cost of his eye. At midnight on December 25th the constellation of Virgo, symbolizing the Mother-goddess in Babylonia, gave birth to the life-giving sun, just as in the Balder myth the avenger of the slain hero (Balder), the good and beautiful son of Odin, appeared on the night of December 24th, rising amid universal rejoicing like the new-born sun to destroy the power of darkness. Indeed, the Syrians and Armenians accused the Latins of sun-worship in transferring the Christmas festival to December 25th, regardless of the fact that their own observance of the feast on January 6th was held at the winter solstice in the Julian calendar, which in Alexandria was also the birthday of Osiris.

Epiphanius identified December 25th with the Roman Saturnalia, but this event ended on December 23rd, though some of its festivities seem to have been incorporated in the Christmas observances. Christ was born, he said, thirteen days after the winter solstice when at Alexandria the Koreian was celebrated in the sacred enclosure of Kore.

'The whole night through they keep watch' [he declared], 'singing to the idol with hymns to a flute accompaniment. Having finished their vigil, when the cocks have crowed, they descend with torches in their hands to an underground chapel and take up a naked image of carved wood. This they set on a litter. On its brow it has a golden seal, as also on both knees, five seals in all worked in gold. They carry this image seven times in procession round the inner temple, with flutes and drums and hymns, and then bring it back to the underground place in a Bacchic rout. If you ask them the meaning of this mystery they reply: "At this hour to-day Kore (that is the Virgin) bore Aeon."'[97]

Therefore, it was 'whilst the heathen were busied with their profane ceremonies', as St Chrysostom opined, that the Christians performed 'their holy rites undisturbed'.[98]

Nevertheless, established beliefs and customs die hard, and Leo the Great (440–61) condemned those current in Rome in his day as indistinguishable from solar worship, in launching his campaign against the current pagan practices connected with the winter solstice. As late as the eighth century, Boniface had to deal with these same abuses in Northern Europe, and three hundred years later, despite constant denunciations in canons, homilies, capitularies and penitentials, Burchardus mentions heathen practices still in vogue in his day. If the praesepe owed anything originally to the cave in which Adonis was born, as Usener suggests, [99] it was so completely Christian-ized that any vestiges of pagan symbolism were eliminated when as 'the cradle of Christ' it became the principal object of devotion in the Christmas festival after it was blessed with incense and holy water at the Midnight Mass, and lighted with candles, to receive the bambino in the manger after the conse-cration. 'The Virgin has brought forth, light increases'—the ancient cry of the celebrant at midnight in Syria and Egypt—throughout the ages has been the theme of the Christmas mystery drama from the Eve of the Nativity to Candlemas. Around it has collected a miscellaneous accumulation of ancient customs and beliefs associated with the winter festival, but only those like the praesepe and the Feast of Lights, that have been relevant to it, have been consecrated by the Church as an integral part of the observance. The rest have been condoned so long as they have not been out of keeping with the annual commemoration of the Nativity of the Son of Mary.

The Conception

From the beginning the virginity of the Madonna was coupled with her immaculate purity so that at the time of the Council of Ephesus she was hailed 'innocent without blemish, immacu-late, inviolate, spotless, holy in soul and body, who has blossomed as a lily from among thorns, unlearned in the evil ways of Eve'.[100] Nevertheless, the Early Fathers were by no means agreed about her sinlessness. On the contrary, although Origen accorded to her a very high degree of sanctity, he included her among those who were offended in Christ at his Passion when the sword of doubt passed through her soul as she stood by his cross.[101] In fact, it was needful, he main-tained, that she should thus sin in order to be redeemed by him. Chrysostom, again, thought that she was guilty of ambi-tion in putting forward her son as a worker of miracles at the marriage feast at Cana,[102] while St Augustine, although he exempted her from actual sin, asserted that she received her physical life *de peccati propagine* through the tainted line of Adam.[103]

Therefore, when the Feast of the Conception of the Blessed Virgin Mary was first instituted, perhaps originally as a monastic observance in Palestine as early as the seventh century, it did not give expression to the later doctrine of her immaculate conception free from all taint of original sin, as promulgated by Pius IX on December 8th, 1854. The first mention of the feast is in a sermon of John Euboea in the middle of the eighth century,[104] and it passed to the West through Greek settlers in Italy in the next century when it appeared in the Neapolitan calendar as the 'Conceptio S. Anne Marie Vir.'. Having spread to Ireland, it reached England by the beginning of the eleventh century, though there is some reason to think that it may have been celebrated in the British Isles before the Norman Conquest, introduced into England possibly in the first in-stance by Archbishop Theodore (668–90), who was a native of Tarsus. Be this as it may, mention is made of 'the day of the Conception of the holy Mother of God, Mary', in a pontifical of Canterbury before 1050, and December 8th is assigned to the observance in two very early calendars of the minsters in Winchester. But it was not until the twelfth century (*c.*1130–40) that it was reintroduced in the Benedictine monasteries in Normandy and Britain, and supported by legendary reve-lations it became widely adopted in spite of the strenuous opposition of Bernard of Clairvaux, who condemned it because he felt it conflicted with the Augustinian doctrine of original sin.[105]

This was the general consensus of opinion among all the theologians of the twelfth and thirteenth centuries—St Victor, Peter Lombard, Albertus Magnus, Bonaventura and St Thomas Aquinas—though they refrained from trying to sup-press the feast on December 8th, explaining it in terms of the sanctification of Mary being alleged to have taken place at the moment of the infusion of her soul in her body, and so making possible the dogma of her immaculate conception as it was set forth by Duns Scotus (*c.* 1264–1308). This English Franciscan having been brought up in the apocryphal tradition of the immaculate conception derived originally from the second-century Joachim and Anna legend in the *Protevangelium of James*, contended that Mary had been preserved from all sin from the moment of her conception by the subtle device of making the sanctification after animation follow in the order of nature not of time so that she was subject to original sin only at one instant, and then that temporal instant resolved itself into a purely logical instant. This was too ingenious to allay the controversy which continued to rage between the Dominicans and Franciscans until in 1439, after a discussion that lasted for two years at the Council of Basle, and in face of the opposition of the University of Paris, the dogma of the Immaculate Conception was declared to be a pious belief consonant with Catholic faith and worship.[106] In 1476 the feast was approved by Sixtus IV, and a proper Mass and Breviary Office assigned to it which in 1708 was extended to the universal calendar by Clement XI as a feast of obligation. So great was the appeal of the Marian cultus that the victory of popular piety over scholastic theology was hailed with delight and approval by the people everywhere. Once the doctrine and its festival had been accorded official status, it was only a question of time before a pious sentiment became an article of faith as defined in 1854.

However the cult is to be interpreted and evaluated theologically, the fact remains that the Madonna of Catholic devotion is very much more than devotion to the simple, wholly dedicated, peasant maiden of Nazareth. She is nothing less than the Mother of God, the Queen of Heaven, the Woman clothed with the sun, having the moon under her feet and a crown of twelve stars above her head; and on earth the immaculate ever-virgin, the Lily of Eden, the Second Eve, the Star of the Sea, the co-redemptress, the compassionate Mother, the bestower of grace, the giver of good counsel, Our Lady of Victory, and now as Notre Dame de Lourdes she has been hailed as the bestower of not a few medically attested miraculous cures at her world-renowned Pyrenaean shrine.

In this unique syncretistic figure almost every aspect of the cult of the Goddess of many names and the Young God finds a place. But the Marian cultus cannot be explained merely in terms of the survival of an outworn relic of paganism. It is a far too vital phenomenon to be so simply dismissed, for however its validity may be assessed, it has been and still is a tremendous force in Western and Eastern Christendom, occupying a unique place in both Catholic and Orthodox piety, and having behind it all the power of a supernatural faith rooted and grounded in remote antiquity. As has been considered, in the beginning the dignity assigned to Mary arose as a result of her relation to Christ in the doctrine of the Incarnation. Prior to the Council of Ephesus she figured mainly in the Christological controversies with which the Church was then preoccupied by virtue of her maternity of Jesus. The attempts by several Gnostic sects to transform her into a goddess were promptly suppressed, and it was not until her position in relation to the humanity and divinity of the Second Person of the Trinity had to be vindicated that the title of Theotokos having been conferred upon her, the cult was definitely established and developed in respect of her several attributes of motherhood— her virginity, her sinlessness, her mediation, and her assumption. It was, however, as the Second Eve bringing forth the Second Adam to reverse the judgment on fallen humanity, not as the Magna Mater and the consort-mother of the Young God, that the Christian Fathers represented Mary and the Church in their respective roles in the new dispensation.

Around these two figures the traits of the pre-Christian myth and ritual were reassembled, not as survivals but as the re-evaluation and representations of very deeply laid beliefs and practices determined by, and deriving their meaning from, fundamental values in the interrelated cultures in which they recurred as a basic structural pattern regulating the behaviour of the members of the community.[107] It may be true that the title 'Lady of Ishtar', current among the West Semitic peoples in the period immediately preceding and following the rise of Christianity, was transferred to the Madonna, as Bel, the κύριος of late Greek writers, may have provided the title *Kyrios Christos* for her Son.[108] But this does not explain the essential nature and significance of the figures around whom many of the ancient beliefs and practices in the cult of the Goddess and the Young God were reassembled, or why they became the distinctive and dominant values of a new culture, reinvested with a present value and vitality which have given them a living function of their own in a faith that has claimed the allegiance of millions all over the world. It was not merely that the cult was Christianized, since the Church took a strong stand against the old beliefs and customs. What it did was to make its own myth and ritual—in this case its central doctrine of the Incarnation —as secure as possible from unorthodox interpretations.

Since the Madonna and the Mater Ecclesia were the principal divine agents in this event, the one responsible for the entry into the world of the Son of God, and the other for the perpetuation of the redemptive process to the end of time, they inevitably occupied the key position in the new dispensation. Whatever was incorporated from the pagan background in defence of their claims was transformed and had a revitalizing effect on the earlier tradition, preventing it from degenerating into merely decadent and effete superstition (i.e. survival). As Maimonides observed in another connexion, 'these things have a pagan and superstitious origin, but they must not be called superstitions, for their origin no longer dominates the meaning attached to these ceremonies'. Every age and culture produce their own beliefs, customs, ideologies, cultic figures and symbols, and only when they become detached from the life of the community in which they occur and cease to exercise their proper functions in it, do they become merely survivals of bygones. But when they are incorporated in recurring structural ritual patterns of great antiquity they acquire a new significance and determination. What is received in the course of the transition is transformed.

Thus, the pagan and Christian traditions represent parallel

but independent developments which without deliberately borrowing the one from the other have coalesced and reacted upon each other inasmuch as both are expressions of certain fundamental attitudes to life, and to the social and religious conditions in which they arose. Old feasts were resuscitated, like the Conception of the Virgin, and given a place in the calendar. This opened the way for the establishment of a cultus that entered into the daily life of the people, providing them with spiritual edification and satisfaction coupled often with relaxation and recreation, but it could hardly expect to escape from the transference of parallel traits in some measure, even though they were brought within the orbit of the established faith and made subservient to its cardinal doctrines (e.g. the Incarnation in Mariology).

The frequent denunciations of current superstitious practices leave no room for doubt that the least edifying survivals did in fact persist in popular belief and practice in spite of the strenuous efforts to eliminate the ephemeral, wanton and transitory elements in the pagan environment in which Christianity had to render its own faith and life explicit. For the most part, however, it was the pagan observances that survived, ritual always being more stable than belief. Thus, as we have seen, the May Day revels appear to have been a folk survival of the Hilaria, the spring festival of Kybele, May 1st on alternate years corresponding to March 25th in the pre-Julian calendar. Whether or not there was any connexion originally between these popular celebrations and the Feast of the Annunciation having been kept at the vernal equinox, they have lost any Christian significance that may have been attached to them, and so have ceased to have a serious purpose. Even the relatively modern devotional dedication of the month of May to Mary has not given so much as a Christian veneer to the folk observances.

CHAPTER VIII

The Goddess and the Young God

THE DIVINE PRINCIPLE OF MATERNITY

FROM the foregoing survey of the Goddess cult in its many forms, phases and manifestations the life-producing Mother as the personification of fecundity stands out clearly as the central figure. Behind her lay the mystery of birth and generation in the abstract, at first in the human and animal world with which Palaeolithic Man was mainly concerned in his struggle for existence and survival; then, when food-gathering gave place to food-production, in the vegetable kingdom where Mother-earth became the womb in which the crops were sown, and from which they were brought forth in due season. With the establishment of husbandry and the domestication of flocks and herds, however, the function of the male in the process of generation became more apparent and vital as the physiological facts concerning paternity were more clearly understood and recognized. Then the Mother-goddess was assigned a male partner, either in the capacity of her son and lover, or of brother and husband. Nevertheless, although he was the begetter of life he occupied a subordinate position to her, being in fact a secondary figure in the cultus.

Motherhood and the Family

Whether or not this reflects a primeval system of matriarchal social organization, as is by no means improbable, the fact remains that the Goddess at first had precedence over the Young God with whom she was associated as her son or husband or lover. A number of causes may have contributed to her enhanced status in society and in the pantheon, but the starting-point in the institution of the family and its wider ramifications in kinship can hardly have been other than the relationship of mother and child in the first instance. That an infant is the offspring of its mother never could be in doubt, however its origin and generation may have been explained, if, indeed, there was any speculation on the subject in its physical aspects. The role of the father might be very obscure and even non-existent, but that of the mother was not open to question, being merely a matter of observation. Therefore, around the maternal centre a network of emotions and senti-ments arose—the care and protection of the offspring and their sense of dependence upon their parents giving rise to respect for parental authority and guidance—all of which were essential for the survival and well-being of the human race and the right ordering of family life. And, as Marett says, 'fear tempered with wonder and submissiveness and thus transmuted into reverence is the forerunner of love'.[1]

Woman with her inexplicable nature and unaccountable attributes and functions, such as menstruation, pregnancy, childbirth and lactation, has been a mysterious person, calling forth a numinous reaction and evaluation, permeated with religious sentiments, rendering her at once sacred and tabu. Regarded as the sole source of the family, the parental instinct doubtless from the first was primarily female, descent invariably following the distaff. This probably explains to a considerable extent the priority of mother-right in primitive society, some-times as a unilateral organization in which the woman may have remained among her own people and the husband was little more than a visitor and stranger in her kin. The mother alone then became the fountain-head and the self-sufficing source of the family, and by implication the personification of the principle of life.

The Earth-mother and Agriculture

When these more extreme forms of matrilocal marriage did not obtain, the husband and the sons would be occupied chiefly with the chase, the pursuit of game, warfare, or tending the

flocks and herds, while the mother and her daughters attended
to the domestic chores, and after the discovery and practice of
agriculture (for which in all probability women were mainly
responsible), hoeing and the cultivation of the crops on a small
scale around the homestead. The fertility of the soil and that of
women has been one of the salient features in agricultural
society at all times, and it was not until sowing and reaping
expanded, involving heavy manual labour, that it was transferred to the male section of the community. It was then that
the plough acquired a phallic significance, being the instrument employed to break up the earth and make it fertile. But
originally the soil was exclusively the domain of Mother-earth,
and to disturb it was a perilous undertaking, usually demand-
ing appeasement by a sacrificial oblation of some kind.[2] Even
when the ground was cleared and farmed by men the breaking
of the soil and the planting was done by women, who as the
child-bearers alone could enable the earth to bring forth
abundantly.

(a) Greece

For the Greeks, as we have seen, it was Ge or Gaia, the Earth-
goddess, who first gave birth to Ouranus, the heavens, and they
then became the primeval pair, begetting the innumerable
family of gods, including the Titans, Cyclops and the mythical
Giants, while by an indirect process of descent, of gods and
men in general. Thus, long before Zeus at Dordona was
coupled with the Earth-goddess, she was the creatrix of all
things in heaven and in the world, and the other goddesses—
Aphrodite, Semele, Artemis, Demeter, etc.—were derived
from or associated with her. It was she who sent up the fruits
of the ground, and to her they were offered in return for her
beneficence. As the cultivated earth she was the Grain-mother
and the Goddess of vegetation as well as of flocks and herds.[3]
And it seems that Kore, the Corn-maiden, originally was
primarily concerned with the seed-corn when it was stored
away in the silos after the harvest. She too, therefore, like her
mother Demeter, had the characteristics of the Earth-goddess,

and these she combined with chthonian attributes and aspects, as was not infrequently the case in her manifestations.

To the primitive religious consciousness the earth in the first instance was experienced as the inexhaustible repository of all the vital forces responsible for the various manifestations of life and maternity, and of cosmic existence, independent of any male intervention and agency. As in the procreation of children so in the origin of all things, it was the self-fertilizing female principle that was the operative cause in fecundity to the exclusion of any 'begetter' exercising paternal functions. It was not until the physiological facts concerning generation became better understood and appreciated in agricultural society that the Earth-mother was associated with a male partner and a chthonian maternity, as the Great Goddess of a seasonal ritual. Then the place of Gaia was taken by Demeter, and the primeval pair personifying Heaven and Earth became the Sky-father and the Earth-mother, Ouranus and Gaia, and their counterparts elsewhere in the Aegean, the Eastern Mediterranean, Western Asia, India, and wherever the cultus occurred. But behind this sacred drama culminating in a *hieros gamos* lay the earlier personification of the principle of birth and maternity as Mother-earth.

Thus, in the *Homeric Hymn* it would seem that the personified Earth was distinct from Demeter, and, indeed, opposed to her, since Kore is represented as having been induced by the Earth-goddess to wander in the Eleusinian meadows in search of Narcissus and so to become an easy victim of the machinations of Pluto.[4] While both Demeter and Kore were concerned with the fruits of the earth they were primarily corn-goddesses, and although the last two syllables of the name of Demeter mean 'mother', the prefix $\Delta\eta$ is not, as was formerly supposed, a dialect-variant for earth.[5] Corn or possibly barley ($\delta\eta\alpha\ell$) would be a rendering more in accordance with her functions and those of Kore, who seems to have been a younger version of herself before she was transformed into her daughter, as the generative power in the corn, and probably originally the wife of Plouton, the god who gave the wealth of the fertile earth.

Nevertheless, the very intimate association of the Corn-goddess and Earth-mother remained, and as Euripides said in reference to Demeter, 'She is the Earth . . . call her what you will!'[6] As the patron of agriculture she controlled the processes of vegetation. Thus, she refused to allow the soil to bear fruit after the abduction of Persephone, and when eventually her release from Hades and their reunion were effected she removed the spell and sent the young prince Triptolemus all over the world to teach men how to cultivate the earth and to perform the rites she initiated at Eleusis. But, in fact, they were older than Demeter, being pre-Hellenic in origin and in all probability, as has been considered,[7] arising out of the practice of storing away the seed-corn in the silos before the drought of summer. If this were so the connexion of the Corn-maiden and the Corn-mother with the earth is not far to seek, and the subsequent re-interpretation of the cultus in terms of a chthonian myth and ritual in which the fruitfulness of the earth was transformed into a seasonal vegetation drama, the sprouting of the new life becoming a symbol of immortality.

Primarily the earth was venerated for its endless capacity to bear fruit, and in Greece Eleusis claimed to be the centre from which knowledge of agriculture was derived.[8] Therefore, if Demeter was not herself the Earth-mother, she stood in this tradition like Ceres, her Roman opposite number whose cult was equated with that of Tellus Mater, the ancient Earth-goddess, and who was as vaguely conceived as Gaia in Greece, having been originally the personified soil in general—the undefined Mother. Under the influence of the practice of agriculture the several expressions of fecundity became more clearly defined in specific divinities, such as Demeter, Kore and Ceres, as corn-goddesses, until at length the Earth-mother virtually passed into oblivion as the Great Goddess of vegetation and the harvest, became increasingly a syncretistic figure.

(b) Mesopotamia

Similarly, in the Ancient Middle East the daughters and wives of the fertility and vegetation gods in all probability had been

Earth-goddesses in the beginning, occupying much the same status and having the same significance as Gaia in Greece and the Tellus Mater in Rome. Thus, in Mesopotamia Ishtar assumed the role usually assigned to such goddesses being the mother of the gods and the controller of vegetation and fertility, whose descent into the nether regions symbolized the death in the soil in winter. As she moved downwards from one stage to another, change and decay took place in the upper world, vegetation languished and died, and all the signs of life ceased. With her return, there was a corresponding emergence in nature from its death-like sleep and the revival of vitality. Thus, Ishtar personified this ceaseless sequence of the seasons—life emerging from the soil, coming to fruition, and then drooping and perishing in the drought of summer, until it was again restored in the spring. So regarded, inevitably she was identified with Mother-earth.

Therefore, in Mesopotamia the Earth cult was brought into relation with the seasonal cycle in a myth and ritual in which the Goddess Inanna-Ishtar represented the source of all genera-tive power in nature and in mankind as the Universal Mother. Being in the first instance the embodiment of fecundity symbol-ized in the fertile soil from which all vegetation springs, before agricultural divinities took the place of the primitive goddesses of the earth she reigned supreme as the author and giver of the productive powers in nature. It appears to have been the same inexhaustible creative activity of motherhood that lay behind such distaff goddesses as Damkina, Lady of the Earth, who became the consort of Ea, or Enki, the god of the waters. Again, Ninlil, the wife of the god of the earth Enlil, who gave birth to Nanna, the Moon-god, and a succession of nether world deities, in all probability was herself an Earth-divinity before Enlil acquired this status and function as a result of his cohabiting with her in the strange manner related in the Sumerian myth.[9] Indeed, in the early lists of the gods, drawn up in the middle of the third millennium B.C., the Earth-goddess, known under a variety of names as Aruru, Nintu, Ninmah and Ninhursag (who may perhaps be identified with

Ki, 'the Earth-mother of the land'), was associated with the first great Triad of deities, Anu, Enlil and Ea (Enki). In each case she was represented as primarily concerned with child-birth and maternal functions while Allatu, the goddess of the underworld (sometimes called 'Irsitu', the earth), the receiver of men, appears to have been another aspect of the Earth-goddess in her chthonian capacity.

In Mesopotamia all life seems to have been conceived as proceeding from a union of earth, air and water, personified as the goddesses. Thus, Nammu, the controller of the primeval waters, gave birth to Anu and Ki as a bisexual combination of heaven and earth. They then produced Enlil, the Storm-and Air-god, and the second member of the Triad, who separated them as male and female—the Heaven-god and the Earth-goddess—with respective capacities and functions. By union with Ki (Ninhursag), Enlil begat Nanna, the Moon-god, and vegetable and animal life from the earth, though man seems to have been a product of Nammu (i.e. Nimah and Ki) and the Water-god Enki. Throughout this succession of creative alliances, although the goddess represented as the mother of the various divine personifications bore different names, they appear to have been merely several designations of one and the same creatrix, be she called Ki, Ninmah, Ninhur-sag, or Nammu. Originally doubtless she was the embodiment of the generative process as a whole and the source of its power alike in nature and in mankind, until, as more clearly defined divinities emerged, the pantheon began to assume its later form with its departmentalized nature and agricultural deities, and the Goddess of many names was assigned one or more male partners. But she always retained to some extent her original predominance.

(c) Syria

In the Semitic region in Western Asia, notably in Syria, the great Mother-goddesses of this region, Anat, Asherah (Astarte) and Atargartis, were, again, all concerned with maternity, fertility and childbirth and while the documentary evidence is relatively late (*c.* 1400–1350 B.C.) and very fragmentary, there is every indication that they too originally were Earth-goddesses. Moreover, like Demeter and Kore, Anat and Baal were associated with a corn cultus. This is clear from the Ugaritic texts, where in the Baal-Anat Epic the vegetation theme is preeminent, whether it be associated with an annual or a septennial ritual. In either case the leading roles in the seasonal drama are played by two goddesses—Asherah and Anat—who as the rival aspirants to the supreme status both sought to become the consorts of the virile Storm- and Weather-god, Aleyan-Baal, the bestower of the fructifying rain, giving life to the earth as the 'Lord over the furrows of the field'. As the wife of the older Supreme Deity, El, Asherah at first was the adversary of Baal, but since she is also represented as joining forces with Anat, his wife and sister, in furthering his cause and fighting his battles, it would seem that Asherah transferred her allegiance to the Young God (Aleyan-Baal). Although he had his own spouse, Anat, he may have been supposed to have annexed Asherah when he became head of the pantheon, as the chief god so often consorted with the chief goddess, either as her brother-husband or her son-lover.

Be this as it may, the two goddesses are the most impressive figures in the texts, and they are so interrelated and brought into juxtaposition that in spite of their contradictory attitudes and allegiances, they would seem to have represented one and the same divinity in the beginning. Nevertheless, when they are encountered in these very imperfectly preserved texts it is always in company with a male partner, be he El or Baal, that they appear. This apparently has conditioned and differentiated their status and characteristic features to a considerable extent, though, as in Mesopotamia, the *Dea Syria* in her several forms always was the predominant figure, combining with fertility and sexuality belligerent traits and propensities. It was Anat who watched over her 'Master' (Baal), and when he escaped from her vigilant eye and left the security of his mountain-home on Sapon to hunt in the plains below, it was she who went in search of him, only to discover that he had fallen a victim of wild, half-human, half-animal creatures called 'the devouring'. With the help of the Sun-goddess she took his corpse back to the holy mountain and buried it. But though she offered seventy animals on six successive occasions to give him nourishment in the nether regions, his demise appears to have become a recurrent event, having reciprocal effects on life in nature. Therefore, if the rains should be delayed wholly or in part, the cause was attributed to the Goddess having repeated her search for the murderer of Baal, designated Mot, meaning 'death', personified as the brother of the deceased god. Having found him, notwithstanding his representing death and sterility, she treated him as the reaped grain, ground him in a mill like flour, and scattered his flesh over the fields to fertilize them. Then Baal was restored to life again and vegetation revived.

THE MALE GOD

If this is a correct rendering of the fragmentary myths, although they are full of contradictions nevertheless a vegetation ritual is depicted in which Anat was the vitalizing power of nature in general, like the Earth-mother, Baal was the male god of fertility, and Mot the 'dead' seed-corn buried beneath the ground to rise again. All this is strictly in line with the seasonal drama that gave expression to the emotional need created by the agricultural situation when the life of mankind depended upon the fertility of the crops and a plentiful rainfall whether or not it was enacted annually or in relation to the recurrent cycles of drought. Nature had to be kept going by the due performance of the rites by which its forces were sustained and renewed at these critical junctures whenever they were likely to occur. They varied according to the climatic conditions in different regions. Palestine, for instance, depended upon the rain for its fertility, whereas in Mesopotamia and Egypt their respective rivers gave life to the soil they watered. But everywhere they were centred in a goddess as the maternal source of generative power and a young male god embodying the sequence of vegetation. From this basic conception of the sacred drama of nature the calendrical myth and ritual developed around these two fundamental figures.

The Young God and the Goddess in Mesopotamia

Thus, in the ancient civilizations of Western Asia and the Fertile Crescent the Earth-mother as the personification of the principle of maternity tended to become obscured when she became the Married Goddess, at once mother and bride, and wife and daughter of a male divinity. As we have seen, this was apparent at a very early period in Mesopotamia when Dumuzi, the Sumerian Shepherd-god and counterpart of the Assyro-Babylonian Tammuz, was associated with Ishtar as her lover-son in the drama of the death and resurrection of vegetation. Since he was regarded as 'the faithful son of the waters that came forth from the earth' (i.e. the Apsu) it was the reunion of Dumuzi-Tammuz with Inanna-Ishtar that reawakened the dormant earth in spring and made it bring forth abundantly. Indeed, it was not confined to the sphere of vegetation. Beyond the domain of plant life it extended to the life, death and rebirth of mankind, and, therefore, the myth and ritual had to be periodically repeated to renew the life-process in the human as well as in the natural order of existence. Thus, the death and resurrection of the vegetation Goddess and the Young God became the archetype of all deaths and of all resurrections in whatever plane they might occur.

It was the Goddess, however, who was the dominant force in this act of renewal whatever form it took. The Young God died in the rotation of the seasons and had to be rescued by her from the nether regions. Moreover, it was she who resuscitated him, and by so doing brought about the revival of life in nature and in mankind. So in the last analysis Inanna-Ishtar was the ultimate source of regeneration, Dumuzi-Tammuz being instrumental as her agent in the process. She was the embodiment of creative power in all its fullness; he was the personification of the decline and revival of vegetation and of all generative force.

When Marduk assumed the role of Tammuz after his city,

Babylon, had become the capital about 1728 B.C., although the New Year Festival was overlaid with accretions, the death and resurrection of the fertility-god and his consort remained the fundamental theme. It was his restoration as 'the resurrected child'—i.e. the Young God—of the Goddess that caused sorrow at his imprisonment in the mountain, symbolizing the land of the dead, to be turned into joy, and defeat into victory. Then the king in what was virtually the Tammuz role, having been reinstated after his ceremonial abduction, engaged in a connubium with the queen (or a priestess), typifying the sacred marriage of the Goddess and the Young God.

By so doing he renewed his reign annually, but it would seem that it was the Goddess who was thought to have taken the initiative throughout. Thus, it was she who invited him to share her couch, and she embraced him in the guise of the Young God.[10] He was subservient to her will and enjoyed the favours she conferred upon him. She was the supreme source of life; he was her servant in the renewal of the repro-ductive forces. From her he took his origin, being called her son, though he was raised to the divine status as her husband. Thus, he became the virile generative force manifest in nature but dependent upon the Goddess. He died annually, was mourned and restored as her offspring, and was subject to the vicissitudes of the seasonal cycle. She, on the other hand, remained the constant source of all life, perpetuating vitality from season to season, and from generation to generation, in order that fecundity and procreation might continue. Therefore, she continued to maintain the status and exercise the functions of the Earth-mother, though she did so in partnership with the youthful male god, who as her instrument died young to rise again.

The Anatolian Weather-god and the Goddess

In the 'Land of Hatti' to the north-east of the Anatolian plateau, in the second millennium B.C. the Hittite kings were the chief-priests of the Storm- and Weather-god, and 'held the hand' of the Goddess, while at the death of the queen-mother the reigning queen succeeded to her office as the priestess of the Goddess. Although the king was never deified in his lifetime, he was called the son of the gods, and through the *tavananna* (queen-mother) he was brought into a relation of sonship with the Goddess.[11] Thus, in the reliefs at Yazilikaya, as we have seen, the chief-goddess of the Hurrian pantheon, Hebat, is depicted standing on a panther or lioness holding a staff in her left hand, and stretching out her right hand to greet a male figure who may be the king in his filial capacity, and offering him symbolic or hieroglyphic signs. If the smaller figure of a beard-less youth standing on a panther behind her represents Sharma, the son of Teshub, he too is her son, who again appears in the small gallery holding King Tudhaliya IV (*c.* 1250 B.C.) in his embrace. It is possible, as we have considered,[12] that it was to this sanctuary that the king and queen repaired at the Spring Festival to engage in a ritual marriage, as in the ziqqurat at Babylon.

But while there can be little doubt about the equation of the Hurrian Goddess with the Hittite Weather-god, the relation of the Hurrian and Hittite Goddess is very obscure. The Sun-goddess of Arinna, as we have seen, was the wife of the Weather-god of Hatti whose Hittite name is still unknown, but who was so intimately connected with the bull, the embodi-ment or symbol of virility, that according to an older conception he was himself a bull. Like Baal and Zeus he controlled the rain and was manifest in thunder and lightning, and, therefore, he was essentially a fertility-god, vegetation in Anatolia being dependent upon the rains. But he was also the divine king as well, owning the land of Hatti as Yahweh claimed to be in possession of Palestine. So numerous, in fact, were his functions that although originally they were almost certainly manifesta-tions of one and the same deity, they came to be treated as virtually localized independent gods.

This also applies to his consort who appears to have been at once the Sun-goddess of Arinna in Hatti and Hebat in the 'Land of the Cedar' (i.e. Hurri),[13] and yet treated as separate goddesses: the Hittite Sun-goddess unlike the Hurrian Hebat being essentially a solar divinity, reigning supreme and giving the king victory over his enemies. The Sun-god was subordinate to her, and he was not her husband; she being the wife of the Weather-god of Hatti, the queen of heaven, the chief goddess of the State, the protector of the reigning sovereign, and, as in the case of the Earth-mother, the guardian of the dead as well as of the crops. But here, again, when the gods and goddesses were grouped in pantheons the supreme Goddess assumed a number of distinct divine personalities, each exercising her own particular role in the Hittite economy.

Similarly, the Anatolian counterpart of Ishtar, known in Hurrian as Shauhkta, the sister of Teshub, combined belligerent qualities with those of sexuality and love. The same applies to the Hurrian goddess, Hebat, who assumed the attributes of the Sun-goddess of Arinna before she developed martial characteristics, and who was identified with Ma Bellona by the Romans. But it was Hannahanna, the 'Grandmother', whose name was written with the ideogram of the Sumerian Mother-goddess, Nintud, who was the Anatolian equivalent of the Magna Mater. It was she in the Telipinu myth who was consulted by the Weather-god when his son vanished in a rage, and, like Dumuzi-Tammuz in Mesopotamia, brought all life to a standstill by his absence. On her advice the bee was sent out to discover the whereabouts of the missing god, and although this device failed, she appears to have been instrumental in securing his return and the restoration of fertility.

Thus, throughout the Ancient Middle East the Goddess cult in association with that of the Young God had the same characteristic features centred in the rhythm of the seasons in which she was the embodiment of generation and procreation in perpetuity, and her youthful male partner personified the transitory life of the ever-changing sequence of the cosmic cycle, each taking on its own autonomous significance. But although in Syria, Mesopotamia, Anatolia and the Aegean the Goddess was the predominant figure, in Egypt the position was reversed.

In the Nile valley when the official priesthoods systematized theological speculation and organized the local cults on the basis of the unified rule of the 'two lands' under the one Pharaoh, the king became the incarnation and physical son of the Sun-god Re at Heliopolis and of Amon at Thebes. In this capacity he reigned as the earthly representative of Amon-Re, the national god of Egypt, and when the Osiris myth was solarized he occupied the throne as the living Horus, the posthumous son of the fertility deity *par excellence* (Osiris). Therefore, he owed his divinity and his status in the nation to the gods he embodied, all of whom were males.

Osiris and Isis in Egypt

Isis originally being the 'throne woman', personified the sacred coronation stool charged with the mysterious power of king-ship. As such she was the source of vitality before she became the prototype of the life-giving mother and faithful wife. She taught her husband-brother the secrets of agriculture, sent him on his civilising mission, searched for him after his assassination, collected his dismembered body, and was responsible for its restoration and mummification. It was by her son Horus, the Young God, that he was revivified, though he remained the dead god who lived in his son as the reigning Pharaoh. But Osiris and the Pharaoh were never subservient to Isis, notwith-standing the prominent position she held in the Osiris myth.

In Egypt the Pharaohs reigned as gods incarnate in their own right, unlike the Babylonian kings, while the gods whom they embodied were equally dominant in their own spheres. There-fore, neither they nor their earthly counterparts were secondary to the Goddess. Indeed, though Isis eventually became the syncretistic 'Goddess of many names' and attributes, in the beginning she did not fulfil the functions of a Mother-goddess. This was rather the role of Hathor, the Cow-goddess of Denderah, with whom she became identified. In fact, the office was split up among several goddesses (e.g. Nut, Neith, Isis), all of whom shared in some of its attributes, but none attained to the dominant position of the Great Goddess of

Western Asia until in Hellenistic times Isis virtually became equated with the Magna Mater in the Graeco-Roman world when her syncretistic mystery was established there from 333 B.C. onwards. Then she became the most popular of all Egyptian divinities, and was identified with all the allied foreign goddesses, Silene and Io, Demeter, Aphrodite and Pelagia, her brother and husband Osiris playing a subordinate role. Always her worship was far more popular than that of Osiris, and when she was incorporated in the Osiris myth her devotion to her husband made a strong emotional appeal in spite of the fact that she was never a tragic figure like Ishtar. It is not surprising, therefore, that at length she became the Great Mother, devoted to her son Horus, and the faithful wife of her husband Osiris, when she captured the popular imagination of the Roman Empire.

The Male and Female Principles in India

In India, again, the worship of the active female principle (*sakti*) as manifest in one or other of the consorts of Shiva (e.g. Uma, Kali, Parvati, Durga) has a long history behind it, having arisen out of the impersonation of feminine energy in the form of the Earth-mother in the pre-Aryan cult of the village-goddesses.[14] Thus, in the *Devi-Mahatmya*, a later popular text, Durga is made to declare, 'then, O gods, I shall nourish (i.e. uphold) the whole universe with these plants which support life and grow from my very body during the rainy season. I shall then become glorious upon the earth like *Sakambari* ("who feeds the herbs") and in that same season, I shall destroy the great *asura* called Durgama (the personification of drought)'.[15] Being at once the goddess of fertility worshipped in a great variety of local vegetation cults, the Durga was the author and giver of life to the fruits of the earth as its primordial essence, the manifestation of cosmic vitality in perpetual process of regeneration, and at the same time a destructive force in the universe, identified with Kali and the malignant *grama-devata*. Thus, in her chthonic aspect she was the chief divinity of death and of the spirits of the dead.

Saktism, in fact, as an offshoot of the Earth cultus, has developed along lines parallel to those of the Goddess in Western Asia and the Aegean. Therefore, in addition to the personification of the female principle a male deity was also an object of veneration, revealed in the figure of the three-faced god at Mohenjo-daro as the prototype of Shiva.[16] This becomes apparent in the association of the Vedic Earth-mother, Prithivi, with the Sky-father Dyaus Pitar, the Aryan Zeus and Juppiter, in the capacity of the universal progenitors of gods and men,[17] having themselves emerged from the cosmic waters, like Nun and Geb in Egypt. Nevertheless, so nebulous is Dyaus in the Vedas that he is little more than the designation of the 'bright sky', and it is to Prithivi alone that one of the hymns in the Rig-veda is devoted.[18] The sky was regarded as omniscient and creative, but throughout the ages Earth has been revered in the morning ritual before sowing, ploughing, and at milking the sacred cow, as the dynamic source of all life. And even as 'the Sky' Dyaus has been replaced by Varuna since the beginning of the Vedic period whose universal sovereignty in this capacity has been supreme. It was he, not Dyaus, who was the guardian of the cosmic order, seeing and knowing everything, absolute alike in the magical and mystical powers, exercising all the prerogatives of royal supremacy.[19]

Therefore, although Dyaus and Prithivi were personifications respectively of heaven and earth from whom the other gods, mankind and the universe were thought to have sprung, their functions were confined to initial generation. Beyond this they played very little part in the course of events, whereas devotion to the Earth-mother has continued to find ritual expression, especially among the Dravidians, all over India and all down the ages. After each successive harvest, the soil having become exhausted has had to be renewed by the performance of fertility dances, sometimes involving revitalization by the sacrifice of human blood, as among the Khonds of Bengal in the well-known offering of the Meriah to Tari Pennu, the Earth-goddess, to obtain 'good crops, good weather and good health'; the flesh of the victim being buried in the fields and the ashes of the burnt bones spread over the plough/lands to ensure a good harvest. So fundamental was this rite that it continued to be practised until it was suppressed under British rule, and then a goat or buffalo was substituted for the human Meriah, who incidentally originally was a voluntary victim born of parents who had themselves fulfilled the role.

In her more benevolent form the Goddess is regarded as the mother of all things producing fertility in man and beast as well as in the fields. Just as fecundity of women has a reciprocal effect on vegetation, so the fertility of the fields assists human mothers in conception. But, as has been considered, the Indian goddesses are at once divinities of fertility and destruction, of birth and of death. Thus, in their benign character they preside over the operations of nature since upon them depend the fecundity of the soil and the health and increase of the commu/nity and its flocks. But, on the other hand, in their malevolent and chthonic aspects they are as terrifying and terrible as in beneficent forms they are auspicious. Thus, Kali 'the black', encircled with snakes, dripping with blood, and adorned with skulls, is a formidable figure, but she is also called 'the gentle and benevolent'. Similarly, her male partner Shiva combines both these elements as the archetype of the polarity of the universe in its rhythmic sequence of birth and death, of renewal and dissolution.

Divine Androgyny

In the process of regeneration through death the Goddess is the central figure by virtue of her life/giving qualities and functions in all their forms and phases. From her identity with the earth has sprung the analogies between women and the soil, sexuality and sowing, death and rebirth, and the conception of the fundamental unity of organic life. From this one and the same principle the male and female duality has developed, creative and destructive, kindly and malevolent, so conspicuous in the Indian cultus. Behind it lies the bisexuality of Shiva and Kali as a single divine entity (*ardhanarisvara*), half male and half female, symbolizing the union of Purusha and Prakriti, and of Dyaus and Prithivi, representing heaven and earth as a single pair, the masculine and feminine designations of one and the same divinity.[20] In the concept of deity male and female elements always have been essential features, and divine androgyny has been a recurrent phenomenon in the Goddess cult everywhere reflecting the primeval cosmic unity from which all creation has been thought to have emerged. From this single ultimate androgynous principle or sacredness the contrast between father and mother, active and passive, was differen/ tiated when an all/embracing motherhood as the life/producer was brought into a nuptial relationship with the paternal figure of the generator. For life may be sacred in either a masculine or feminine aspect. Under matriarchal conditions the emphasis naturally will be on maternal potencies, whereas in patriarchal society the male will tend to predominate in his works and ways. Sex, however, in its respective characteristics and attributes may not always have been clearly determined and firmly fixed in independent divine personalities, the village/goddesses some/ times being more or less hermaphrodites, partly male and partly female in their features and functions, just as they are ambivalent in their characters.

The Bucranium

Nevertheless, the sacredness of female life in its various aspects has played the principal role in agricultural society and vegeta/ tion ritual, the male partner in the first instance being the lover/son, or young god, rather than a heavenly father. When greater importance has been attached to authority than to generation the term father has had a connotation of the elder as opposed to the younger in an age/group, not to paternity in its sexual significance. Then Sky/gods have been brought into relation with the Great Goddesses, primarily as fecundators. Thus, under the symbol of the bull their virility as Weather/gods frequently has found expression in the iconography, as, for example, in Anatolia and Mesopotamia where the bucranium is so prominent, going back to the fourth millennium B.C.

in the Tell Halaf pottery motifs, and in the bronze figure of bulls in the Aladjahüyük graves.[21] That it survived in relation to the Goddess cult is shown by the reliefs on the sphinx gate at Aladjahüyük at the end of the New Empire, where the Goddess is depicted in association with her consort, the Weather-god, who is represented as a bull. In the Late Hittite period he appears standing on the hill while these sacred animals are attached to his chariot, as in all probability they were in Hurrian mythology to that of Teshub, under the names of Sheri and Hurri, 'Day' and 'Night'.[22] Moreover, at Aladjahüyük the Hittite king is represented worshipping the Weather-god in the image of a bull.[23]

Similarly, in the Ugaritic texts El is likened to a 'mighty bull', and Baal is said to have fallen like a bull.[24] In the Rig-veda, Dyaus is described as a bull,[25] and Indra in his fertility capacity is called 'the bull of the world'.[26] Rudra united with the Cow-goddess in his procreative activities,[27] just as in Egypt Min was 'the bull of his mother'. It is not improbable that the Cretan myth of the unnatural love of Pasiphas, the wife of Minos, for the Minotaur was of Egyptian origin.[28] Though we cannot be sure that the bull was actually venerated by the Minoans,[29] he seems to have been identified with the sun as a fertilizing agent in Crete,[30] and it is very difficult to dissociate his Cretan manifestations from his firmly established role as the dynamic force of fertility throughout Asia Minor where in association with the Goddess he was regarded as the fecundator alike of flocks and herds and of vegetation. In Mesopotamia Frankfort has suggested that the bull symbolized drought, as seven lean years are said to follow his onslaught, and showers of rain are shown on a seal as a result of his having been slain.[31]

On a ring from a chamber-tomb near Arkhanes, south of Knossos, an ithyphallic figure of a bull occurs in a scene portraying the bull-games in which he seems to represent the reproductive force in nature. In front of him are objects which Evans interprets as 'sacral knots' as a sign of consecration, and he has no doubt about the religious character of the sports which he believes were held under the patronage of the Goddess whose pillar shrine overlooked the arena. It was for this reason that well-bred girls took part in these highly skilled, dangerous feats as votaries of the Goddess.[32]

While Minoan influences were very strongly felt in the cultus on the mainland, there are no indications that the bull-games were practised in Greece, though they may be detected in the Theseus saga in the seven youths and maidens delivered from their fate as sacrificial victims of the Minotaur, the bull of Minos. Whether or not anything approaching the Dionysian *Omophagia* as a 'feast of raw flesh' was in fact held in Crete, as is suggested in the fragment of the play of Euripides, *The Cretans*,[33] Dionysus, so intimately associated with vegetation, was believed to be embodied in the bull, and was identified with growth, decay, and death leading to rebirth, as evidenced by the seasonal cycle.

In the Thracian orgies the devouring of the raw flesh of the bull or of a goat in which Zagreus dwelt was the culmination of the mountain madness of the maenads,[34] thereby becoming possessed by the deity as Bacchoi. So crude and primitive a rite must have had a long history behind it, and after it had been sobered under Delphic influences and obtained a place in the Olympian tradition in the Graeco-Oriental Mysteries, the nocturnal frenzies and Bacchanalia could not be suppressed completely among the private *thiasoi*. Indeed, sometimes they continued to secure a measure of official recognition so that the wife of the Archon of Athens engaged in a ritual marriage with Dionysus in a former residence of the ruler which was called the *Bukolion* (the 'ox-stall' of the 'mighty bull', i.e. Dionysus).[35] The suppression of the cultus by the Roman Senate in 187 B.C. shows how firmly established it must have been in the Graeco-Roman world in the first century B.C., since Bacchic bands of women still assembled annually with their *thyrsoi*, and in the manner of the maenads raved in the presence of Dionysus,[36] who remained the principal vegetation god among the Greeks, worshipped in all the vigour of his manhood as at once a bull and a young man of great beauty and virility.

When at length Dionysus gained a place in the Olympian pantheon he became the son of Zeus, the much-married 'father of gods and men', himself having been originally a Sky- and Weather-god controlling the rainfall among his celestial functions. Therefore, Zeus was readily identified with the indigenous fertility divinities and their cultus when he became the dominant figure in the Olympian tradition, and, in fact, of the invading Greeks when they settled in Thessaly. Even so essentially Hellenic a deity as Poseidon, who eventually assumed the status of a major god as the brother of Zeus (i.e the son of Kronos), in his original capacity was the moisture of the earth and the consort of Gaia. Therefore, he gave life to the soil. For this reason bulls were sacrificed to him[37] as the male god of fertility dwelling in the earth, and he was often associated with Demeter in myth and ritual for cult purposes.[38]

In this role, however, like most other male partners of the Goddess, he occupied a relatively unimportant position, and it was not until he was given rule over the ocean when the universe was divided between the sons of Kronos that he came into greater prominence, especially among those who 'went down to the sea in ships and occupied their business in great waters'. It was always the Mother of the gods in one of her aspects and manifestations who was predominant because she was at once the protector and giver of life. But notwithstanding the fact that she was the embodiment and mistress of fecundity in general, she exercised her regenerative functions in union with her male partner. Therefore, as the ploughed earth was regarded as the Mother who bore the crops sown in her in due season, so she had to contract a sacred marriage in order to become fertile. Thus, in India the furrow was identified with the *yoni* (vulva), and the seeds in it with the *semen virile*,[39] while an ancient Anglo-Saxon spell used when the land was barren declared, 'Hail, Earth, Mother of men, be fertile in the god's embrace, be filled with fruit for man's use.'[40]

When this was effected by the sky pouring its life-giving rain on the earth, the process of regeneration was interpreted in terms of a sacred marriage between the Sky-father and the Earth-mother, as is clearly stated in a fragment of the play of Aeschylus, the *Danaides*.[41] There Aphrodite is made to say,

> The pure Sky yearns passionately to pierce the Earth,
> And yearns likewise for her marriage.
> Rain falls from the bridegroom Sky makes pregnant the Earth.
> And she brings forth her brood for mortal men—
> Pastures of flocks and corn, Demeter's gift,
> While trees from that same watery brilliance grow
> Their fruits to fulness.

Thus, the earth is represented as the embodiment of the Mother-goddess, bearing its fruits in human fashion fertilized by the sky whose seed is imparted in the rain that descends upon the ground.

While it is very doubtful whether Hera, the legitimate wife of Zeus, was an Earth-goddess,[42] nevertheless their nuptial relations were intimately associated with the productivity of the soil, and of the flocks and herds under her protection, as well as of mankind, in her capacity of the patroness of marriage and birth. But Zeus, having attained pre-eminence in the Olympian pantheon, unlike many of the consorts of the Goddess elsewhere, he was no longer subservient to his spouse. On the contrary, he contracted liaisons with goddesses at will, to say nothing of his 'affairs' with less exalted mortal females. But the Mother of the Gods, by whatever specific name she might be called, and however she exercised her functions, was the oldest, the most revered and the most mysterious of divinities, extolled by the poets[43] and supplicated by the people for their daily needs, especially to promote the growth of the crops.[44]

THE MOTHER OF THE GODS

The Mountain-mother

Thus, in Greek temples the *omphalos*, or navel of the world, was a symbol of both the earth and of all birth, taking the form of an eminence representing the sacred mountain which emerged out of the waters of chaos (i.e. the primordial hill[45]). Being regarded as the point where heaven and earth met at the centre of the world, on it was located the abodes of the gods (e.g. Heliopolis, Olympus, Sinai, Meru, Himingbjorb, Geni-zim). Therefore, it is not surprising that the earliest representa-tions of the Minoan Mother are the seal-impressions showing her standing on a hill in her flounced skirt, holding a sceptre or lance, and flanked by guardian lions, near a pillar shrine with horns of consecration.[46] In these scenes she is shown alone as the Earth-goddess in all her majestic strength and power with a male worshipper in a state of ecstasy before her, or with a youthful male god in process of descending from the sky; evidently in a completely subordinate status, and doubtless for the purpose of fertilizing her as Mother-earth. There are no indications in these Minoan intaglio impressions of the pre-dominance of the male god as the supreme Sky-father so that in Crete, unlike Thessaly, it was the Mountain-goddess rather than the Olympian god who was personified in attitudes that leave no room for doubt concerning her supremacy, while the presence of a sacred tree in these peak sanctuaries, together with pillars, horns of consecration and the double axe, suggest the nature of her cultus.

That it was one Great Goddess of the mountains, who was also the Earth-mother, the Mistress of the animals, the Patroness of fertility, the underworld, and the goddess of war and of the seas, who was venerated first in Crete and then on the mainland in the Minoan-Mycenaean cult is highly probable in spite of Nilsson's contention that these several figures represent a plurality of independent divinities, each with her own parti-cular individual functions and attributes. It seems much more likely that Evans was correct when he affirmed that 'we are in the presence of a largely monotheistic cult in which the female form of divinity held the supreme place'.[47]

It is, as he says, substantially the same form of religion as that so widespread throughout the Anatolian and Syrian regions. There, as we have seen, it prevailed in Western Asia from Carchemish to Ephesus, from Kadesh to the Black Sea and the Mediterranean. Originally a nature cult derived in the first instance from the productivity of the earth capable of self-reproduction as the Universal Mother, in due course it incorporated the Young God as a satellite of the Goddess. From the fertile plains of Mesopotamia it was introduced into Asia Minor through the influence of Hittite peoples, the Goddess appearing as Kybele in Phrygia, Artemis in Ephesus, Ma in Comana, Anat and Asherah in Syria, the Sun-goddess at Arinna, and Hebat and Shaushka in the Hurrian region, in association with her youthful consort, Attis, Adonis, Baal, or Teshub, whose virility was necessary to complete her maternity.

Before the Mother of the Gods and her partner, whether as mother and son or as wife and husband, in their several aspects and varied symbolism, celestial, chthonic, sexual and fertility, became differentiated with individual functions by fusion with local deities as syncretistic figures, they would seem primarily to have personified the bestowal of fecundity through rain, as in Mesopotamia, in the capacity of a universal Nature-goddess and a Weather-god respectively. So long as divinities were thought to resemble human beings and their relationships no one deity, male or female, was a single unifying principle absolute in power. At first it would appear the female form of divinity held the supreme place for the reasons which have been discussed, and even in the urban civilization of Greece it was the goddesses who presided over the destinies of cities who were venerated and honoured chiefly by all who enjoyed their patronage.

Nevertheless, when the highly complex Zeus, who combined many strands in his personality derived from a number of different sources, Indo-European, Hellenic, Cretan, Cypriote and Western Asiatic, attained to pre-eminence in the Olympian pantheon he occupied a unique position. From being a Sky-, Weather- and Mountain-god he became 'the father of gods and men' until at length, when in the latter part of the sixth century B.C. the idea arose of 'one God, the greatest among gods and men, like unto mortals neither in form nor in thought',[48]

Zeus gradually reached the status of a single primary Being and Life-force, from whom all existence emanated and to whom all things were destined to return. Throughout his long and checkered career, from his Indo-European origins as a Rain-, Cloud-, Thunder- and Mountain-god and despotic ruler on high Olympus, to his heroic Mycenaean eminence and his subsequent overwhelming power and righteousness in the classical age of Aeschylus, and his Hellenistic identification with the Reason pervading and animating the universe, only in Crete was he subservient to the Goddess. There as the son of Rhea, the Earth-mother, who hid him in a cave to prevent his being swallowed up by his father Kronos, he was a more primitive figure than the Indo-European Sky- and Weather-god, representing the Minoan conception of the year-god. In the Olympian tradition enthroned on his sacred mountain he usurped the position elsewhere occupied by the Mountain-mother and all she signified in the Goddess cult, until at length he became ground of all creation, the source and renewer of life pantheistically conceived by the poets.

The Mother of the gods, on the other hand, remained a syncretistic figure, personifying the female principle in its manifold manifestations, symbols and attributes, absorbing first one divinity and then another in this locality and in that, wherever her cult was diffused. If she was not actually herself the earth, she was so intimately associated with the Earth-goddesses as to be virtually indistinguishable from them, as, for example, in the case of Gaia in Greece, or Prithivi in India, or Ninil in Mesopotamia, until eventually, when she had annexed the young male god, she became the Anatolian Magna Mater, Kybele. Alike in Asia Minor and the Aegean, she appeared under her several names and exercised her various functions as the pre-eminent divinity. But while she reigned supreme she was never a monotheistic deity, whether as the Mountain-mother, the Mistress of animals or as the Phrygian Great Mother. She always tended to be blended with a son or consort and with the goddesses she absorbed whose identity was never completely lost.

Thus, although Rhea was a somewhat nebulous figure, when she came to be identified with Kybele[49] in the fifth century B.C., and the orgiastic Phrygian cultus was transferred to her with its cymbals, drums and pipes,[50] she retained her identity in the Greek theogonies.[51] As the mother of the Cretan Zeus by Kronos, who may well have been an ancient pre-Hellenic agricultural deity, perhaps, as Nilsson suggests, a god of the harvest, she stood in the same vegetation tradition as Kybele and her counterparts elsewhere. Therefore, behind both divinities lay the universal concept of the Goddess representing the ultimate source and embodiment of life and fertility, personi-fying the female principle, rather than a single monotheistic divine being. Like the Theotokos of Christian tradition, how-ever, in spite of having given birth to so illustrious a son who was destined to become the self-existent Creator and unifying principle of the universe, Rhea never attained the unique status of Zeus any more than Mary ever officially was assigned equality with her divine Son whom, as it is affirmed, she conceived by the Holy Ghost.

The Mother of the Mysteries

Nevertheless, in popular esteem the Mother of the Gods and the Virgin Mother were held in such veneration as the personi-fication of maternity in all its aspects, that it was to them rather than to the more remote transcendent Deity that devotion was paid among the masses. Thus, as we have seen, in Western Asia and India, in the Eastern Mediterranean, Crete and Aegean, and in the Graeco-Roman world, the Goddess cult was widely practised, either in its mystical or mystery guise. The main purpose of the rites was to secure the union of the votary with the Great Mother in one or other of her forms, not infrequently by the aid of frenzied dancing, wild music and the sexual symbolism of the sacred marriage, in the hope that a condition of abandonment and communion with the source of all life and vitality might be obtained.

Whether or not this was prompted by some unconscious desire to return to the maternal womb, either of the actual mother or of that of a symbolic womb of the earth, it would seem to have been an urge to return to a biocosmic unity inherent in the maternal principle in order thereby to acquire a renewal of life at its very source and centre. Therefore, the principal occasion of the cultus invariably was the spring when nature was in process of reawakening from its nocturnal slumber during the long dark night of winter. Then mankind sought to be reborn to newness of life and vigour by a ritual orgy and a mystery regeneration and reintegration. Thus, although May Day customs and the associated popular obser⁄ vances have long since lost their original significance, Easter has remained the queen of festivals with life through death as its theme, and the most popular season for weddings, thereby preserving the very close bond between marriage, maternity and vegetation. Similarly, the in⁄gathering of harvest at the autumnal turn of the year continued to be marked by so much debauchery that at the beginning of the Chris⁄ tian era harvest festivals were condemned altogether, and at the Council of Auxerre in A.D. 590 were prohibited. Even so, the licence continued well into the Middle Ages, and still survives here and there in Central and Southern Europe.

The Madonna

It was this aspect of the Goddess cult, so very deeply laid and so fundamental in its fertility and sexual significance, that was largely responsible for the reticence of the Early Church to adopt or countenance its incorporation in Christian faith and practice, and especially in the Marian cultus. As has been considered, Mariology was inseparable from Christology. The first feasts dedicated to Mary in the fourth century, those of the Annunciation and the Presentation, were chiefly festivals of Christ. It was not until the next century that the Nativity and the Assumption appeared in the East, and they were not observed in the West until the seventh century. Churches had begun to be dedicated to her in Rome in the fourth century (e.g. Santa Maria Maggiore, Santa Maria in Trastevere, Santa

Maria Antiqua), and this practice fostered the cultus. Once established, it grew rapidly, stimulated by the Christological controversies in which she became the crucial figure as the Theotokos, until at length in the Middle Ages she was represented as the final glory of the Mystical Body of Christ, the Church, and the mediatrix, or co-redemptrix, in the process of redemption. But here, again, it was within the context of theological speculation concerning the nature and function of the Mater Ecclesia that the Marian cultus developed without reference to the Goddess cult.

This applies also to the doctrine of the Immaculate Conception in which the freedom from all sin on the part of the Virgin Mother was a corollary of the essential holiness of the Church. And in this connexion it is not without significance that the final formulation of the dogma in the West in 1854 coincided with that of papal infallibility in 1870. Behind it lay the perfections and status of Christ rather than those of the Mother of the gods, however much the earlier cult may have prepared the way for and anticipated the position eventually assigned to Mary in Catholic theology and devotion, first in the East and then in the West. But it was her divine maternity inherent in the doctrine of the Incarnation that gave her her unique status in Christendom, and in Marian typology it was to the Jewish signs and symbols (e.g. the burning bush, the fleece of Gideon, the temple, Wisdom's tabernacle, the Ark of the Covenant, Sinai and the rainbow), and to Hebrew archetypes (e.g. Eve, Hannah, Sarah, Deborah, Esther, Judith), not to those of the Graeco-Oriental cult that appeal was made, in spite of the fact that the Old Testament symbolism and typology were much less relevant than those of the pagan Goddess mysteries.

In the highly patriarchal Hebrew tradition the divine female principle was a relatively inconspicuous feature by comparison with its prominence in the surrounding cultures. When it did occur it was as a foreign accretion, or a survival of the indigenous agricultural ritual. Therefore, at any rate in prophetic and mono-Yahwist circles, it was not regarded with favour, and so far as possible it was suppressed, notwithstanding the prevalence of sacred prostitution and the worship of the Queen of Heaven in popular practice. Mary as a chaste Jewish maiden could hardly be equated with any of these fertility figures and the associated cultus. Therefore, her antecedents were confined to Eve and the prototypes mentioned, to the Emmanuel sign (Is. vii. 10–14), and to other prophetical harbingers of the Incarnation, for clearly she stood completely outside the Israelite sexual cult with its Western Asiatic affinities.

In Anatolia, on the other hand, the culture had been built up very largely on the supreme importance of motherhood, and this was reflected in the matriarchal character of its social structure and in the worship of the Goddess before the Phrygians introduced the Father-god, who when the civilizations were fused became the consort of the Mother-goddess. In Israel the Goddess cult was only incorporated unofficially and syncretistically in that of Yahweh who alone was regarded as the legitimate god of the land. In Asia Minor the worship of the Mother of the gods was so firmly established that in its diffusion in the West it became the dominant influence in the Aegean and the Graeco-Oriental world, having made its way through Anatolia to the Troad, Crete and Greece, and then into the Balkans. At Troy, Frankfort has called attention to face-urns as images of an owl-eyed Mother-goddess which at the fourth city of Thermi go back to the middle of the third millennium B.C., together with a limestone stele showing a crude female face flanked with slabs and carved in low relief, standing just outside the gate of the city.[52] These symbols of the Ishtar cult so widely distributed throughout Syria, Anatolia, Egypt, the Troad and the Cyclades, unquestionably were of Northern Mesopotamian origin, as has been demonstrated beyond reasonable doubt, going back to the Brak 'eye-idols' and the Hassuna painted face vessels to the fourth millennium B.C., and behind them to the Palaeolithic female figurines and the stylized engravings in the decorated caves of Pech-Merle and Combarelles.

The Origin, Function and Persistence of the Cult

While it is uncertain whether the earliest images represented the Mother-goddess as such, they were indicative of the recognition and veneration of maternity as a divine principle. Since they are most abundant as amulets in the West Asiatic sites of the Gravettian culture, it is the Southern Russian loess plain that constitutes the most probable original diffusion-centre of the cult, extending thence to the Danube basin, to Southern France and North-west Europe. Thus, it was from this Eurasian cradleland that it was diffused, both in easterly and westerly directions in the succeeding Chalcolithic period and the Bronze Age when the Mother-goddess and her cultus had become a predominant feature of the culture from India to Britain. In the flourishing Neolithic civilization at Arpachiyah near Nineveh it had become firmly established in the fifth millennium B.C. There the squatting female figurines are in the direct line with the Palaeolithic Lespugne, Wisternitz and Willendorf technique, [53] and are combined with bulls' heads suggestive of the bucranium. But in the Neolithic the male god personifying virility and paternity does not appear to have been in evidence, the Mother-goddess still retaining her earlier status as the fertile Earth, the womb from which all life was born.

Mixed farming, however, in which agriculture and domestication were combined in the maintenance of the food-supply, seems to have produced in due course the growing consciousness of the duality of male and female in the generative process. It was then that the Young God, embodied in man and the bull, became the son and consort of the Goddess in the seasonal drama. Nevertheless, while Mother-earth retained her status and significance, and continued to reign supreme as the Mountain-mother from Western Asia to Minoan Crete, it was in their dual capacities that they usually appeared when the cult in its developed form was dispersed from its area of characterization through Cappadocia to the Eastern Mediterranean, and across the Iranian plateau and Baluchistan to India.

In the background, however, there was also the shadowy

cosmic figure of the Sky-father, the Supreme Being who controlled the weather and particularly the rainfall, and was manifest in the thunder and lightning and displayed his power in hurricanes and storms. As he came into greater prominence, especially under patriarchal conditions, as the personification of transcendence *par excellence*, he was destined to become in Greece 'the father of gods and men' as the head of the Olympian pantheon. In Egypt, Re-Atum, the self-created Creator, made his first appearance alone in the primordial waters of Nun and began to rule that which he had created before heaven and earth were separated or the rest of the gods have been brought into being. In Hebrew tradition Yahweh being absolute in transcendence and autonomy, neither the earth nor the sun nor the sky was divine. He stood over and against every phenomenon of nature to the exclusion of any legitimate partner, male or female, once Hebrew monotheism was fully established. He was a Sky-god and a Storm-god, it is true, but unlike other Supreme Beings he was the absolutely sovereign and omnipotent Creator of the entire universe and its processes so that he was never merely the spouse of the Great Goddess, even though in the popular cultus from time to time goddesses may have been associated with him.

Christianity having arisen in the first instance as a sectarian movement within post-exilic Judaism, its conception of the triune Godhead was essentially monotheistic, though in its doctrine of the Incarnation emphasis was laid also on divine immanence. Moreover, since it was claimed that the Logos was made flesh through a human mother, when the Jewish sect became the Catholic Church centred at Rome and Constantinople rather than in Jerusalem, and in this status was destined to be the unifying dynamic of the disintegrating empire, the ancient cult of the Goddess and the Young God was re-established in a new synthesis. Within the context of one single and supreme transcendent Deity, the creator and ground of all existence, the Incarnate Lord was represented at once as the Son of God and the Son of Mary the Madonna, while the Church and his Bride and mystical Body was the

Mater Ecclesia. In this spiritualized and impressive theological setting the age-long widely diffused quest of life in a continual process of renewal, bound up with the resurrection of vegetation and the mystery of birth and generation, acquired a new significance which gave the ancient theme and its ritual, shorn of their earlier fertility motifs, a permanent place and function in Christendom.

Such a persistent tradition surviving and reviving throughout the ages, continually undergoing innumerable transformations, fusions, accretions and abstractions, yet always retaining inherently a permanence of structure and content, can be explained only on the assumption that it has given expression to a vital element in religious experience and in the endeavour of mankind to go forth on life's pilgrimage with hope and confidence in a strenuous, precarious and often adverse environment. Its symbolism constitutes the earliest evidence available in the archaeological data of a concept of divinity with vaguely defined traits, going back to Palaeolithic times before agriculture and herding were practised and the archetypal Earth-mother or the Great Goddess had emerged as a syncretistic personality.

With the rise of husbandry and the development of the techniques of farming, agriculture and pastoral ways of life in their various aspects, the cult and its figures and symbols were adapted to the cultural conditions, just as with ever-deepening spiritual perceptions and mysticisms in the religious consciousness they assumed corresponding qualities, attributes and modes of representation. The manifestations often may have been vastly different, but there has been no break in continuity from the earliest to the latest, the lowest to the highest attitudes to one and the same fundamental quest, be it in the material or in the spiritual sphere of operation, in which in an evolving world of human experience and understanding new modes of thought and perception, of empirical knowledge and philosophic and theological insight, were continually arising, making possible new ways of embracing reality. The factors in the process were many and various, cultural, technical, economic, social, intellectual, ethical and spiritual; but they one and all opened new vistas in which the generally benign but sometimes malign figure of the Mother-goddess in her manifold forms and phases, accretions and transformations, occupied a dominant position because she and her cult met certain of the vital needs of mankind at all times.

NOTES

CHAPTER I

1. *L'Anthropologie*, xxxiv, 1924, pp. 346ff.; Salmony, *Jahrbuch für Prähistorische und Ethnographische Kunst (I.P.E.K.)*, vol. vii, 1931.
2. *I.P.E.K.*, xi, 1926, p. 288.
3. *L'Anthrop.*, xxxii, 1922, p. 365, fig. 2, pls. i–iii.
4. *The Illustrated London News*, November 30, 1929, figs. 25–32.
5. *Ibid.*, October 2, 1937, pp. 550ff.
6. Antonielli, *I.P.E.K.*, xi, 1926, pp. 46ff.; *L'Anthrop.*, xxxvi, 1926, p. 431; *Bulletin Soc. Anthrop.*, 1902, p. 772; Burkitt, *Eurasia Septentrionalis Antiqua*, vol. ix, Helsinki, 1934, pp. 113ff.; Passemard, *Les Statuettes féminines dites Vénus stéatopyges*, Nîmes, 1938, pl. ii, fig. 8, pl. iii.
7. Lalanne and Breuil, *L'Anthrop.*, xxii, 1911, pp. 257ff.; xxiii, 1912, pp. 129ff.; Passemard, *op. cit.*, pp. 121f.; Capitan, *Rev. de l'école d'anthrop.*, xxii, 1912, pp. 316ff.; Luquet, *Art and Religion of Fossil Man*, New Haven, 1930, pp. 16, 85, 110.
8. Verneau, *Les Grottes de Grimaldi*, vol. xi, Monaco, 1906, pp. 23, 260, 277f.
9. *Ibid.*, pp. 298ff.
10. *Ibid.*, pp. 33, 298, fig. 4, p. 12.
11. *Comptes-Rendus de l'Acad. des Sciences*, lxxiv, 1872, pp. 1060f.; Boule, *Les Hommes Fossiles*, Paris, 1923, p. 266.
12. J. W. Jackson, *Shells as Evidence of the Migrations of Early Culture*, Manchester, 1917, pp. 138ff.; Elliot Smith, *The Evolution of the Dragon*, Manchester, 1919, pp. 150ff.
13. Capitan, *Les Combarelles aux Eyzies*, 1924, pl. vi.
14. Bégouen, *L'Anthrop.*, xxiii, 1912, pp. 657ff.; *Comptes-Rendus de l'Acad. Inscrip. et Belles-Lettres*, 1912, pp. 532ff.; *I.P.E.K.*, xi, 1926, pp. 219ff.
15. Bégouen, *Antiquity*, iii, 1929, p. 12.
16. Breuil, *Quatre cents siècles d'art parietal*, Montignac, 1954, p. 176.
17. Malinowski, in *Science, Religion and Reality*, 1926, p. 44.
18. Cf. Obermaier, *Fossil Man in Spain*, pp. 117, 122.
19. H. Martin, *Antiquity*, iii, 1929, pp. 45ff.
20. Breuil and Calve Aguilo, *L'Anthrop.*, xx, 1909, p. 1.
21. The technique indicates a Caspian origin of this type of Eastern Spanish art which in North Africa in its early phase corresponded to the Middle Aurignacian and Gravettian though it continued until the Neolithic.
22. Cf. S. Hartland, *Primitive Paternity*, 1909; Malinowski, *The Father in Primitive Psychology*, 1927; *Sexual Life of Savages in North-western Melanesia*, 1929, pp. 146ff.

23. M. E. L. Mallowan and J. Cruikshank Rose, *Iraq*, vol. ii, pt. i, 1935, pp. 79 ff.

24. *Ibid.*, p. 95, cf. p. 87.

25. *A.A.S.O.R.*, xxi–xxii, 1943, pp. 23 ff.; *The Archaeology of Palestine and the Bible*, New York, 1932, p. 109.

26. *Iraq*, vol. ii, pt. i, 1935, p. 87.

27. Seton-Lloyd and Fuad Safar, *J.N.E.S.*, iv, 1945, p. 269, pls. x, 1, 14; xi, 1, 5–7.

28. *Ibid.*, pl. xviii, 2.

29. Mallowan, *Syria*, vol. iii, 1936, pp. 19 f., fig. v, 1–12; pl. 1. At Tell Brak in the Khabur valley in Eastern Syria face-idols with very large eyes have been found in abundance, probably closely related to the Goddess cult (*c.* 3000 B.C.); cf. Mallowan, *Iraq*, vol. ix, 1947, pp. 156 ff.; van Buren, *Iraq*, vol. xii, 1950, pp. 141 ff.; O. G. S. Crawford, *The Eye Goddess*, 1957, pp. 25 ff., 139.

30. A. H. Tobler, *Excavations at Tepe Gawra*, vol. ii, Philadelphia, 1950, pp. 163 f.; pl. lxxxi; vol. cliii, figs. 1–10.

31. *Ibid.*, pl. lxxx, d. no. 5.

32. *Ibid.*, pl. cliii, fig. 5.

33. *Ibid.*, p. 165.

34. Woolley, *Antiq. Journal*, x, no. 4, 1930, pp. 338 f., pl. xcviii; *The Development of Sumerian Art*, 1935, pp. 37 f., pls. 6a–f, b; Hall and Woolley, *Ur Excavations*, Oxford, 1927, vol. i, p. 153.

35. *Proceedings of Society of Antiquaries*, 1919, p. 33, fig. 13; *J.E.A.*, ix, 1923, pl. xxxvii, 2.

36. *Deutsche Forschungsgeneinschaft in Uruk-Warka*, vol. vii, Berlin, 1936, pl. 47; vol. viii, pp. 50, 52, pl. 49e; Heuzey, *Catalogue des Figurines Antiques de terre culte du Musée du Louvre* (new ed., 1923), p. 22.

37. Frankfort, *Fifth Preliminary Report Iraq Expedition*, 1936, p. 73, pl. 57; Perkins, *The Comparative Archaeology of Early Mesopotamia*, Chicago, 1949, p. 153.

38. *Oriental Institute Publications*, lviii, Chicago, 1942, p. 26, fig. 23; lx, 1943, p. 1, pl. 1; xliv, 1939, pp. 19–27.

39. *Oriental Institute, Chicago*, no. 2, pp. 33 f.

40. E. F. Schmidt, *The Alishar Hüyük Seasons 1928, 1929*, Chicago, 1932, pt. i, p. 128, fig. 157.

41. *Ibid.*, p. 131, fig. 161; cf. pt. ii, season 1927, p. 36, fig. 27.

42. *Ibid.*, p. 53, fig. 62.

43. Garstang, *Prehistoric Mersin*, Oxford, 1953, p. 217, fig. 136.

44. *Ibid.*, p. 71, fig. 39.

45. R. Ghirshman, *Fouilles de Sialk*, Paris, 1938, vol. i, p. 19.

46. E. F. Schmidt, *Excavations at Tepe Hissar*, Philadelphia, 1937, p. 300.

47. R. Ghirshman, *Fouilles du Tepe-Giyan*, Paris, 1933, p. 50, pl. vi.

48. D. E. McCown, *The Comparative Stratigraphy of Early Iran*, Chicago, 1942, pp. 19, 43 ff.

49. Contenau, *Syria*, vol. viii, 1927, p. 198, figs. 2, 3; *La Déesse nue babylonienne*, Paris, 1914, p. 59, fig. 58; cf. p. 62, fig. 59; J. de Morgan, *Délégation en Perse, Memoires*, vol. i, 1900, p. 127, fig. 296; cf. p. 130, pls. vii, 14, viii, 19.

50. Pézard et Pottier, *Les Antiquités de la Susiane*, Paris, 1913, p. 129.

51. *Ibid.*, p. 149.

52. *De Morgan Collection*, Ashmolean Museum, no. 276.

53. *De Morgan, op. cit.*, vol. i, p. 130, pls. vii, 10; Pézard, *op. cit.*, p. 129; Contenau, *La Déesse*, fig. 60.

54. Pumpelly, *Explorations in Turkestan*, 1904, vol. i, Washington, 1908, p. 171, pls. 46, 60, figs. 13, 14, 11; 10*a*, 10*b*.

55. McCown, *op. cit.*, pp. 57f.

56. H. Schmidt, in Pumpelly, *op. cit.*, p. 200, pl. 55.

57. S. Piggott, *Prehistoric India*, 1950, pp. 72ff.; *Ancient India*, no. 1, 1946, pp. 8ff.; no. 3, 1947, pp. 113ff.; cf. McCown, *J.N.E.S.*, v, 1946, pp. 284ff.

58. *J.N.E.S.*, v, 1946, pp. 291ff.

59. Piggott, *Prehistoric India*, pp. 107ff., 126ff.; Stein, *Memoirs of Arch. Survey of India*, no. 37, 1925, pp. 38, 42, 60, 75; pls. ix, p.w. 9, p. 262; xii, k. 14; xvi, d.n.d., S.J. 68.

60. *Op. cit.*, p. 60.

61. *Prehistoric India*, p. 127.

62. Stein, *op. cit.*, pl. ix, P.C. 17.

63. Cf. Marshall, *Mohenjo-daro and the Indus Civilization*, 1931, vol. iii, pl. clvb; Mackay, *Further Excavations at Mohenjo-daro*, 1937, vol. ii, pls. lxxiii, 6; lxxii, 5, 6; lxxv, 1, 5; lxxvi, 21, 22.

64. Mackay, *op. cit.*, vol. ii, pls. lxxii, 4; lxxiii, 3, 4, 6; lxxv, 1, 4, 6, 21–23; Marshall, *op. cit.*, vol. iii, pls. xciv, 12, 14; xcv, 8, 26, 28.

65. Mackay, *op. cit.*, vol. i, pp. 260f.

66. *Ibid.*, vol. ii, pls. lxxii, 7; lxxiii, 1, 5; lxxv, 10, 14, 17.

67. *Ibid.*, pl. lxxiv, 14, 16.

68. *Ibid.*, pl. lxxiii, 8, 8; xci, 12; xcii, 1.

69. *Ibid.*, vol. i, p. 267; vol. ii, pl. lxxvi, 5.

70. *Ibid.*, vol. ii, pls. lxxiv, 21, 22, 25; lxxvi, 1.

71. Gen. xxxi. 19ff.

72. Brunton and Caton-Thompson, *The Badarian Civilization*, 1928, p. 29; Woolley, *Antiq. Journal*, xi, 1931, p. 368; Zammit, *Archaeologia*, lxx, p. 197.

73. Marshall, *op. cit.*, vol. i, p. 339.

74. Mackay, *op. cit.*, vol. i, p. 259.

75. Marshall, *op. cit.*, vol. iii, pl. xciv, 11; Mackay, *op. cit.*, vol. ii, pls. lxxii, 7; lxxvi, 5; Vats, *Excavations at Harappa*, vol. ii, 1940, pls. lxxvi, lxxvii; cf. vol. i, pp. 293ff.

76. As will be considered later (cf. Chapter IV), although in the Vedas goddesses play an insignificant part, this literature being essentially a product of the Aryan invasion and therefore in fundamental opposition to the indigenous cultus, in popular practice they have remained predominant. Hence the prominence of female imagery of fecundity in Hindu icono graphy, often realistic (cf. the Black Rock Temple in Chittagong) but sometimes symbolic and mystical (e.g. the inverted triangle and various forms of *yoni*).

77. Marshall, *op. cit.*, vol. iii, pl. xciv, 11.

78. Mackay, *op. cit.*, vol. ii, pls. lxxvi, 6, 23, 24; lxxii, 8–10.

79. Marshall, *op. cit.*, vol. i, pp. 52ff., pl. xii, 17.

80. Mackay, *op. cit.*, vol. i, p. 335; vol. ii, pls. lxxxviii, 222, 235; xciv, 420.

81. Marshall, *op. cit.*, vol. iii, p. 337, pl. xcix, *A*.

82. Cf. Vats, *op. cit.*, vol. i, pp. 51, 53, 56, 116, 368 ƒƒ

83. Marshall, *op. cit.*, vol. i, pls. xiii, 1; xiv, 2, 4.

84. *Ibid.*, pl. xiii, 7; Vats, *op. cit.*, vol. i, pp. 140, 371.

85. Vats, *op. cit.*, p. 370.

86. Petrie, *Prehistoric Egypt*, 1920, pp. 8ff., pls. iv, 1, 9; v, 1–3; cf. 11, 31; Brunton and Caton Thompson, *op. cit.*, pp. 29ff.

87. Petrie, *op. cit.*, p. 9.

88. Quibell, *Hierakonpolis*, 1900, pt. i, p. 7, pls. xi, xviii, 3; Petrie, *Abydos*, 1903, pt. ii, p. 24, pl. 11.

89. *Abydos*, p. 9.

90. Hogarth, *Ionia and the East*, Oxford, 1909, p. 86.

91. Dikaios, *Khirokitia*, Oxford, 1953, pp. 296ff., pls. xcv, cxliii, cxliv. A slight indication of female genitalia occurs on two squatting examples, pl. xcv, 680, 948.

92. Dikaios, *Excavations at Erimi*, Cyprus, 1936, pl. xxix; *Iraq*, vol. vii, 1940, pp. 78f.

93. Contenau, *La Déesse nue babylonienne*, Paris, 1914, pp. 77ff.

94. C. W. Blegen, *American Journal of Archaeology*, xli, 1937, p. 569, pl. xx; Blegen, Caskey, Rawson and Sperling, *Troy*, i, Princeton, 1950, pp. 45, 48f., pl. 216.

95. Childe, *Dawn of European Civilization*, 1947, p. 42, fig. 19; *New Light on the Most Ancient East*, 1934, p. 197, fig. 75.

96. Blegen, *Troy*, i, 1950, pp. 27f., fig. 127; cf. 216; W. Lamb and R. W. Hutchinson, *B.S.A.*, xxx, 1932, pp. 30ff., pl. viii; Lamb, *Excavations at Thermi in Lesbos*, Cambridge, 1936, pp. 149ff., pls. xx–xxiii; p. 177, pl. xxvi.

97. Bent, *J.H.S.*, v, 1884, pp. 49ff.

98. A. J. B. Wace and M. S. Thompson, *Prehistoric Thessaly*, Cambridge, 1912, pp. 70, 83.

99. *Ibid.*, pp. 41, 69, 83, 125.

100. Vassits, *B.S.A.*, xiv, 1907-8, pp. 321ff.; W. A. Heurtley, *Prehistoric Macedonia*, Cambridge, 1939, pp. 139, 165.
101. Evans, *The Palace of Minos*, vol. i, 1921, pp. 45ff., figs. 12, 13.
102. Homer, *Odyssey*, 125f.; Hesiod, *Theogony*, 969; Diodorus, vol. v, 25 ff.; J. E. Harrison, *Themis*, Cambridge, 1912, pp. 54, n. 7, 164; *Prolegomena to the Study of Greek Religion*, Cambridge, 1903, p. 456.
103. Evans, *op. cit.*, vol. i, pp. 500ff., figs. 359, 362; Nilsson, *The Minoan-Mycenaean Religion*, 1950, pp. 309ff.; B. E. Williams, *Gournia*, Philadelphia, 1908, pp. 47ff., pl. xi.
104. Evans, *op. cit.*, vol. iv, p. 559, fig. 522; cf. *B.S.A.*, vii, 1900, p. 29, fig. 9.
105. *Op. cit.*, vol. i, p. 52.
106. Zammit, *Prehistoric Malta*, Oxford, 1930, p. 45; Hawkes, *Prehistoric Foundations of Europe*, pp. 153f.
107. Zammit, *op. cit.*, pp. 13, 15, 44, 80, 94f., pl. xxvi; cf. Zammit and Singer, *J.R.A.I.*, liv, 1924, pp. 75ff., pls. v, 6, 7, 9; xix, 20; Battaglia, *I.P.E.K.*, 1927, pp. 135ff., figs. 1-10.
108. Zammit, *The Hal-Saflieni Prehistoric Hypogeum*, Malta, 1910, p. 40; *J.R.A.I.*, liv, 1924, pl. ix, 22.
109. *Ibid.*, pl. x, 23.
110. Cf. Childe, *Dawn of European Civilization*, 1947, pp. 247f.
111. Siret, *Revue préhistorique*, 1908, pp. 10, 21; *Les premiers Âges du métal dans le sud-est de l'Espagne*, Paris, 1888.
112. Correia, *Comisión de investigaciones paleontológicas y prehistoricas*, Madrid, 1921, pp. 27, 63ff., figs. 50, 56, 58.
113. Siret, *Revue préhistorique*, 1908, pp. 6ff.
114. Correia, *op. cit.*, p. 75.
115. *Junta superior para excavaciones arqueológicas*, Madrid, 1930, Mems. x, § 112.
116. Le Rouzic, *Carnac, Menhirs-Statues avec signes figuratifs Amulettes ou Idoles des Dolmens du Morbihan*, Nantes, 1934, pp. 13ff.; Kendrick, *The Archaeology of the Channel Islands*, vol. i, 1928, p. 12; *Antiq. Journal*, v, 1925, pp. 429ff.
117. Piggott, *Neolithic Cultures of the British Isles*, 1954, p. 88, figs. 14, 1-4, 10.
118. Curwen, *Sussex Archaeological Collections*, vol. lxx, 1929, p. 56, fig. 175.
119. Drew and Piggott, *P.P.S. N.S.*, vol. ii, 1936, pp. 86ff.
120. Cf. Piggott, *Neolithic Cultures of the British Isles*, p. 42, pl. iv; J. and C. Hawkes, *Prehistoric Britain*, 1947, p. 39.

CHAPTER II

1. *Tammuz and Ishtar*, Oxford, 1914, p. 5.
2. Kramer, *Sumerian Mythology*, Philadelphia, 1944, pp. 56ff.; *A.N.E.T.*, pp. 37ff.; Jacobsen, *J.N.E.S.*, iv, 1946, p. 150; Thureau-Dangin, *Revue d'assyriologie et d'archéologie orientale*, xix, Paris, 1884, pp. 175ff.

3. Kramer, *A.N.E.T.*, pp. 41f.; Jacobsen, *Intellectual Adventure of Ancient Man*, Chicago, 1946, pp. 166f.
4. Kramer, *Proceedings of the American Philosophical Society*, lxxxv, 1942, pp. 293ff., pls. i–x; *A.N.E.T.*, pp. 52f.
5. *A.N.E.T.*, p. 52.
6. Speiser, *A.N.E.T.*, pp. 107ff.
7. Langdon, *Tammuz and Ishtar*, Oxford, 1914, pp. 11, 14f.; Wetzel, *Analecta Orientalis*, vol. x, 1935, pp. vif.; A. Moortgat, *Tammuz*, Berlin, 1949, pp. 81ff.; Ezek. viii. 14.
8. Langdon, *J.R.A.S.*, 1926, pp. 16ff., 35ff.; col. vi, 6ff.
9. *Kingship and the Gods*, p. 297.
10. Frankfort, *Cylinder Seals*, 1939, pp. 117f., pl. xix, *a*, *b–d*.
11. Pallis, *The Babylonian Akitu Festival*, 1926, pp. 124ff., 173, 198f.
12. Pallis, *op. cit.*, pp. 109, 197ff.; S. Smith, *J.R.A.S.*, 1928, pp. 849ff.; Tallquist, *Sumerischakkadische Names der Totenwelt*, Helsingfors, 1914, p. 26, n. 4.
13. Zimmern, *Berichte über die Verhandlungen der Kgl. Sächsischen Gesellschaft der Wissenschaften, Phil-hist. Klasse*, vol. lxviii, 1916.
14. Sethe, *Urgeschichte und Aelteste Religion der Aegypter*, Leipzig, 1930, p. 85; M. A. Murray, *J.R.A.I.*, xlv, 1915, pp. 308ff.
15. *P.T.*, 1479, 1521.
16. *P.T.*, 1248, 1479; cf. Budge, *The Gods of the Egyptians*, vol. i, 1904, pp. 322ff.
17. Budge, *From Fetish to God in Ancient Egypt*, Oxford, 1934, pp. 173, 256; Badawi, *Der Gott Chnum*, Glückstad, 1937, pp. 56ff.
18. Gauthier, *Les fêtes de dieu Min*, Cairo, 1931, pp. 194, 235.
19. *P.T.*, 282c.
20. *P.T.*, 900a.
21. *P.T.*, 316a.
22. A. Scharff, *Aegyptische Sonnenlieder*, Berlin, 1922, p. 39.
23. *P.T.*, 580, 827f.; Budge, *The Book of the Dead*, p. 59.
24. *P.T.*, Pepi I, 593.
25. Wiedemann, *Religion of the Ancient Egyptians*, 1897, p. 143.
26. *Der Schende und blinde Gott*, München, 1942, pp. 40f.
27. *P.T.*, 466a.
28. Newberry, *Ancient Egypt*, 1914, p. 155.
29. Budge, *The Gods of the Egyptians*, vol. i, pp. 450ff.
30. Budge, *The Book of the Dead*, chap. xlii, 11; lxvi, 2.
31. Mallet, *Le Culte de Neit à Saïs*, Paris, 1888, pp. 140, 252.
32. Mallet, *op. cit.*, p. 191; Budge, *The Gods of the Egyptians*, vol. i, p. 459.
33. Budge, *The Gods of the Egyptians*, vol. i, p. 463.
34. Cf. Frankfort, *The Intellectual Adventure of Ancient Man*, p. 17.
35. Cf. Plutarch, *De Iside et Osiride*, p. 15.
36. Cf. C. E. Sander-Hansen, *Das Gottesweib des Amun*, Copenhagen, 1940.

37. Junker, *Die Onurislegende*, Wien, 1917, pp. 116f.
38. Erman, *A Handbook of Egyptian Religion*, 1907, pp. 215ff.
39. Junker, *Die Onurislegende*, p. 116.
40. Blackman, *Luxor and its Temples*, 1923, pp. 70ff.; W. Wolf, *Das schöne Fest von Opet*, Leipzig, 1931, pp. 73ff.
41. Blackman, *J.E.A.*, xi, 1925, p. 250, n. 3.
42. Gayet, *Le Temple de Louxor*, 1894, pls. lxiiiff.
43. Sethe, *Urkunden des Aegyptischen Altertums*, vol. iv, Leipzig, 1903, p. 227; *P.T.*, 196–203; Naville, *The Temple of Deir el-Bahari*, vol. ii, pls. l–liii; Moret, *Du caractère religieux de la royauté pharaonique*, Paris, 1902, pp. 53ff.
44. Sethe, *Urkunden*, vol. iv, pp. 219ff.
45. *Ibid.*, pp. 244f.; Moret, *op. cit.*, pp. 53ff.
46. Naville, *The Temple of Deir el-Bahari*, vol. iii, pls. lxff.; Moret, *op. cit.* pp., 79ff.
47. *P.T.*, 282c.
48. *P.T.*, 990d.
49. Sethe, *Urkunden*, vol. iv, pp. 26, 29, 34, 77; Breasted, *Ancient Records of Egypt*, vol. ii, Chicago, 1906, § 14, 33, 110, 360f.; Erman, *op. cit.*, p. 73.
50. Breasted, *op. cit.*, vol. iv, § 957.
51. Brugsch, *Egypt under the Pharaohs*, 1902, p. 420.
52. Breasted, *op. cit.*, vol. iv, § 935ff., 988ff.; Erman, *Life in Ancient Egypt*, 1894, pp. 165ff.
53. Breasted, *op. cit.*, vol. iv, § 988D.

CHAPTER III

1. Cf. chap. i, p. 24; J. B. Pritchard, *Palestine Figurines*, New Haven, 1943, pp. 5ff.
2. *Syria*, vol. x, 1929, pl. 54, 2, pp. 289ff.; vol. xiii, 1932, pl. 9, 1, c, e, pl. 9, 1, d, pp. 8ff.; vol. xviii, 1937, pl. 18.
3. A. Rowe, *The Topography and History of Beth-Shan*, 1930, pp. 19ff. pl. 48, 2.
4. Sethe, *Zeitschrift für Aegyptische Sprache und Altertumskunde*, 64, 1929, pp. 6ff.
5. C. H. Gordon, *Ugaritic Handbook*, Rome, 1947, no. 2010, p. 275.
6. Gaster, *Thespis*, New York, 1950, pp. 57ff.; Driver, *Canaanite Myths and Legends*, Edinburgh, 1956, pp. 11ff.; *Syria*, vol. xiii, 1932, pp. 113ff.
7. Gaster, *op. cit.*, p. 181; cf. Gen. vii. 11, viii. 2; 2 Kings vii. 2, 19; Mal. iii. 10 for lattices and rain.
8. *The Cuneiform Texts of Ras Shamra-Ugarit*, 1939, p. 68.
9. *Anat-Baal Texts (A.B.)*, II, 39ff.; 49: IV, 27, 29; Krt. text, 126, col. iii, 1, 5ff.

10. *A.B.*, 67: II, 3 ff.

11. *A.B.*, 49: II, 5 ff. (IV, *A.B.*, ii. 28). As Anat is associated with the cow, and Baal is said to have mated with a heifer in the fields of Shlmmt to produce a male offspring, they are both connected with the cow-symbolism of the Mother-goddess elsewhere in Western Asia and Egypt; cf. Dussaud, *Revue de l'histoire des Religions*, iii, 1935, pp. 15, 44 ff.

12. *A.B.*, 67: VI, 8 ff.

13. *A.B.*, 62: I, 15.

14. *A.B.*, 62: I, 18 ff.

15. *A.B.*, 49: I, 11–15, 34.

16. *A.B.*, 49: II, 10 ff.

17. Cf. Frazer, *Golden Bough*, pt. vii, pp. 216 ff.; V. Jacobs, *Harvard Theological Revue*, 38, 1945, pp. 80 ff.

18. Gaster, *op. cit.*, p. 124.

19. I *A.B.*, II, 15–20.

20. *A.B.*, 49: III, 6 f., 12.

21. *A.B.*, 51: VII, 42; 67: II, 10 ff.

22. *A.B.*, 49: V, 1 ff.; VI, 15 ff.

23. Gordon, *op. cit.*, Ginsberg, *A.N.E.T.*, 1955, pp. 129–42; Virolleaud, *Syria*, vol. xvi, 1935, pp. 29–45; vol. xvii, 1936, pp. 150–73.

24. *'nt.* pl. vi: IV, 6 ff.; cf. II Aqht: vi, 48 ff., III Aqht: rev. 1 ff.

25. Engnell, *Studies in Divine Kingship*, Uppsala, 1943, pp. 77 f.

26. *Syria*, vol. xiv, 1933, fasc. 2, pp. 128 ff.; Ginsberg, *J.R.A.S.*, 1935, pp. 45 ff.

27. Gaster, *J.A.O.S.*, 1946, pp. 50, 54, 67.

28. Pope, *El in the Ugaritic Texts*, Leiden, 1955, pp. 39 ff.

29. *A.B.*, II, 49b–64a; cf. II *A.B.*, iii, 41; vi, 55.

30. Gaster, *J.A.O.S.*, p. 72; Gordon, *Ugaritic Literature*, p. 57.

31. *A.B.*, 76: IL, 1 ff.

32. *A.B.*, 76: 11: 25–111: 20; 67: V, 18 ff.

33. *A.B.*, 67: V, 17–22.

34. *A.B.*, 52: 45; 51: V, 47 f.; V, 66 f.

35. Pope, *op. cit.*, pp. 32 ff.; A. S. Kapelrud, *Baal in the Ras Shamra Texts*, Copenhagen, 1952, pp. 32 ff.

36. Albright, *Archaeology and the Religion of Israel*, 1946, pp. 75 f.

37. *A.B.*, 51: 1: 22; 111: 25 f.; 29 f., 34 f.; IV, 31 f.

38. *A.B.*, 75: 1: 26 ff.

39. *Syria*, vol. xvi, 1935, pp. 246–66; Montgomery, *J.A.O.S.*, lvi, 1936, pp. 226 ff.; Ginsberg, *Journal of the Palestine Oriental Society*, 1936, pp. 138 ff.

40. *A.B.*, 49: 1: 11–18.

41. *A.B.*, 51: 11: 21 ff.

42. *A.B.*, 51: IV: 43 ff.

43. *A.B.*, 51: VI: 47 f.

44. Obermann, *Ugaritic Mythology*, New Haven, 1948, pp. 12, 64, 73, 85f.

45. *A.B.*, 51: 11: 13ff.; 49: 1: 11ff.

46. *Op. cit.*, pp. 12f.

47. A Cowley, *Aramaic Papyri of the Fifth Century B.C.*, Oxford, 1923, pp. 65ff.; Mercer, *Egyptian Religion*, vol. iii, New York, 1935, pp. 198ff.; W. C. Graham and H. G. May, *Culture and Conscience*, Chicago, 1936, pp. 90, 166, 283.

48. 2 Kings xxiii. 4; Jud. ii. 13; x. 6; 1 Sam. vii. 4; xii. 10.

49. Jud. vi. 25, 28, 30; Deut. vii. 5; xvi. 21; 1 Kings xv. 13; xvi. 33; 2 Kings xiii. 6; xvii. 10; xviii. 4; xxiii. 4, 6, 14; Jer. xvii. 2.

50. Alt, *Festschrift Georg. Beer*, 1935, pp. 1–18; Eissfeldt, *Zeitschrift für die Alttestamentliche Wissenschaft*, 1939, LVII, pp. 1–31.

51. 1 Kings xviii. 19.

52. *A.B.*, 1: 197–205.

53. Albright, *B.A.S.O.R.*, no. 94, 1944, pp. 30f.; J. Gray, *The Krt Text in the Literature of Ras Shamra*, Leiden, 1955, pp. 12, 43f.; Gordon, *Ugaritic Literature*, 1949, p. 72.

54. 1 Kings xix. 14.

55. 1 Kings xii. 28; cf. Gen. xlix. 24.

56. Jud. vi. 25–32.

57. Jud. ix. 27; xxi. 19ff.; 1 Sam. i. 3, 21; ii. 19

58. Macalister, *Gezer*, vol. ii, 1912, pp. 419ff.

59. A. Rowe, *Beth Shan: Topography and History*, Philadelphia, 1930, pl. 48.

60. *Mélanges Dussaud*, i, pp. 118ff.; Albright, *Archaeology and the Religion of Israel*, p. 114; Macalister, *op. cit.*, vol. iii, pls. ccxx, ccxxi; Petrie, *Gerar*, 1928, pls. xxxv, xxvi; May, *Oriental Institute Communications*, vol. xxvi, Chicago, 19—, pls. xxiii–xxxi.

61. Graham and May, *op. cit.*, p. 138.

62. W. F. Bade, *Quarterly Statement of the Palestine Exploration Fund*, lxii, 1930, pp. 12ff.; *Palestine Institute Publications*, California, 1928, pp. 30ff., no. 1.

63. Gustav Holscher, *Die Profeten, Untersuchung zur Religionsgeschichte Israels*, x, Leipzig, 1914, p. 160; Vincent, *La religion des Judeo-Araméens d'Elephantine*, Paris, 1937; Dussaud, *Revue de l'Histoire des Religions*, vol. cv, Paris, 1932, pp. 245ff.; Gaster, *Quarterly Statement Pal. Explor. Fund*, lxvi, 1934, pp. 141ff.

64. Jer. vii. 18.

65. Jer. xliv. 15ff.

66. Jer. xliv. 20ff.

67. Amos v. 4–6; Hos. x. 9ff.

68. Albright, *Archaeology and the Religion of Israel*, p. 173.

69. 1 Sam. ii. 22.

70. Amos ii. 7ff.

71. Jer. v. 7; iv. 30.
72. Isa. lvii. 8; Ezek. xxiii. 17; Cant. iii.
73. Ps. xlv. 9 ff.
74. Isa. viii. 3; cf. J. M. P. Smith, *Zeitschrift für die Alttestamentliche Wissenschaft*, vol. xxxiv, p. 222.
75. 1 Kings xv. 12; Hos. iv. 14 ff.
76. Deut. xxiii. 17 ff.
77. Gen. xxxiv. 31; xxxviii. 15, 21; Joshua ii. 1 ff.
78. Judges xi. 1.
79. 2 Kings xxiii. 7.
80. Deut. xxiii. 18.
81. Hos. ii. 16 ff.
82. Hos. ii. 2 ff.
83. Cf. Eissfeldt, *Molk als Opferbegriff im Punischen und Hebraïschen und das Ende des Gottes Moloch*, 1935.
84. Ezek. viii; xviii. 4; xxi. 2–7; 2 Kings xxiii. 3–14.
85. R. S. Hardy, *A.J.S.L.*, lviii, 1941, pp. 178 ff.
86. Gen. xv. 19 ff.; xxiii; xxvi. 34; xxxvi. 1–3; Num. xiii. 20; Joshua i. 2–4; iii. 10.
87. 1 Kings xi. 1; 2 Kings vii. 6 f.; 2 Chron. i. 17.
88. R. Dussaud, *Religion des Hittites et des Hourrites*, Paris, 1945, pp. 338 ff.; E. Laroche, *Journal of Cuneiform Studies*, vi, 1952, pp. 115 ff.; *Recherches sur les noms des dieux hittites*, Paris, 1947, pp. 47 f., 106; Gurney, *Annals of Archaeology and Anthropology*, 27, Liverpool, 1940, pp. 10, 22 ff.; Garstang, *The Hittite Empire*, 1929, pp. 95 ff.; *The Land of the Hittites*, pp. 211 ff., pls. lxiv–lxxi; B. Bittel, R. Naumann, H. Otto, *Yazilikaya*, Leipzig, 1941.
89. Garstang, *The Land of the Hittites*, pp. 211 ff., 256 ff.; Ramsay, *J.R.A.S.*, N.S., xv, 1883, pp. 113 ff.; G. Perrot and Ch. Chipier, *Histoire de l'Art dans l'Antiquité*, vol. iv, pp. 633 ff., 666 ff.
90. Garstang, *The Land of the Hittites*, pp. 328 ff.; *The Syrian Goddess*, 1913, pp. 7 ff.
91. *The Land of the Hittites*, pp. 116 ff.
92. W. M. Muller, *Mitteilungen der Vorder-asiatischen Gesellschaft*, vol. vii, 1902, no. 5, pp. 193 ff.; *A.N.E.T.*, pp. 199 f.; *K.U.B.*, xxi, no. 27.
93. Bossert, *Altanatolien*, pp. 297–306.
94. *K.U.B.*, vi, 45; Goetze, *Handbuch der Altertumskunde*, 1933, p. 130.
95. Gurney, *op. cit.*, pp. 10 f., 22 ff.; *K.U.B.*, xxxi, 127; F. Sommer, *Zeitschrift für Assyriologie*, 46, 1940, N.S., pp. 22, 34.
96. Laroche, *Recherches sur les noms des dieux hittites*, p. 106; *Journal of Cuneiform Studies*, i, 1947, pp. 208 ff.
97. *K.U.B.*, xxi, no. 27; Goetze, *Kleinasien*, p. 129.
98. Gurney, *The Hittites*, 1952, p. 141.
99. Laroche, *Journal of Cuneiform Studies*, i, p. 96.

100. Gurney, *The Hittites*, pp. 139ff.
101. Gurney, 'Hittite Prayers of Mursili II', *Annals of Archaeology and Anthropology*, 27, Liverpool, 1940, pp. 23ff.
102. Burrows, *J.R.A.S.*, 1925, pp. 279ff.
103. *K.U.B.*, xvii, 10; xxxiii, 1-12; *A.N.E.T.*, pp. 126ff.; Gaster, *Thespis*, pp. 353ff.; Otten, *Die Uberlieterungen des Telipinu-Mythes* (*M.V.A.G.*, 46, 1), Leipzig, 1942.
104. Gaster, *Thespis*, pp. 317ff.
105. Goetze, *A.N.E.T.*, pp. 120f.; *K.U.B.*, xxxiii, 120.

CHAPTER IV

1. Chap. i, pp. 30f.
2. R. Ghirshman, *Iraq*, 1954, pl. viii.
3. *S.B.E.*, xxiii, pp. 52ff.; *Yasht*, v.
4. *Yasht*, v. 5; *Vendidad*, vii. 16.
5. Clement of Alexandria, *Protrept*, 5; Herodotus, i, 131; iv, 52; Pliny, *Hist. Nat.*, vi, 27, 135; Plutarch, *Vit. Artax.*, 27; Polybius, x, 27, 12.
6. Weissbach-Bang, *Die altpersischen Keilinschriften*, 1893, 44, 46.
7. Clement of Alexandria, *op. cit.*, 5, § 65; *Yasht*, v.
8. Cf. Chap. iii, pp. 77.
9. Strabo, xi, 512, 532; xii, 559, 537.
10. Herodotus, i, 131.
11. Sarre and Herzfeld, *Iranische Felsreliefs*, p. 128.
12. A. U. Pope, *A Survey of Persian Art from Prehistoric Times to the Present*, vol. iv, 1939, pl. 160B.
13. *Agathangelos*, 5th ed., Venice, 1862, pp. 51f., 61.
14. Strabo, xi, 532C.
15. Strabo, xii, 537C, 559C; xv, 733C.
16. H. C. Tolman, *Cuneiform Supplement*, New York, 1910, 65-67; cf. *Ancient Persian Lexicon and Texts*, New York, 1908, p. 55.
17. Herzfeld, *Archaeological History of Iran*, 1935, p. 8.
18. Keith, *Indian Culture*, vol. iii, p. 421.
19. *Yasht*, x. 13.
20. Cumont, *Les Mystères de Mithras*, vol. i, Paris, 1899, pp. 334ff.
21. Rig-veda, vi, 27, 8; x, 33, 2; *Atharva-veda*, v, 22, 5, 7, 9.
22. The earliest example of a definitely Aryan type of speech occurs in the names of the gods Mitra, Varuna and Nasatyas in the treaties between the Hittite king Shubbiluliuma and the Mitanni king Mattinaza about 1400 B.C.; cf. *Cambridge History of India*, vol. i, 1922, p. 72.
23. Vats, *Excavations at Harappa*, vol. i, New Delhi, 1940, pp. 203ff.
24. Cf. chap. i, p. 34.

25. Cf. P. T. Srinivasa Ivengar, *Pre-Aryan Tamil Cultures*, Madras, 1920; Caldewell, *Comparative Grammar of the Dravidian Languages*, 3rd ed., 1913, pp. 113f.

26. Cf. S. Shivapadasundarum, *The Saiva School of Hinduism*, 1934, p. 15.

27. G. Grierson, *Imperial Gazetteer of India*, vol. ii, 1909, p. 422.

28. *Mohenjo-daro and the Indus Civilization*, vol. i, p. vii.

29. C. Eliot, *Hinduism and Buddhism*, vol. ii, 1921, p. 144.

30. *Taittiriya Aranyaka*, x, 1, 7.

31. *Satapatha Brahmana*, vi, 1, 1, 7; cf. i, 9, 2, 29.

32. *Manu*, ix, 1, 13, 85, 100.

33. Rig-veda, i, lxv; *S.B.E.*, vol. xlvi, 54, 220.

34. Rig-veda, x, 45, 1; 121, 7; vi, 8, 2; xi, 113, 7, 8.

35. Rig-veda, iii, 3, 10; x, 51, 3; 26, 9; 27, 9.

36. E. Moor, *The Indian Pantheon*, Madras, 1897, pl. xxxi.

37. Ivengar, *Dravidic Studies*, vol. iii, p. 62.

38. *Ibid.*, p. 126.

39. *Yajurveda*, VI, ii, 4.

40. A. E. Haydon, *Biography of the Gods*, 1941, pp. 105f.

41. Rig-veda, i, 22, 16–24; 154.

42. Crooke, *Popular Religion and Folk-lore of Northern India*, vol. ii, 1896, p. 299.

43. *Vishnu Purana*, bk. 80.

44. *Kurma Avatara*, p. iii; *Vishnu Purana*, bk. i, chap. ix.

45. *Satapatha Brahmana*, xi, 4, 3.

46. *Vishnu Purana*, bk. 59.

47. *Ibid.*, p. 80.

48. Rig-veda, x, 129, 1–6.

49. Rig-veda, vii, 96, 4, 6.

50. Rig-veda, x, 75, 5; 135, 5, 6; Muir, *Original Sanskrit Texts*, vol. v, 1872, pp. 338ff.

51. xxv, 10, 6.

52. Rig-veda, iii, 23, 4. Although it has become the Indian counterpart of the Egyptian Nile, it does not appear to have been held in particularly high esteem in the Rig-veda, where it is only twice mentioned. Its goddess, Ma-Ganges, however, was the elder daughter of Hinavat, Uma being her younger sister, its waters issuing from the foot of Vishnu and falling on the head of Shiva. So now it is the holiest of all rivers.

53. Rig-veda, vi, 52ff.; x, 17, 10.

54. *Manu*, ii, 17f.

55. *Satapatha Brahmana*, xiv, 4, 2, 4; *Brihad-aranyaka Upanishad*, 3.

56. *Santiparva*, 12920.

57. *Taittiriya Brahmana*, ii, 8, 8, 5.

58. Rig-veda, x, 110, 9; iii, 3, 11; ii, 155, 3.

59. N. Brown, *J.A.O.S.*, lxii, 1942, pp. 85ff.

60. Rig-veda, i, 32, 1; 95, 8; iii, 34, 9.

61. Rig-veda, i, 159, 1; 160, 2.
62. *Aittareya Brahmana*, iv, 27.
63. Rig-veda, i, 160; iv, 30, 5; viii, 36, 4.
64. Rig-veda, i, 159; 1, 2.
65. Rig-veda, v, 84, 1 ff.
66. Rig-veda, i, 22, 1, 5.
67. Rig-veda, x, 18, 10.
68. Rig-veda, i, 43, 2.
69. Rig-veda, i, 72, 9; *Atharva-veda*, xiii, 1, 38; *Satapatha Brahmana*, ii, 2, 1, 19.
70. Rig-veda, i, 8, 9, 10.
71. A. Barth, *The Religions of India*, 1914, pp. 173 ff.
72. Cf. chap. iii, p. 72.
73. Monier-Williams, *Religious Thought and Life in India*, 1885, pp. 226 ff.
74. Crooke, *op. cit.*, vol. ii, pp. 118 ff.
75. W. T. Elmore, *Dravidian Gods in Modern Hinduism*, New York, 1915, pp. 18 ff.
76. Cf. Whitehead, *Madras Government Museum*, bulletin v, no. 3, 1907, pp. 129 ff.
77. Whitehead, *Village Gods of South India*, Oxford, 1916, pp. 69 ff.
78. Thurston, *Castes and Tribes of Southern India*, vol. iv, Madras, 1909, pp. 295 ff.; E. R. Clough, *While Sewing Sandals*, New York, 1899, pp. 62 ff.
79. Elmore, *op. cit.*, pp. 97 f.; Clough, *op. cit.*, pp. 74 ff.
80. *The Village Gods of South India*, p. 25.
81. Cf. Frazer, *Folk-lore in the Old Testament*, vol. i, 1918, pp. 66 ff.
82. Barth, *op. cit.*, p. 173.
83. Rig-veda, x, 146.
84. A. A. Macdonell, *Vedic Mythology*, Strassburg, 1897, p. 154.
85. Thurston, *op. cit.*, vol. vi, p. 62.
86. *North Indian Notes and Queries*, vol. iii, pp. 23 f.
87. T. T. Dalton, *Descriptive Ethnology of Bengal*, Calcutta, 1872, pp. 261 ff.
88. Crooke, *op. cit.*, vol. iv, pp. 34 f.
89. P. H. Buchanan, *Eastern India*, vol. xii, 1838, p. 51.
90. Thurston, *op. cit.*, vol. iv, pp. 415 f.
91. Gait, *Census Report, Bengal*, vol. i, 1901, pp. 187 ff., 190, 191, 193.
92. C. E. Luard, *Ethnographical Survey, Central India*, Art. 'Bhil', p. 29.
93. *Bombay Gazetteer*, vii, 1883, p. 527.
94. *Op. cit.*, viii, 1884, pp. 660 f.
95. *Op. cit.*, xxiii, 1884, pp. 676 f.
96. E. T. Atkinson, *Himalayan Gazetteer*, ii, 1883, p. 792.
97. Burgess, 'Elura Cave Temples', *Archaeol. Survey of Western India*, vol. v, 1883, pp. 41 f.
98. J. Burgess, *The Rock-Temples of Elephanta or Gharapuri*, Bombay, 1871; J. Fergusson and J. L. Burgess, *The Cave Temples of India*, 1880, p. 471.
99. *Manu*, viii, 10, 22–29; Harvard Oriental Series, viii, 514.

100. *Vishnu Purana*, bk. i, chap. xiii.
101. Monier-Williams, *op. cit.*, p. 318.
102. *Mahabharata*, xiii, pp. 74f.
103. *Ibid.*, 77.
104. *Satapatha Brahmana*, vii, 5, 2, 6.
105. *Ibid.*, xiii, 80, 1–3; 78, 24f.; Hillebrandt, *Rituallit, Grundriss d. Indo-Arischen Philologie*, iii, 2, Strassburg, 1897, p. 83.
106. Crooke, *op. cit.*, vol. ii, p. 232.
107. Rig-veda, vii, 93, 15.
108. *Satapatha Brahmana*, iii, 1, 2, 21.

CHAPTER V

1. Cf. chap. i, pp. 37f.
2. Evans, *Palace of Minos*, vol. i, 1921, p. 51.
3. *Ibid.*, p. 52.
4. *Ibid.*, pp. 500ff., frontispiece.
5. B. E. Williams, *Gournia*, Philadelphia, 1908, pp. 47f., pl. x; Nilsson, *The Minoan-Mycenaean Religion*, 2nd ed. Lund, 1950, p. 82, fig. 14.
6. *Op. cit.*, vol. iv, pp. 138ff., 159.
7. Evans, *op. cit.*, p. 159; *The Earlier Religion of Greece*, 1931, p. 25.
8. O. Froedin and A. W. Persson, *Asine*, 1938, p. 298, fig. 20b; Nilsson, *op. cit.*, p. 113.
9. Paribeni, *Monumenti Antichi*, vol. xix, 1908, pp. 1ff.; Nilsson, *op. cit.*, pp. 428ff.; F. v. Duhn, 'Sarkophag aus Hagia Triada', *Archiv. für Religionsviss*, vol. xii, 1909, pp. 161ff.; Evans, *Palace of Minos*, vol. i, pp. 438ff.
10. *Der kretische Bildersarg. Arch. Jahrbuch*, xxiv, 1909, pp. 162f.
11. *Themis*, Cambridge, 1912, pp. 178f.
12. Nilsson, *op. cit.*, pp. 584ff.
13. *Palace of Minos*, vol. i, pp. 439, 447f.
14. Gen. xxviii. 18; C. Tsountas, *Praktika*, 1896, pp. 29ff.; Evans, *Mycenaean Tree and Pillar Cult*, 1901, p. 19, figs. 12, 13.
15. Evans, *Mycenaean Tree and Pillar Cult*, pp. 3, 19, figs. 1, 14.
16. *Ibid.*, pp. 7ff., 15.
17. Nilsson, *op. cit.*, pp. 245f.; B. E. Williams, *op. cit.*, p. 53.
18. A. B. Cook, *Transactions of the Third Congress for the History of Religions*, ii, p. 184; Dussaud, *Les civilisations préhelléniques*, Paris, 1914, pp. 338, 350.
19. Cf. *Odyssey*, xix, 188; Strabo, x, 476.
20. Marinatos, *Praktika*, 1929, p. 94; 1930, pp. 91f.; Nilsson, *op. cit.*, pp. 58, 518f.
21. Hesiod, *Theogony*, 477; Hogarth, *B.S.A.*, vi, 1900, pp. 94ff.
22. Evans, *J.H.S.*, xvii, 1897, pp. 350ff.; *Palace of Minos*, vol. i, pp. 625ff.; *Earlier Religion of Greece*, 1931, p. 6; Nilsson, *op. cit.*, pp. 62ff.

23. The cave of Zeus on Mount Ida was not a cult centre in Minoan times, and it is very uncertain that that of Kamares on the summit facing Phaestos was used as a sanctuary, though it contained Middle Minoan pottery; cf. *B.S.A.*, xix, 1913, pp. 1ff.

24. *Palace of Minos*, vol. i, pp. 159f.

25. *Ibid.*, vol. i, pp. 161f.

26. *Ibid.*, vol. ii, pp. 838ff.

27. Nilsson, *op. cit.*, p. 267.

28. Evans, *Archaeologia*, vol. xv, 1914, pp. 10f., fig. 16.

29. Deedes, *The Labyrinth*, 1935, pp. 27ff.

30. Evans, *Tree and Pillar Cult*, pp. 78f., fig. 52.

31. Evans, *Palace of Minos*, vol. ii, p. 842; vol. iii, p. 142; Nilsson, *op. cit.*, pp. 342f.

32. Persson, *The Religion of Greece in Prehistoric Times*, California, 1942, p. 34.

33. Evans, *B.S.A.*, vii, 1900–1, pp. 28f., fig. 9.

34. *Ibid.*, ix, 1902–3, pp. 59f., figs. 37, 38.

35. Nilsson, *op. cit.*, p. 356; Evans, *Tree and Pillar Cult*, p. 3, fig. 1; p. 19, figs. 12–14; pp. 66f., figs. 44–46.

36. Evans, *B.S.A.*, vii, 1900, pp. 101f.; *Tree and Pillar Cult*, p. 65, fig. 43.

37. Evans, *Palace of Minos*, vol. iv, p. 467.

38. *Tree and Pillar Cult*, p. 77, fig. 51; *Palace of Minos*, vol. iii, pp. 463f., fig. 324.

39. *Antike Gemmen*, vol. iii, p. 36, fig. 14; Nilsson, *op. cit.*, pp. 351f.; Persson, *op. cit.*, pp. 69f.

40. *Palace of Minos*, vol. iii, pp. 143, 438ff., fig. 305; *The Earlier Religion of Greece*, p. 32, fig. 14.

41. *Palace of Minos*, vol. iii, pp. 471ff., fig. 328.

42. Ch. Tsountas, *Ephemeris Archaiologika*, 1887, pl. x, 3; Rodenwaldt, *Athenische Mitteilungen*, 37, 1912, pp. 129ff., pl. viii.

43. *Palace of Minos*, vol. iv, pt. ii, p. 956, fig. 925.

44. *Ibid.*, vol. ii, p. 277; Marinatos, *Ephemeris Archaiologika*, 1937, p. 290; Persson, *op. cit.*, p. 123; Farnell, *Essays to Sir Arthur Evans*, Oxford, 1927, p. 11; Wace, *Mycenae*, Princeton, 1949, p. 115.

45. *Op. cit.*, pp. 392ff.; *History of Greek Religion*, Oxford, 1925, p. 18.

46. *Minoan-Mycenaean Religion*, pp. 543ff.; cf. Hesiod, *Theogony*, 453ff.; *Antoninus Liberalis*, chap. 19.

47. Strabo, x, 466ff.

48. Cf. R. S. Bosanquet, *B.S.A.*, xl, 1943, pp. 66ff.; Harrison, *Themis*, pp. 3ff.

49. Cf. Homer, *Iliad*, viii, 281ff.; *Odyssey*, xiv, 199ff.

50. Aeschylus, *Danaides, frag.*, ed. Nauck, 44; Euripides, *Frag.*, 898, 7ff. (ed. Nauck); Proclus, in *Plato Timaeus*, iii, 176, 26.

51. Pausanias, ll, 38, 2; viii, 22, 2; Plato, *Laws*, 774A; Aeschylus, *Eumenides*, 1, 217f.; Farnell, *Higher Aspects of Greek Religion*, 1912, pp. 37ff.; Rose, *Handbook of Greek Mythology*, 1933, pp. 103f.

52. Aristophanes, *Thesmophoriazusae*, 973; Pausanias, ii, 17, 3; ix, 3, 1; Aeschylus, *Eumenides*, i, 214; cf. Farnell, *C.G.S.*, vol. i, pp. 244f.

53. Plutarch, *de Daedalis Plataeensibus*, 6; Pausanias, ix, 31ff.; Farnell, *C.G.S.*, vol. i, pp. 192ff.; Nilsson, *J.H.S.*, xliii, 1923, pp. 144ff.

54. *Op. cit.*, p. 103; cf. *Iliad*, xiv, 346f.

55. Rose, *op. cit.*, p. 52.

56. *Iliad*, xiv, 294ff.; cf. Farnell, *C.G.S.*, vol. i, pp. 253f.

57. Diodorus Siculus, v, 72, 4.

58. Farnell, *C.G.S.*, vol. i, p. 179.

59. Aristophanes, *Thesmorphoriazusae*, 973.

60. *Iliad*, xi, 270f.; Hesiod, *Theog.*, 921f.

61. Pausanias, ii, 38, 2; cf. A. B. Cook, *Zeus*, vol. iii, Cambridge, 1914, p. 224, n. 3.

62. *Iliad*, i, 540ff.

63. *Odyssey*, vii, 80; cf. ii, 547.

64. Nilsson, *Minoan-Mycenaean Religion*, pp. 487ff.; *History of Greek Religion*, p. 26.

65. D. Levi, *American Journal of Archaeology*, xlx, 1945, p. 298.

66. *Odyssey*, ii, 120.

67. Nilsson, *Minoan-Mycenaean Religion*, pp. 489ff.

68. *Iliad*, xvii, 398.

69. Hesiod, *Theog.*, 886ff.; cf. Rose, *op. cit.*, p. 108.

70. Liddell and Scott, *Greek-English Lexicon*, new ed., 1925, παλλάς; Dummler, *Real-Encyklopädie* (Pauly-Wissowa, Kroll), vol. ii, 2007.

71. Herodotus, i, 105; Pausanias, i, 14, 7; *Iliad*, v, 330; *Odyssey*, viii, 362f.; Hesiod, *Theog.*, 192.

72. *Iliad*, v, 312, 338; *Odyssey*, viii, 270, 362; Pindar, *Pyth.*, 4, 87.

73. *Odyssey*, viii, 266–336.

74. Virgil, *Hymn. Hom. Venus*, 5.

75. Lucian, *De Dea Syria*, 6–9; the boar incident may be a later importation; cf. Baudissin, *Adonis und Esmun*, Leipzig, 1911, pp. 142ff.

76. *J.H.S.*, ix, 1888, pp. 193ff.; Tacitus, *Annals*, iii, 62; Herodotus, i, 199; Strabo, xvi, 1, 20, 745.

77. Theocritus, *Idylls*, 15; Gow, *J.H.S.*, lviii, 1938, p. 182.

78. Plutarch, *Alcibiades*, 18.

79. Plutarch, *De sera numinis vindicta*, 17; cf. Frazer, *The Golden Bough*, pt. v, pp. 236ff.

80. Ovid, *Metamorphoses*, 4, 288.

81. Plutarch, *Theseus*, 21.

82. Pausanias, v, 11, 8; Lucretius, *Homeric Hymns*, 1, 4; Hesiod, *Theog.*, 188–206.

83. Lucretius, 1, 4.

84. Plutarch, *Quaest. Rom.*, 269b.

85. *Odyssey*, xx, 73; xxii, 22, 444; Hesiod, *Works and Days*, 521; Hesiod, *Frag.*, 143; Lucretius *Homeric Hymns*, 4, 1 ff.
86. Lucretius, 1, 10 ff.
87. *Iliad*, xiv, 214.
88. Nilsson, *Minoan-Mycenaean Religion*, pp. 503 f.
89. *Iliad*, xxi, 470 f.
90. Aeschylus, *Agamemnon*, 134 ff.
91. Nilsson, *Minoan-Mycenaean Religion*, p. 130.
92. *Iliad*, xi, 270 f.; cf. Hesiod, *Theog.*, 921 f.
93. Nilsson, *Greek Popular Religion*, New York, 1904, p. 16.
94. Farnell, *C.G.S.*, vol. ii, p. 456.
95. Harrison, *Prolegomena to the Study of Greek Religion*, 3rd ed., 1922, p. 497; Farnell, *C.G.S.*, ii, pl. xxix; P. Kern, *Mitt. Deutsch. Arch. Inst. Athens*, 50, 1925, p. 160, fig. 1.
96. Picard, *Ephese et Claros*, Paris, 1922, pp. 310 ff., 344.
97. Timotheos of Miletus, Bergk, *Poetae lyrici Graeci*, iii, 620.
98. Solinus, ii, 8; Hesychios, βριτόμαρτις, βριτύ; Roascher, *Lexikon*, art. 'Britomartis'.
99. Callimachus, *Hymns*, iii, 189; Pausanias, ii, 30, 3.
100. Farnell, *C.G.S.*, vol. ii, pp. 512 ff.
101. Hesiod, *Theogony*, 409 ff.
102. *Scholia Apoll. Rhod.*, 3, 467.
103. Bacchylides, *Frag.*, 40, Bergk.; Euripides, *Phoenissae*, 108.
104. *Scholia Lycophr.*, 1180.
105. Farnell, *C.G.S.*, vol. ii, p. 503.
106. Aristophanes, *Plut.*, 595. Scholia on 594; *Apoll. Rhod.*, iii, 1211 ff.
107. *The Homeric Hymns*, ed. by T. W. Allen, E. E. Sikes and T. W. Halliday, Oxford, 1936, 3rd ed.
108. Farnell, *C.G.S.*, vol. iii, 1907, pp. 29 f.
109. Mannhardt, *Mythologische Forschungen*, Strassburg, 1884, pp. 29 ff.
110. *Greek Popular Religion*, New York, 1940, p. 51.
111. Scholia, Sophocles, *Oedipus Coloneus*, 681; cf. *C.G.S.*, vol. iii, pp. 32 ff.
112. Allen, Sikes, Halliday, *op. cit.*, pp. 10 ff.
113. K. Kourouniotis, *Eleusis*, Athens, 1936, pp. 14 ff.; G. Mylonas, *The Hymns to Demeter and Her Sanctuary at Eleusis*, 1942; Kourouniotis-Mylonas, *American Journal of Archaeology*, xxxvii, 1933, pp. 271 ff.
114. Farnell, *C.G.S.*, vol. iii, pp. 75 ff.
115. Sophocles, *Fragmenta*, 719; Pindar, *Frag.*, 121; Plato, *Phaedo*, 69C; Cicero, *De Legibus*, ii, 14; Farnell, *C.G.S.*, p. 197.
116. Plutarch, *Alcibiades*, xix-xxii.
117. Aristophanes, *Frags.*, 324 ff.; Origen, *Contra Celsus*, 111, 59.
118. Kourouniotis, *Eleusis*, p. 15.
119. Farnell, *C.G.S.*, vol. iii, p. 256, pl. xxxib.
120. *Minoan-Mycenaean Religion*, p. 502.

121. Clement of Alexandria, *Protrept*, 11, 21.

122. *Hibbert Journal*, ii, 1904, p. 316.

123. *Refutatio omnium haeresium*, v, 8.

124. Foucart, *Les Grands Mystères d'Eleusis*, Paris, 1900, pp. 475 ff.; Asterius, *Encomium in Sanctos Martyres*, 111B.

125. *C.G.S.*, vol. iii, pp. 177, 183.

126. Produs, ad Plato, *Timaeus* (Lobeck), p. 293.

127. *C.G.S.*, vol. iii, p. 185.

CHAPTER VI

1. Strabo, 3, 17; i, xiv, 1, 20; cf. Julian, *Orat.*, v, 159.

2. Pausanias, vii, 17, 10–12; cf. Arnobius, *Adversus Nationes*, v, 5–7.

3. Servius, on Virgil, *Aeneas*, ix, 115.

4. Pausanias, vii, 17, 10–12, cf. Scholiast, on Nicander, *Alexipharmaca*, 8.

5. While the details are changed in several of the accounts the self-castration is a permanent feature; cf. Ovid, *Fasti*, iv, 221–4.

6. Polybius, 22, 20.

7. Clement of Alexandria, *Protrept.*, ii, 15, p. 13 (ed. Potter); Firmicus Maternus, *De errore profanarum religionum*, chap. 18.

8. *Peristephan*, x, 1034–9, 1076; Firmicus Maternus, *op. cit.*, 27, 8; Wissowa, *Religion und Kultus der Römer*, Munich, 1902, pp. 323 ff.

9. Dessau. *Inscriptiones Latinae Selectae*, nos. 4152, 4271.

10. Dessau, *op. cit.*, nos. 4145, 4147, 4151, 4153; cf. *C.I.L.*, xiii, 1751.

11. Strabo, xii, ii, 3.

12. *C.I.L.*, vi, 490; ix, 3146.

13. *Revue d'Histoire et de Littérature religieuses*, vol. vi, no. 2, 1901, p. 97.

14. *The Oriental Religions in Roman Paganism*, 1911, p. 67.

15. Pausanias, vii, 17, 9.

16. Ovid, *Fasti*, iv, 223 f.

17. Lucian, *De Dea Syria*, 15.

18. Diodorus Siculus, iii, 58 f.; Clement of Alexandria, *Protrept.*, viii, 78 f.

19. Stobaeus, *Floril.*, lxxiv, 61.

20. *History of Greek Religion*, 31.

21. Diodorus Siculus, iii, 59, 7.

22. Hepding, *Attis, seine Mythen und sein Kult*, Giessen, 1903, p. 131; Rapp., in Roscher's *Lexikon der griech. und röm Mythologie*, 'Kybele', vol. ii, 1638 ff.

23. Woolley, *Carchemish*, pt. ii, 1921, pl. B, 19a; J. Lewy, *Die Kültepetexte aus der Sammlung Frida Hahn*, Leipzig, 1930, p. x.

24. Lucian, *De Dea Syria*, 49, 52.

25. Farnell, *C.G.S.*, vol. iii, pp. 306f.; *Greece and Babylon*, 1911, pp. 256f.
26. Livy, xxix, 10f.
27. Julian, *Orat.*, v, 159; Ovid, *Fasti*, iv, 255ff.; Arnobius, *Adversus Gentes.*, vii, 46.
28. Livy, xxix, 10-14; Ovid, *Fasti*, iv, 257-72, 291-348.
29. Livy, xxxvi, 36, 4.
30. Pliny, *Nat. Hist.*, xviii, 16.
31. Livy, xxix, 14.
32. Livy, xxxiv, 54.
33. Livy, xxxvi, 36.
34. Dionysius, Hal. *Ant. Rom.*, ii, 19, 4.
35. Aulus Gellius, ii, 242; xviii, 2, 11; Ovid, *Fasti*, iv, 353, 4; Cicero, *de Senect.*, 13, 45.
36. *Fasti*, iv, 377.
37. Juvenal, xi, 193.
38. Cicero, *de Senect,.* 45.
39. Lucretius, *De rerum nat.*, ii, 600-30 (ed. by C. Bailey, Oxford, 1947), pp. 267ff.
40. Dionysius, Hal., *Ant. Rom.*, ii, 19, 5.
41. Diodorus Siculus, xxxvi, 6; Plutarch, *Marius*, 17.
42. That the Emperor was Claudius Gothicus in A.D. 258; cf. Domaszewski, *Journal of Roman Studies*, i, 1913, p. 56.
43. Showerman, *The Great Mother of the Gods*, 1901, p. 277; *Classical Journal*, xi, 1906, p. 29; Graillot, *Le Culte de Cybéle*, Paris, 1912, pp. 117f.
44. Arnobius, *Adversus Gentes.*, v, 7, 16, 39, 167f.; Julian, *Orat.*, v, 168; Hepding, *op. cit.*, Giessen, 1903, pp. 86, 92f., 96, 152ff.
45. Cf. Tertullian, *Apolgeticus*, 25; Apuleius, *Metamorphoses*, viii, 28.
46. Firmicus Maternus, *De errore profanarum religionum*, 22; Hepding, *op. cit.*, p. 167; Graillot, *op. cit.*, p. 131.
47. Macrobeus, *Saturnalia*, i, xxi, 10.
48. Ovid, *Fasti*, iv, 337-46; Arnobius, *Adversus Gentes*, vii, 32, 49; Lucretius, *De rerum nat.*, ii, 608-12.
49. Minucius Felix, *Octavius*, 22, 1.
50. Tacitus, *Hist.*, iv, 81; Plutarch, *Moralia*, 361f-362e.
51. *Metamorphoses*, xi, 22.
52. Dia Cassius, xlvii, 15, 4; liii, 2, 4; Tertullian, *Apol.*, 6; *ad nat.*, 1, 10 (Varro).
53. Virgil, *Aeneas*, viii, 698-700.
54. Mommsen, *C.I.L.*, i, 2, pp. 333f.; Apuleius, *Metamorphoses*, xi, 26.
55. Minucius Felix, *Octavius*, 22, 2.
56. *Metam.*, xi, 21; cf. Plutarch, *de Iside et Osiride*, 8.
57. *Metam.*, xi, 5, 6, 16, 21.
58. *Metam.*, xi, 23-30.

59. Propertius, iv, 5, 34; Tibullus, i, 3, 23–26; Ovid, *Amores*, iii, 9, 33.
60. *Metam.*, xi, 21.
61. *de Iside et Osiride*, 8.
62. *Metam.*, xi, 2, 5, 22, 25 f.
63. Chap. ii, p. 61.
64. Plutarch, *de Iside et Osiride* 53.
65. *Codex Parisinus*, 8084, 98–101.
66. Tertullian, *Ad Nationes*, i, 10; *Apologeticus*, 6; Arnobius, *Adversus Gentes.*, 73; Dion. Cassius, xl, 47; liii, 2; Tacitus, *Annales*, ii, 85; Suetonius, *Tiberius*, 36; Hegesippus, ii, 4.
67. Livy, viii, 9, 6; x, 19; Ovid, *Fasti*, vi, 201.
68. *C.I.L.*, vi, 490; ix, 314*b*; cf. Wissowa, *op. cit.*, p. 291.
69. *The Syrian Goddess* by Strong and Garstang, 1913, pp. 41 ff.
70. *Metam.*, viii, 24–27.
71. *Bulletin de Correspondance Hellénique*, iii, 407; vi, 495 ff.; vii, 477; viii, 132; xvi, 748, 785.
72. Ovid, *Metam.*, iv, 44–46; Cornelius, *de Nat. Deor.*, 6.
73. Lucian, *De Dea Syria*, 10, 31 f.
74. Macrobius, *Saturnalia*, chap. xxiii; cf. Lucian, *De Dea Syria*, 30.
75. *Op. cit.*, 12–29.
76. *Op. cit.*, 13, 33, 48.
77. *Op. cit.*, 15.
78. Apuleius, *Metam.*, viii, 170; Macrobius, *Sat.*, i, 23, 18; Tertullian, *Ad nat.*, ii, 8; *Apol.*, 24.
79. Cumont, 'Gallos' Pauly-Wissowa, *Real-Encyklopädie*, vol. vii, p. 697; Strong and Garstang, *The Syrian Goddess*, 1913, pp. 11 ff.
80. Garstang, *Land of the Hittites*, 1910, p. lxviii.
81. J. Toutain, *Les cultes païens dans l'empire romain*, vol. ii, Paris, 1911, pp. 73 f.
82. Herodotus, i, 34 ff.
83. Cf. C. B. Lewis, *A Miscellany of Studies to L. E. Kastner*, 1932, pp. 338 ff.
84. Graillot, *op. cit.*, 1912, pp. 121 ff.
85. *De errore profanarum*, chap. xxvii, 1 ff.
86. R. Chambers, *Book of Days*, vol. i, 1886, p. 577, col. 1; F. Thistleton Dyer, *British Popular Customs*, 1876, pp. 251 ff.; W. Hone, *Every Day Book*, vol. xi, 1820, pp. 615 ff.; Brand, *Popular Antiquities*, vol. i, 1882, pp. 212 ff.; Mannhardt, *Antike Wald- und Feldkulte*, Berlin, 1877, pp. 160 ff., 583 f.; Frazer, *Golden Bough*, pt. ii, pp. 60 ff.; A. B. Cook, *Zeus*, vol. i, Cambridge, 1914, p. 339.
87. Stubbes, *The Anatomie of Abuses*, 1877–82, p. 149.
88. Graillot, *op. cit.*, p. 123.
89. Thistleton Dyer, *British Popular Customs*, pp. 270 ff.; A. R. Wright, *British Calendar Customs*, 1938, pp. 224 ff.

90. W. H. D. Rouse, *Folk-lore*, vol. iv, 1893, pp. 50ff.; Mannhardt, *Der Baumkultus der Germanen und ihrer Nachbarstämme*, Berlin, 1875, p. 322.
91. C. B. Lewis, *op. cit.*, pp. 330ff.
92. Frazer, *Golden Bough*, pt. ii, p. 88.

CHAPTER VII

1. Irenaeus, *Adversus Haereses*, i, 29, 57; ii, 18; iii, 15.
2. *Hauptprobleme der Gnosis*, Göttingen, 1907, pp. 26, 58–83.
3. *Op. cit.*, 4, 1, 1; 2, 146.
4. Gal. iv. 21–31; Isa. i. 26, l.; i, li., 17f.; lxvi. 6ff., 11ff.
5. St Matt. xxiii. 37; St Luke xiii. 34f.; xix. 43f.
6. Rev. xix. 7; xxi. 9f.; Rom. vii. 4; Eph. v. 23; 2 Cor. xi. 2–4; Eusebius, *Hist. Eccl.*, iv, 26, 8; v, 1, 10.
7. Chavasse, *The Bride of Christ*, 1940, pp. 19–48; E. Mura, *Le corps mystique du Christ*, vol. i, Paris, 1936, pp. 65f.; vol. ii, pp. 483ff.
8. Hippolytus, *Philosophumena*, v, 9; cf. Clement of Alexandria, *op. cit.*, ii, 16.
9. Chap. v, pp. 193 ff.
10. *Op. cit.*, xxxviii.
11. Cerinthus, ii.
12. Bousset, *Hauptprobleme der Gnosis* (Göttingen, 1907; Reitzenstein, *Poimandras*, Leipzig, 1904.
13. E. de Faye, *Gnostiques et gnosticisme*, Paris, 1913.
14. Rev. ii, 6, 15.
15. *Adv. Haer.*, xxxv.
16. Clement of Alexandria, *Strom.*, ii, 20; iii, 4; Tertullian, *Adv. Marc.*, i, 29.
17. Acts vi. 5; Rev. ii. 6; Irenaeus, *op. cit.*, i, 26; iii, 11, 1; Hippolytus, *Philos.*, vii, 36; Tertullian, *Praesc. Haer.*, 33; *Adv. Marc.*, i, 29; *De Pudicitia*, 19.
18. John xiv. 12–18; Matt. xxiii. 34.
19. Eusebius, *Hist. Eccl.*, xvi, 7, 14.
20. *Ibid.*, V, xvii, 1; V, iii, 4; cf. xvi, 22.
21. *Cities and Bishoprics of Phrygia*, pt. ii, Oxford, 1897, pp. 573ff.
22. Origen, *Ap.* Cramer, *Cat.* v, 279; Cyprian, *Ep.* lxxv, 10; Epiphanius, *Haer.*, xlix, 2f.
23. *de Virg. Vel.*, 9.
24. Irenaeus, *Adv. Haer.*, III, xi, 9; IV, xxxiii, 6f.; Eusebius, *Hist. Eccl.*, V, viii, 4; cf. P. de Labriolle, *La crise monteniste*, Paris, 1913, pp. 225ff.; *Les Sources de l'histoire du Montenisme*, Paris, 1913, pp. 194ff.
25. *Hist. Eccl.*, V, iii, 4.

26. Tertullian, *De Oratione*, II; *De Monogamia*, VII; Eusebius, *Hist. Eccl.*, V, i, 3; 402, 12f.; J. C. Plumpe, *Mater Ecclesia*, Washington, 1943, pp. 35ff.

27. *Syriac Fragment*, 30: 2, 461 (Harvey); cf. H. Jordan, *Texte und Unter-suchungen zur Geschichte der altchristlichen Literatur*, vol. xxxvi, 3, 1913, 3–5; *op. cit.*, iii, 38, 131 (Harvey); V, 35, 2; 2, 425 (Harvey).

28. *De Pudicitia*, xviii; *De Anima*, xi, xxi.

29. *Ibid.*, xliii, 43.

30. *Paedagogus*, i, 6, 42; cf. Stahlin, *Die griechischen christlichen Schriftsteller der ersten drei Jahrhunderte*, Clement of Alexandria, *op. cit.*, vol. i, 115, 10–24.

31. *Paed.*, III, 12, 99, 1.

32. *Ibid.*, I, 6, 40f.

33. *Canticum Canticorum*, lib. I; III, 232ff.; *De Orat.*, 20, 1.

34. In Matt. 17, 21; Migne, *P.L.*, 13, 1559.

35. Sel, in Gen. Migne, *P.G*, 12, 1432A.

36. Eph. ii; Migne, *P.G.*, 34, 416.

37. *Spiritual Homily*, 4, Migne, col. 375.

38. His provenance is very uncertain in spite of Jerome, who alleges that he was bishop of Olympus in Lycia and afterwards bishop of Tyre, *De Viris illustribus*, lxxxiii; cf. F. Diekamp, *Theologische Quartalschrift*, 109, 1928, pp. 285ff.

39. *Symposium*, 3, 8, 74f.; 37, 9–15.

40. *Op. cit.*, 3, 9, 75; 37, 16–25.

41. *Op. cit.*, 8, 5, 183f; 86, 19–87, 14.

42. *Op. cit.*, 8, 6, 186f.; 88, 5–18.

43. *Op. cit.*, 8, 8, 190f.; 90, 6–19.

44. *Op. cit.*, 8, 11, 197; 93, p. 12.

45. *Op. cit.*, 7, 3, 156; 74, 8ff.

46. Cf. P. Batiffol, *Le catholicisme de saint Augustine*, Paris, 1920, pp. 270ff.

47. Meek, *The Song of Songs, a Symposium*, 1924, pp. 48–79.

48. *Hom.*, i, John ii. 2.

49. *Hom.*, Ps. xlv. 3; cf. *Hom.* Ps. xix. 6.

50. *Hom.*, St. John viii. 4.

51. *De Virginstate*, 2; *De Natura et Gratia*, cap. 36.

52. *Panarion*, 78: 11, 24; 79: 4, 7.

53. *De Spiritu Sancto*, iii, cap. II, n. 80.

54. Cf. K. Prümm, *Der christliche Glaube und die altheidnische Welt*, vol. i, Leipzig, 1935, pp. 285ff.

55. E. Neumann, *The Great Mother* (E.T. by R. Manheim, 1955).

56. F. C. Conybeare, *Proceedings of the Society of Historical Theology*, Oxford, 1902, pp. 13f.

57. Luke i. 27ff., 34, 42–45; Matt. i, 20.

58. Rom. v.; 1 Cor. xv. 22, 45.

59. Rom. viii. 18ff.

60. Eph. v. 22f.; cf. iv. 32.
61. Rom. viii. 18ff.
62. Rom. iv. 17ff.; Gal. iv. 26.
63. Irenaeus, *op. cit.*, III, xxii, 4.
64. Justin Martyr, *Dial. cum Trypho*, 100, 3.
65. Origen, *Comment. on Matt.*, 10, 7; Tertullian, *De Monogamia*, 8.
66. Tertullian, *De Carne Christi*, 7, 20.
67. *Op. cit.*, xxi, 10; cf. xix, 3; *P.G.*, vii, 955, 941.
68. Athanasius, *Epistola as Epictetum*, 4, 5, 7ff. (*P.G.*, xxvi, 1056ff.).
69. *Op. cit.*, lxxix, 7.
70. *Ep.* lix, *ad Epict.* 2.
71. Hefele-Leclercq, *Histoire des Conciles*, vol. ii, Paris, 1908, pt. i, p. 242.
72. Epistula, ii, *Nestorii ad Coelestium.*
73. Acts xix. 35.
74. *Homily*, 4, *Acta conciliorum oecumenicorum*, Leipzig, 1914, i, 1, 2, 102–3.
75. Niceph. Callist., xiv, 2; xv, 14.
76. Cf. Martigny, *Dictionnaire des Antiquités Chrétiennes*, Paris, 1877, pp. 792ff.
77. *de Trinit.*, viii, 5 (*P.L.*, xlii, 952).
78. C. Cecchelli, *Mater Christi*, vol. i, Rome, 1946, pp. 83, 88, 217, 235.
79. Cecchelli, *op. cit.*, vol. i, pp. 89, 198f.
80. *Hist. Eccl.*, xvii, 28.
81. *Bibliotheca Patrum Maxima*, ii, pt. ii, p. 212.
82. *Panarion*, 78, 11, 24.
83. Duchesne, *Christian Worship*, 1912, pp. 273f.
84. J. D. Mansi, *Sacrorum Conciliorum Collectio*, vol. ii, Florence, 1759, 572.
85. *P.L.* (Migne), lxxxv, 170, 734.
86. Duchesne, *op. cit.*, pp. 118, 262.
87. *P.L.*, lxxi, 713.
88. Luke xii. 2–8; ii. 22ff.
89. Dom Férotin, *Peregrinato Egeriae*, Paris, 1903.
90. *Historiarum Compendium*, Paris, 1647, p. 366.
91. *Historia Miscellanaea*, vol. xvi, Milan, 1723, p. 108.
92. *Martyrologicum Romanum*, p. 87.
93. Cf. chap. v, p 157.
94. Plutarch, *Symp.*, iii, 7, 1; viii, 10, 3.
95. Brand, *Popular Antiquities*, vol. i, p. 50; J. Ramsay, *Scotland and Scotsmen of the Eighteenth Century*, vol. ii, Edinburgh, 1888, p. 447.
96. Usener, *Religionsgeschichtliche Untersuchungen*, pt. i, Bonn, 1889; Duchesne, *op. cit.*, pp. 257ff.
97. *Panarion*, li, 22.
98. *Hom.*, xxxi.
99. *Op. cit.*, pp. 280ff.

100. Theodotus of Ancyra, *Homily*, 6 (*P.G.*, 77, 1427).
101. *Hom. in Lucam*, xvii.
102. *Hom.*, xliv. In Matt., *Hom.*, iv.
103. *De Genesi ad litteram*. x: cap. 18, 32; *Contra Julianum*, iv, cap. 122.
104. *P.G.*, xcvi, 1499.
105. Epist. clxxiv, *Op.* tom., i, p. 169, Paris, 1690.
106. Mansi, xxxix. 182.
107. Cf. R. Benedict, *Patterns of Culture*, 1935.
108. Cf. Zimmern, Belti ('Beltija, Beletja) eine, zunächst Sprachliche, Studie zur Vorgeschichte der Madonnakults', *Paul Haupt Anniversary Volume*, pp. 281ff.

CHAPTER VIII

1. *E.R.E.*, xii, p. 183.
2. Sophocles, *Antigone*, 339f.
3. Pausanius, X, xii, 10; I, xxxi, 4.
4. *Hymn to Demeter*, 8ff.
5. Farnell, *C.G.S.*, vol. iii, pp. 29ff.
6. *Bacchae*, 274.
7. Cf. chap. v, pp. 153f.
8. Callimachus, *Hymnus in Cererum*, 20–22; *Metam.* 5, 645.
9. Chap. ii, pp. 48f.
10. Cf. chap. ii, pp. 51f.
11. Cf. chap. iii, pp. 85f.
12. Chap. iii, p. 86.
13. *K.U.B.*, xxxi, no. 27; Gurney, *Annals of Archaeology and Anthropology*, 27, Liverpool, 1940, pp. 10f., 22ff.
14. Chap. iv, pp. 102f.
15. Chap. xvii, 43f.
16. Chap. iv, pp. 34, 101f.
17. Rig-veda, i, 106, 3; 159, 1; 185, 4; iv, 56, 2.
18. Rig-veda, v, 84.
19. Dumezil, *Ouranos-Varuna*, Paris, 1934, pp. 39ff., 42ff., 53ff.
20. Rig-veda, x, 90.
21. H. Z. Kosay, *Ausgrabungen von Alaca Hoyuk, 1936*, Ankara, 1944, pp. 113f., 131ff., 212.
22. Malten, *Jahrbuch des deutschen archaologischen Instituts*, vol. lxiii, 1928, p. 107.
23. Gurney, *The Hittites*, 1952, p. 66, pl. 16, fig. ii.
24. Dussaud, *R.H.R.*, cxiii, 1936, p. 19.
25. Rig-veda, x, 160, 3; v, 6, 5; v, 58, 6.
26. *Atharva-veda*, xii, 1, 6.
27. Rig-veda, ii, 34, 2.
28. Picard, *Revue de Philologie*, 1933, pp. 344ff.
29. Nilsson, *Minoan-Mycenaean Religion*, pp. 373f.

30. Cook, *Zeus*, vol. i, Cambridge, 1914, p. 468.

31. Frankfort, *Stratified Cylinder Seals from the Diyala Region*, Chicago, 1955, Oriental Institute Publications, lxxii, p. 43.

32. *Palace of Minos*, vol. iii, pp. 220 ff., fig. 154.

33. Guthrie, *Orpheus and Greek Religion*, 1935, pp. 111, 199; Harrison, *Prolegomena to the Study of Greek Religion*, 1922, p. 479; Nilsson, *op. cit.*, pp. 578 f.; Porphry, *De abstinentia*, iv, 19.

34. Euripides, *Bacchae*, v, 141 f., 726, 736 ff.

35. Aristotle, *Ath. Pol.*, 3.

36. Diodorus, iv, 3.

37. Farnell, *C.G.S.*, vol. iv, p. 95, n. 112.

38. *Op. cit.*, vol. x, iv, pp. 6 f.; Plutarch, *Quaest. Com.*, 668e.

39. *Satapatha Brahmana*, vii, 2, 2, 5.

40. Krappe, *Études de mythologie et de folklore germaniques*, Paris, 1928, p. 62.

41. *Tragg. Graec. Frag.* (Nauck), 44; cf. Euripides, *Frag.*, 898, 7 ff.

42. Cf. chap. v, pp. 144 f.

43. Sophocles, *Antigone*, 339 (Storr); Aeschylus, *The Suppliant Women*, 890 ff. (Murray).

44. Frazer, *The Golden Bough*, pt. ii, pp. 98 ff.

45. Cf. chap. ii, p. 56.

46. Chap. v, pp. 134 f.

47. *The Earlier Religion of Greece*, 1931, p. 41.

48. Xenophanes, *Frag.* 19 (Diehl).

49. Euripides, *Bacchae*, 58 ff., 127 ff.

50. *Hymn Homer*, xiv; xxx, 17.

51. Gruppe, *Griechische Mythologie*, Munich, 1906, p. 1521; Rapp., 'Kybele' in *Lex. der Mythol.*, vol. ii, p. 1659; cf. vol. iv, pp. 91 ff.; Nilsson, *Minoan-Mycenaean Religion*, p. 464.

52. *J.N.E.S.*, viii, 1949, pp. 194 ff.; cf. Blegen, *American Journal of Archaeology*, xli, 1937, p. 569, pl. xx; A. E. D. van Buren, *Iraq*, vol. xii, 1950, pp. 139 ff.; Crawford, *The Eye-Goddess*, 1957, pp. 29 ff.

53. Mallowan and Cruikshank, *Iraq*, vol. ii, i, 1935, pp. 85 f.

ABBREVIATIONS

A.A.S.O.R.	*Annual of the American Schools of Oriental Research,* New Haven.
A.B.	*Anat-Baal Texts.*
A.J.S.L.	*American Journal of Semitic Languages and Literatures,* Chicago.
A.N.E.T.	*Ancient Near Eastern Texts relating to the Old Testament.* J. B. Pritchard, Ltd., 1955.
L'Anthrop.	*L'Anthropologie,* Paris.
B.A.S.O.R.	*Bulletin of the American Schools of Oriental Research,* New Haven.
B.S.A.	*Annual, British School of Athens.*
C.G.S.	*Cult of the Greek States,* by L. R. Farnell, Oxford.
C.I.L.	*Corpus Inscriptiones Latinarum.*
E.R.E.	*Encyclopaedia of Religion and Ethics* (Hastings).
I.P.E.K.	*Jahrbuch für Prähistorische und Ethnographische Kunst,* Cologne.
J.E.A.	*Journal of Egyptian Archeology.*
J.H.S.	*Journal of Hellenic Studies,* London.
J.A.O.S.	*Journal of the American Oriental Society,* New Haven.
J.N.E.S.	*Journal of Near Eastern Studies,* Chicago.
J.R.A.S.	*Journal of the Royal Asiatic Society,* London.
J.R.A.I.	*Journal of the Royal Anthropological Institute,* London.
K.U.B.	*Keilschrifturkunden aus Boghazköi.*
M.V.A.G.	*Mitteilungen der Vorderasiatisch-Aegyptischen Gesellschaft.*
P.G.	*Patrologia Graeca* (Migne).
P.L.	*Patrologia Latina* (Migne).
P.P.S.N.S.	*Proceedings Prehistoric Society. New Series.*
P.T.	*Pyramid Texts.*
R.H.S.	*Revue d'histoire des religions,* Paris.
S.B.E.	*Sacred Books of the East,* Oxford, 1879–1910.

BIBLIOGRAPHY

CHAPTER I

Albright, W. F., *The Archaeology of Palestine and the Bible*, New York, 1932.

Breuil, H., *Quatre cents siècles d'art pariétal*, Montignac, 1954.

Brunton, G., and Caton-Thompson, G., *The Badarian Civilization*, 1928.

Childe, V. G., *New Light on the Most Ancient East*, 1934; *The Dawn of European Civilizatiou*, 1947.

Contenau, G., *La Déesse nue babylonienne*, Paris, 1914.

Crawford, O. G. S., *The Eye Goddess*, 1957.

Evans, Sir Arthur, *The Palace of Minos*, vols. i–iv, 1921–35.

Garstang, J., *Prehistoric Mersin*, Oxford, 1953.

Ghirshman, R., *Fouilles de Sialk*, Paris, 1938; *Fouilles du Tepe-Giyan*, Paris, 1933.

Hartland, S., *Primitive Paternity*, 1909.

Hawkes, C. F. C., *The Prehistoric Foundations of Europe*, 1940.

James, E. O., *Prehistoric Religion*, 1957.

Levy, G. R., *The Gate of Horn*, 1948.

Luquet, G. H., *The Art and Religion of Fossil Man*, New Haven, 1930.

McCown, D. E., *The Comparative Stratigraphy of Early Iran*, Chicago, 1942.

Mackay, E. J., *Further Excavations at Mohenjo-daro*, Delhi, 1937.

Malinowski, B., *The Father in Primitive Psychology*, 1927.

Mallowan, M. E. L., 'Excavations at Brak and Chagar Bazar', *Iraq*, vol. ix, pp. 157 ff., 1947.

Marshall, Sir John, *Mohenjo-daro and the Indus Civilization*, 1931.

Obermaier, H., *Fossil Man in Spain*, Yale Press, New Haven, 1925.

Perkins, A. L., *The Comparative Archaeology of Early Mesopotamia*, Chicago, 1949.

Petrie, Sir Flinders, *Prehistoric Egypt*, 1920.

Piggott, S., *Prehistoric India*, 1950.

Pumpelly, R., *Explorations in Turkestan*, 1904, vol. i, Washington, 1908.

Schmidt, E. F., *Excavations at Tepe Hissar*, Philadelphia, 1937.

Stein, Sir Aurel, *Memoirs of the Archaeological Survey of India*, no. 37, 1925.

Tobler, A. J., *Excavations at Tepe Gawra*, Philadelphia, 1950.

Van Buren, A. E. D., *Clay Figurines of Babylonia and Assyria*, Yale Press, 1930.
Verneau, R., *Les Grottes de Grimaldi*, Monaco, 1906.
Vats, M. S., *Excavations at Harappa*, 2 vols., Delhi, 1940.
Zammit, T., *Prehistoric Malta*, Oxford, 1930.

CHAPTER II

Blackman, A. M., *Luxor and its Temples*, 1923.
Breasted, J. H., *Ancient Records of Egypt*, Chicago, 1906.
Budge, E. A., *The Gods of the Egyptians*, 1904; *From Fetish to God in Ancient Egypt*, Oxford, 1934.
Erman, A., *A Handbook of Egyptian Religion*, 1907.
Frankfort, H., *Kingship and the Gods*, Chicago, 1948; *Cylinder Seals*, 1939; *The Intellectual Adventure of Ancient Man*, Chicago, 1946.
James, E. O., *Myth and Ritual in the Ancient Near East*, 1958.
Junker, H., *Die Onurislegende*, Wien, 1917.
Kramer, S. N., *Sumerian Mythology*, Philadelphia, 1944.
Langdon, S., *Tammuz and Ishtar*, Oxford, 1914.
Mercer, S. A. B., *Religion of Ancient Egypt*, 1949.
Moortgat, A., *Tammuz*, Berlin, 1949.
Moret, A., *Du caractère religieux de la royauté pharaonique*, Paris, 1902.
Naville, E. H., *The Temple of Deir el-Bahari*, 1894.
Pallis, S. A., *The Babylonian Akitu Festival*, 1926.
Sethe, K., *Urgeschichte und Aelteste Religion der Aegypter*, Leipzig, 1930; *Urkunden des Aegyptischen Altertums*, Leipzig, 1903.
Wiedemann, A., *Religion of the Ancient Egyptians*, 1897.

CHAPTER III

Albright, W. F., *Archaeology and the Religion of Israel*, Baltimore, 1946.
Cook, S. A., *The Religion of Ancient Palestine in the Light of Archaeology*, 1930.
Driver, G. R., *Canaanite Myths and Legends*, Edinburgh, 1956.
Dussaud, R., *Religion des Hittites et des Hourrites*, Paris, 1945.
Garstang, J., *The Hittite Empire*, 1929; *The Land of the Hittites*, 1910; *The Syrian Goddess*, 1913.
Gaster, T. H., *Thespis*, New York, 1950.

Gordon, C. H. *Ugaritic Handbook*, Rome, 1947.

Graham, W. C., and May, H. G., *Culture and Conscience*, Chicago, 1936.

Gray, J., *The Krt Text in the Literature of Ras Shamra*, Leiden, 1955.

Gurney, O. R., *The Annals of Archaeology and Anthropology*, 27, Liverpool, 1940; *The Hittites*, 1952.

Kapelrud, A., *Baal in the Ras Shamra Texts*, Copenhagen, 1952.

Laroche, E., *Recherches sur les noms des dieux hittites*, Paris, 1947.

Leslie, E. A., *The Old Testament in the Light of its Canaanite Backgrounds*, New York, 1936.

Obermann, J., *Ugaritic Mythology*, New Haven, 1948.

Pritchard, J. B., *Palestine Figurines*, New Haven, 1943.

Schaeffer, C. F. A., *The Cuneiform Texts of Ras Shamra-Ugarit*, 1939.

CHAPTER IV

Barth, A., *The Religion of India*, 1914.

Burgess, J., *The Rock-Temples of Elephanta or Gharapuri*, Bombay, 1871.

Cambridge History of India, vol. i, Cambridge, 1922.

Clough, E. R., *While Sewing Sandals*, New York, 1899.

Crooke, W., *Popular Religion and Folk-lore of Northern India*, 1896.

Cumont, F., *Les Mystères de Mithras*, Paris, 1899.

Eliot, Sir C., *Hinduism and Buddhism*, 1921.

Elmore, W. T., *Dravidian Gods in Modern Hinduism*, New York, 1915.

Fergusson, J., and Burgess, J. L., *The Cave Temples of India*, 1880.

Gait, E. A., *Census Report, Bengal*, vol. i, 1901.

Ghirshman, R., *Iraq*, 1954.

Haydon, A. E., *Biography of the Gods*, 1941.

Herzfeld, E. E., *Archaeological History of Iran*, 1935.

Ivengar, P. T. Srinivasa, *Pre-Aryan Tamil Cultures*, Madras, 1920.

Macdonell, A. A., *Vedic Mythology*, Strassburg, 1897.

Marshall, Sir John, *Mohenjo-daro and the Indus Civilization*, 1931.

Monier-Williams, Sir Monier, *Religious Thought and Life in India*, 1885.

Moor, E., *The Indian Pantheon*, Madras, 1897.

Risley, H. H., *Castes and Tribes of Bengal*, 1891.

Shivapadasundarum, S., *The Saiva School of Hinduism*, 1934.

Thurston, E., *Castes and Tribes of Southern India*, Madras, 1909.

Vats, M. S., *Excavations at Harappa*, New Delhi, 1940.

Whitehead, H., *Village Gods of South India*, Oxford, 1916.

CHAPTER V

Allen, T. W., Sikes, E. E., Halliday, T. W., *The Homeric Hymns*, Oxford, 1936.

Baudissin, W. W., *Adonis und Esmun*, Leipzig, 1911.

Cook, A. B., *Zeus*, Cambridge, 1914.

Evans, Sir Arthur, *Palace of Minos*, 1921, vols. iii, iv; *The Earlier Religion of Greece in the Light of Cretan Discoveries*, 1931; *Mycenaean Tree and Pillar Cult*, 1901.

Farnell, L. R., *Cult of the Greek States*, vols. i, ii, iii, Oxford, 1907; *Higher Aspects of Greek Religion*, 1912.

Foucart, P., *Les Grands Mystères d'Eleusis*, Paris, 1900.

Frazer, J. G., *The Golden Bough*, pt. v, 1914.

Guthrie, W. K. C., *The Greeks and Their Gods*, 1950; *Orpheus and Greek Religion*, 1935.

Harrison, J. E., *Themis*, Cambridge, 1912; *Prolegomena to the Study of Greek Religion*, Cambridge, 1922 (3rd ed.).

James, E. O., *Myth and Ritual in the Near East*, 1958.

Kourouniotis, K., *Eleusis*, Athens, 1936.

Losbeck, C. A., *Aglaophamus*, Leipzig, 1829.

Mylonas, G., *Hymns to Demeter and Her Sanctuary at Eleusis*, St Louis, 1942.

Nilsson, M. P., *Minoan-Mycenaean Religion*, Lund, 2nd ed., 1950.

Persson, A. W., *The Religion of Greece in Prehistoric Times*, California, 1942.

Rhode, E., *Psyche* (E.T. by W. B. Hillis), 1925.

Rose, H. J., *Handbook of Greek Mythology*, 1933; *Greek Religion*, 1947.

Williams, B. E., *Gournia*, Philadelphia, 1908.

CHAPTER VI

Apuleius, *Metamorphoses*.

Bailey, C., *Phases in the Religion of Ancient Rome*, 1932.

Brand, J., *Popular Antiquities of Great Britain*, 1822–3.

Chambers, R., *Book of Days*, 1886.

Cook, A. B., *Zeus*, Cambridge, 1914.

Cumont, F., *The Oriental Religions in Roman Paganism*, 1911.

Dyer, J. F. Thistleton, *British Popular Customs*, 1876.

Farnell, L. R., *Cult of the Greek States*, vol. iii, Oxford, 1907.

Frazer, Sir J. G., *The Fasti of Ovid*, 5 vols., 1929; *Golden Bough*, pt. ii, 1911.

Garstang, J., and Strong, H. A., *The Syrian Goddess*, 1913; *The Land of the Hittites*, 1910.

Graillot, H., *Le Culte de Cybèle*, Paris, 1912.

Hepding, H., *Attis, seine Mythen un sein Kult*, Giessen, 1903.

Lucian, *De Dea Syria*.

Macrobius, *Saturnalia*.

Mannhardt, W., *Antike Wald- und Feldkulte*, Berlin, 1877.

Plutarch, *de Iside et Osiride*.

Showerman, G., *The Great Mother of the Gods* (Bulletin of the University of Wisconsin, no. 43, phil. and lit. series, i, 3, 1901).

Toutain, J., *Les Cultes païens dans l'empire romain*, Paris, 1911.

Wissowa, G., *Religion und Kultus der Römer*, Munich, 1902.

Wright, A. D., *British Calendar Customs*, 1938.

CHAPTER VII

Bousset, W., *Hauptprobleme der Gnosis*, Göttingen, 1907.

Cecchelli, G., *Mater Christi*, Rome, 1946.

Duchesne, L., *Christian Worship* (E.T. by M. L. McClure), 1912.

Faye, E., *de Gnostiques et gnosticisme*, Paris, 1913.

Hippolytus, *Philosophumena*.

Irenaeus, *Adversus Haereses*.

Legge, F., *Forerunners and Rivals of Christianity*, Cambridge, 1915.

Methodius, *Symposium*.

Miegge, G., *The Virgin Mary* (E.T. by W. Smith), 1955.

Mura, E., *Le corps mystique du Christ*, Paris, 1936.

Plumpe, J. C., *Mater Ecclesia*, Washington, 1943.

Prumm, K., *Der christliche Glaube un die altheidnische Welt*, Leipzig, 1935.

Ramsay, W., *Cities and Bishoprics of Phrygia*, Oxford, 1897.

Reitzenstein, R., *Poimandras*, Leipzig, 1904.

Usener, H., *Religionsgeschichtliche Untersuchungen*, pt. i, Bonn, 1889.

CHAPTER VIII

Aeschylus, *The Danaids*.

Callimachus, *Hymnus in Cererum*.

Cook, A. B., *Zeus*, Cambridge, 1914.

Dumezil, G., *Ouranos-Varuna*, Paris, 1934.

Euripides, *Bacchae*, *Cretes*.

Evans, Sir Arthur, *The Palace of Minos*, vol. iii, 1930; *The Earlier Religion of Greece in the Light of Cretan Discoveries*, 1931.

Farnell, L. R., *Cult of the Greek States*, vols. iii, iv, Oxford, 1907.

Frankfort, H., *Stratified Calendar Seals from the Dyala Region*, Chicago, 1955.

Frazer, Sir J. G., *The Golden Bough*, pt. ii, 1911.

Gurney, O. R., *The Hittites*, 1952; *Annals of Archaeology and Anthropology*, 27, Liverpool, 1940.

Guthrie, W. K. C., *Orpheus and Greek Religion*, 1922.

Harrison, J. E., *Prolegomena to the Study of Greek Religion*, Cambridge, 1922.

James, E. O., *Myth and Ritual in the Ancient Near East*, 1958.

Krappe, A. H., *Études de mythologie et de folklore germanique*, Paris, 1928.

Nilsson, M. P., *Minoan-Mycenaean Religion*, 2nd ed., 1950.

Sophocles, *Antigone*.

INDEX

A figure in bold type in the entry for a subject refers to the page number of a sub-section where that subject is treated at some length.